MASS MEDIA IN NEW WORLD ORDER

MASS MEDIA IN NEW WORLD ORDER

A N SHAMSI

2006

SBS Publishers & Distributors Pvt. Ltd.
New Delhi

ISBN : 81-903098-2-X

Indian Price - Rs 745

First Published in India in 2006
Reprint 2006

Published by:
SBS PUBLISHERS & DISTRIBUTORS PVT. LTD.
2/9, Ground Floor, Ansari Road, Darya Ganj,
New Delhi - 110002, INDIA
Tel: 23289119, 41563911
Email: mail@sbspublishers.com

Contents

Preface

With growing globalisation, a new world-order is in the offing. Early signs hold pointer to the fact that values are under change. The phenomenon can be experienced both at micro and macro levels. Society consists of people and people are the soul of Mass Media. Consequently, it puts on a new garb—in its new *avtar*.

Freedom of speech is one of the fundamental rights of man. This right gets fullest expression in Mass Media. A person linked with this discipline is supposed to be honest and bold. Honesty demands impartiality, boldness and courage to call a spade a spade.

But in changing scenario, these principles sound somewhat archaic. Why? probably due to the modern and advanced technology used in the sphere. In this context, a micro-camera is more powerful than a sword. In fact, the invention and development of camera is one of the most tremendous successes, man has ever achieved. It not only captures the past but also solves an intricate riddle pertaining to the life, hereafter (parts of body give evidence).

Another important aspect of camera-reporting is that it cannot be belied. The man with the camera remains or can remain behind the curtain. A live footage saves time and energy. The more a film is screened, the more layers of reality come up.

All this—and a lot more—constitute the subject matter of this well-prepared book, aimed at providing the concerned and general readers with the latest info on the topic.

The undersigned anticipates and solicits readers' views on this piece of work.

— Author

1

Fundamental Aspects

Journalism as a craft, a profession and even as a trade or business, is over two centuries old. It was made possible by the coming together of a number of technologies as well as several social, political and economic developments. The main technologies that facilitated the development of large-scale printing and distribution of print material were the printing press and the railways.

As a craft Journalism involves specialisation in one area (editorial, design, printing); for the reporters and the sub-editors for instance, it entails writing to a deadline, following routines in a conveyor-belt like work-place, while respecting the division of labour in the newsroom and the printing press. In earlier times, knowledge of type-writing and shorthand were the main skills demanded; today, computing and DTP skills are in demand for all areas of Journalism. Also, the divisions among the different areas have become blurred. As a profession, it is markedly different from other established professions like law, medicine, engineering, management or teaching. While the established professions require some specialised educational qualifications and training to be recruited to them, Journalism does not make any such requirement essential. There is no bar to anyone entering the profession, no matter what one's educational background or professional experience is. From the very beginning, Journalism (like the other media professions such as Advertising, Public Relations, Film, Television, Theatre, and Publishing) has been, and still remains, an 'open' profession.

Further, journalism has no distinct body of knowledge that defines the profession and marks its relationship with its clients (readers, advertisers, advertising agencies, public relations officials and others) and other professions. It may be argued that journalism is 'a way of knowing different from that produced in social science' or that it has its own specific approach to reality. However, there is no consensus in the journalistic community on this. Nor is there a universally accepted Code of Conduct or Code of Ethics, and where it does exist, is rarely enforced. Opinions vary on whether journalism is a 'calling', a public service, an entertainment, a cultural industry motivated by profit, or a tool for propaganda, public relations and advertising. Journalism can be a combination of all these, or each of these separately. Opinions are not so varied about the other professions. As a business and trade, Journalism involves publishing on a regular basis for profit, with news considered as the primary product. Hence the need to attract advertisers and readers, through marketing strategies which focus on circulation and readership.

Who then is a 'Journalist?' And what is 'Journalism?' The words 'journalist', 'journal' and 'journalism' are derived from the French 'journal', which in its turn comes from the Latin term 'diurnalis' or 'daily.' The Acta Diurna, a handwritten bulletin put up daily in the Forum, the main public square in ancient Rome, was perhaps the world's first newspaper. In later periods of history, pamphlets, tracts, reviews, periodicals, gazettes, news books, news sheets and letters came to be termed 'newspapers.' Those who wrote for them were first called 'news writers' or 'essayists' (even 'mercurists') and later 'journalists.' The Mughal rulers in India employed 'vaquia-navis' and 'confianavis' as public and secret news-writers to record once a week in a 'vaquia' (a sort of gazette or mercury) the events of importance in the empire. These news letters were read to the king every evening by the women of the court. The British colonial rulers used a system of 'informers' for their intelligence networks.

Journalism has come a long way since then. Today, a journalist is anyone who contributes in some way to the gathering, selection, and processing of news and current affairs for the press, radio, film, television, cable and the internet; and Journalism is the profession to which they belong. Thus, editors, correspondents, assistant editors, reporters, sub-editors, proof-readers, cartoonists, photographers ('photo-journalists') are journalists; so are, camera crew, audio and video editors, news readers, producers, directors and managing editors. 'Stringers' are part-time journalists, while 'free-lance' journalists are those who are occasional contributors.

Various Dimensions

Journalists work for the 'broadsheet' (or 'quality' or 'serious') press and the 'tabloid' (or 'popular' or 'sensational') press. The terms 'broadsheet' and 'tabloid' usually describe the two main formats of newspapers, but the labels also connote two kinds of news stories selected, and more importantly, the presentation, treatment and style as well.

However, this distinction is blurred, especially when the serious or quality papers (such as The Times of India, the Indian Express and The Asian Age) choose to highlight the private lives of public figures and the tabloids (such as the Blitz and the Midday) to publish serious investigative stories of corruption in high places. 'Tabloid television' follows the pattern of selection, treatment and style of the tabloid press. Segments of STAR News, 'The World This Week', and the video news magazines such as 'News track' and 'Eyewitness' can be included in the tabloid tradition. Similarly, the 'Entertainment Today' (ET) and newspapers like the Blitz and The Daily as well as the evening papers not only in format but content as well, can be put in the same slot.

'Tabloid Journalism' is frequently termed 'yellow journalism' primarily because of its tendency to sensationalize and trivialise events, issues and people. The staple of the 'tabloids' is the private lives of famous people, crime, accidents, disasters, public corruption, sex, etc. Tabloid journalists are believed to indulge in 'Cheque book Journalism' which implies that the subjects of the news stories are bribed to sell their 'true confessions.' Such journalists are also believed to indulge in 'keyhole journalism' in their attempts to probe the private sexual infidelities and peccadilloes of well-known people. These journalistic practices raise several ethical questions about the privacy of individuals and the public's right to information. In most democracies, reasonable restrictions are imposed on these intrusions on privacy, especially if they are not in any way related to the 'public interest'.

Thus, the nature of journalism and one's approach to what Journalism is, depends on one's perspective of news and news values. 'News is the account of an event, not something intrinsic in the event itself. Hence 'news' is the written, audio or visual construction of an event or happening or person. There is nothing in the event itself that makes it news; the event is not the news. Rather, the 'news' is the write-up or the audio or visual presentation of the event. Further, such a presentation or 'representation' or 'construction' of an event has to be in a particular format and is selected according to a certain professional value-system to make it 'news.'

It needs to be emphasised that 'news is the end-product of a complex process which begins with a systematic sorting and selecting of events according to a socially constructed set of categories.' So, it is not the event which is reported that determines the form, content, meaning or 'truth' of the news, but rather the 'news' that determines what it is that the event means. Its meaning results from the cultural discourse that 'news' employs. As one social linguist puts it: News is a social institution and a cultural discourse which exists and has meaning only in relation to other institutions and discourses which exist and have meaning only in relation to other institutions and discourses operating at the same time.'

Like language, news is a map, not the terrain which the map represents. A map uses codes, conventions, signs and symbols which have to be 'read' or interpreted. So does news; news as it were 'maps' the world. News selects, processes, produces and shapes an event or happening, but it is we as readers who make our own sense of the news.

Mainstream journalism treats news as a commodity to be bought and sold in the market place of information. Newspapers and other media subscribe to news agencies for news stories and visuals, and their primary sources of revenue are advertising and circulation. The media are run, like any other business or industrial enterprise, in the tradition of Western-style journalism. The focus is on the 'exceptional' and the 'elitist' and the preferred format is the 'inverted pyramid' news structure.

Applied Reporting

Where news is used primarily for publicity of an organisation or a product or of a particular perspective on issues national and international, the kind of journalism that results may be termed "public relations." The chief objective is not the reaping of profits but in advancing causes and perspectives, or in fighting a 'cold war.' Most overseas broadcasts like that of the Voice of America, the BBC World Service, Radio Deutsche Welle, and AIR's external service are examples of the use of broadcasting for public relations. Governments and corporate groups the world over spend millions of dollars to do public relations under the cover of journalism. They present views and perspectives as 'facts' in the form of news stories. Newspapers in India, especially the local and business sections, are packed with reports and features that have their source in 'press releases' and 'backgrounders' issued by social, political and business groups who wish to publicise their activities.

In recent years, newspapers and magazines have begun publishing glossy sections which are interestingly termed 'response features' or 'space marketing' supplements. Such supplements are no more than a marketing ploy to woo advertisers and to involve the corporate world in the newspaper business. Take *The Times of India's* supplement *'Ascent'* for instance. Its main writers are from the corporate world; so are those who contribute to 'space marketing' supplements. Several journalists too write for such supplements; however, they do not equate this with journalism, but rather with public relations and publicity.

Different Angles

Shelton Gunaratne describes development journalism as an integral part of a new journalism that involves 'analytical interpretation, subtle investigation, constructive criticism and sincere association with the grassroots (rather than with the elite).' Development or 'alternative' journalists reject the 'mainstream' Western-style approach to news and news values. They argue that 'mainstream' journalism is subservient to government and private business interests. They also argue that Western-style journalism aims at upholding, supporting and justifying confidence in the status quo. Development (or developmental) journalism rejects the 'famous five' of traditional journalism: balance, consensus, impartiality, objectivity and value-neutrality. It also rejects the traditional news values as the criteria for news selection: timeliness, immediacy, proximity, oddity, conflict, mystery, suspense, curiosity and novelty. This 'man-bites-dog' approach to journalism, according to development journalists, promotes sensationalism, elitism and conservatism, and thus indirectly suppresses the voice of the silent and oppressed majority. Development journalism is thus deliberately pro-Third World, pro-development/liberation, and pro-marginalised and poor groups.

The main sources of information for Development Journalism are the poor, the rural, the weak, the marginalised, the voiceless, not the powerful, the elite or the rich. The language of alternative journalism differs from 'the laconic, sterile staccatto of the wire-service ticker and ventures boldly into innovative forms of creative prose.' Further, such an approach rejects the format of the 'inverted pyramid' structure for news reporting, opting instead for the analytical essay or feature-type of writing, with context and the background of issues always spelt out at length. For the development journalist it is not the 'sound bite' or the 'scoop' or the information 'leaks' that make for news as much as social issues and developments in their global and national contexts.

Rather than present news as a series of isolated events with little or no explanation, the development journalist is concerned with explaining 'why?' and asking 'so what?' Development Journalism is thus not propaganda and certainly not government propaganda, as mainstream Anglo-American journalists tend to believe it is.

Rather, it could be a partner of government in discovering what sort of development the people want and need, and what sort of policies the authorities might pursue. Beyond this relationship, development journalism is equally an independent investigator of what type of development is taking place; and it is an honest and free critic in pointing out what may be going wrong and what dangers may be building up as a result. Development or alternative journalism is practised by Inter Press Service (IPS), the Rome-based international news agency, and other news services such as Depthnews, Gemini and South-north News.

Various Parts

Prior to Independence, the press in India had a clear-cut role to play in the nation's struggle against British rule. It had put up a brave fight in its heroic effort to expose the brutality of the regime, particularly in its suppression of the freedom movement. Many editors of the Indian language press defied censorship regulations to keep the nation informed (and agitated) about the progress of the movement, and especially of the plight of national leaders like Gandhi and Nehru.

With the goal of Independence being achieved at long last, the Indian press seemed to have lost its moorings. It was in a quandary. Should it play the role of an adversary to the government in power-the role it had played with remarkable success or, should it transform itself into an ally, and support the government in its efforts at national development? That quandary of the press has yet to be resolved.

Girilal Jain, the late editor of The Times of India believed that one is an 'Indian first, and a journalist next.' According to the First Press Commission, the press should help secure and protect a social order in which justice (social, economic and political) would prevail.

But the role of the press in India need not be that of an adversary or of an ally of the government. The press should be a watch-dog and act as a catalytic agent to hasten the process of social and economic change.

The perspective of an adversary role for the press derives from the assumption that the press is the voice of the public, is above corruption, and that the government, though deriving power from the people, might misuse it. It must be noted that the press is part of the political process, craves for power, is made up of people with personal ambitions and aversions, preferences and prejudices. As perhaps the largest advertiser, the government supports and strengthens the press. Both the government and the press represent the 'power elites,' and therefore reflect their interests. This is why the interests of the poor are rarely on the agenda of public discussion.

The press is so obsessed with politics that even a silly rumour hits the front page. What the press urgently needs is creative, investigative and development reporting chiefly on non-political themes like unemployment, malnutrition, exploitation of the poor, miscarriage of justice, police atrocities, development schemes and the like. The exposure of the blinding incidents at Bhagalpur, which would have never come to light but for the alert press, is just one example of the heights the Indian press can sometimes scale. Recent examples include the Bofors pay-offs, the Harshad Mehta securities scam, the 'hawala' payments to top politicians, and the animal husbandry scandal in Bihar.

But follow-up investigations of these public scams are lacking, and are rarely pursued to the end. The press whips up interest in a scam to a crescendo, then forgets about it when another scam is unearthed. Such 'crisis' reporting sells newspapers but does little to bring the guilty to book or to educate the public about the contexts of corruption.

Credibility is indeed the very life-blood of the press, no matter which government is in power. The period of the Emergency showed how the credibility of the press could suffer. There are other reasons why credibility suffers, the chief being the unduly heavy dependence on official press handouts by business and government. When, for example, there is a strike or riot, the Police Department's handout is printed without comment. On-the-spot investigative reports are few and far between.

Further, journalists are inclined to accept many favours from government such as subsidised housing and medical facilities, and it is therefore not surprising that they rush to the same government when they have differences with editors, and with management, or when they demand higher salaries and better working conditions. "An awesome responsibility", remarks the veteran editor, S. Nihal Singh, "rests on the shoulders of journalists because in the final analysis they are the custodians of the freedom of the press. If they prefer careerism to standing up for their rights, they are letting down their profession." However, the press is much too important in a democracy to be entrusted entirely to journalists; a vigilant public, the courts and the Press Council are needed to keep a watchful eye on it.

For Strength

The 'power' of the press to bring about social and political change or economic development is extremely limited. In capitalist societies, the press is primarily like any other business or industry: it exists to raise advertising revenue and circulation with the aim of making profits. 'Public service' and 'public interest' are not the main concerns.

This is not to suggest that the press does not make attempts to exercise its 'power' in favour of one political or economic ideology over another, or of one group or class or caste over another. These attempts, it must be acknowledged, are sometimes successful and at other times disastrous failures. At most times, however, the attempts are not paid much heed to, unless it affects some group's interests in a radical manner.

In the ultimate analysis, the 'power' of the press depends on its credibility among readers, as well as on how the news reported is understood and interpreted. Different groups 'read' the same news item in varied ways depending on their own social backgrounds. How news is read is not entirely in the hands of journalists. Indeed, the press often succeeds only in reinforcing widely held beliefs and the status quo rather than bringing about change and development.

Does the press 'set the agenda' for us and for society? There is no doubt that the press keeps us informed about selected events, issues and people. But the public too has a role in 'setting the agenda' of the press. The public has interests, beliefs and expectations that are catered to by the press. While the press tells us what to think about, and also what to think, it has little power to change our ideas, beliefs and attitudes even when it attempts to do so. Only when there is a general consensus on an issue among all the elements of the press and the other media, and this consensus fits in with a community's needs, is there some likelihood of a change being effected. Even in this case, several other factors would have to come into play before any real change can be felt.

The public attitude to the 'internal emergency' imposed by the Indira Gandhi regime is a case in point. One could argue, however, that it was not so much the press that brought about the downfall of that regime as the people's hostility to the crackdown on their fundamental rights. The press, after all, was easily silenced during the emergency. In the post-emergency period, the press only reflected the public's seething anger against the regime.

By and large, then, the press rarely initiates change, innovation and development. Because of its dependence on commercial interests and the dominant groups, it is of necessity conservative and status-quoist. The widespread support that the anti-Mandal riots and the 'liberalisation' policies of the Government have received from the 'national' and the 'regional' press is a reflection of that dependence. The current news values of Indian journalists are no different from the news values of their counterparts in the West. These are timeliness, immediacy, proximity, oddity, conflict, mystery, suspense, curiosity and novelty. The new development/alternative journalists, however, challenge-these elite and immediacy-oriented values, and the man-bites-dog approach to news. They believe that the voice of the silent, suffering majority should be heard through the press. Not politics, business, finance, sports should be the staple of news but rather what is of value in terms of equality, social justice and peace.

Chief Characteristics

In past, the Indian Press, besides Indian literature, played a distinctive role as a medium of public opinion. The Indian Press was not necessarily Indian-owned. Some of these were either owned by Europeans or staffed by individuals, who had some sympathy for the Indian aspirations. Their pro-Indian bias often found expression in editorial columns and in feature articles. The authorities were not slow in coming down heavily on them. Several of the European editors, William Duane, Charles Mclean, James Silk 'Buckingham, Sandford Arnot were some of the victims of deportation under orders of the Government. But they were exceptions. On the whole, the Anglo-Indian English language papers gave unstinted support to all moves by the authorities that be, in practising racial discrimination, acts of social injustice, denial of the right to education, economic disparities and hindrances to the growth of nationhood.

Local Press

The Vernacular language papers as also Indian-owned News papers in English, however, gave publicity to nearly all misdeeds of racial arrogance and never fought to expose the lapses of officials, as a corollary to a policy based of discrimination and denial. As Hunter put it, they raised their voice despite risks of deportation and under menace of the censor's rod. Surendranath and Tilak, as is well-known, suffered imprisonment while eminent journalists from Harish Chander Mukherjee to Ramananda Chatterjee consistently braved the wrath of the authorities. From the beginning of the 20th century their role become more positive and their ideas tended to expand.

Their writings were freely punctuated with Swaraj or self rule, constitutional rights, democratic norms and civil liberties. The Pioneer, the Indian Herald, the Independence, the Hindu Patriot, the Indu Prakash, the Indian Mirror and the Amrit Bazar Patrika, to name only a few, did enormously contribute to the education of public opinion, convincing the people that even good government cannot be a substitute for 'Self-Government'. The growing influence of the Press alarmed the rulers and to curb it, they chose to strike at the vernacular language papers at the first instance. The series of repressive measures adopted by the Government, as we know, could not stifle the Press. It survived all onslaughts and continued to serve the people by instilling in them nation list outlook and by stressing the need of constituting themselves into well-knit organisations. The efforts of the Government to muzzle the press was bound to be a failure as the other media, like schools and colleges, remained unaffected.

As Bhupendranath Bose observed: You will have to stop the

printing of unlicensed books. The possession of a copy of Milton or Burke or Macaulay or of Brights speeches and all the flashing array of writers and authors who are the glory of our grand, and our noble English tongue, the possession of anyone of these books will on this peculiar and puerile notion of Government to be like the possession of a bomb, and we shall have to direct the passing of an Explosive Books Act.

Press Abroad

Qualitatively, it may be presumed, the impact of the English language papers was more important, but from the quantitative point of view, the vernacular papers were not only read but also read out to many who were not literature. One may reasonably argue that in spite of all that it had done, the Press did not exhort enough and failed to satisfy the Nationalists or the Extremists.

A colonial Press could ill-afford to take on a positively hostile role. Even then the importance their role cannot be underestimated. Their role was on the whole effective if not in restraining the rulers to the extent desired, certainly in pressing for civil rights, democratic norms and a clean and just administration. The various measures of repression by the British authorities bring to our mind the truth of a statement attributed to Napoleon Bonaparte:

A journalist is a grumbler, a censurer, a giver of advice, aregent of sovereign, a tutor of nations. Four hostile newspapers are more to be feared than a thousand bayonets.

One is also likely to be reminded of the couplets composed by James Montgomery:

The Press

"What is the Press-I cried;

When thus a wonderous voice replied;

"In me all human knowledge dwells; the oracle a oracles;

Past, present, future, I reveal,
Or in oblivious silence seal,
What I preserve can perish never,
What I forget is lost for ever."

Liberty of Expression

Theoretically viewed, the Press in India is free today. It is also true that the newspapers have developed new techniques with the object of coming into closer contact with public. Inactivate programmes like general knowledge tests, cross word puzzles, comic sketches and illustrations are regular features. Advertisement is assigned a sizeable space in any news paper worth its name. This follows from the fact that newspaper advertising is today a vital factor in national industry and salesmanship. An advertising agent, it has been said, instead of being a mere conduit type has become a highly scientific expert. Newspapers have reaped the benefit of originality, resource, thought and enterprise which advertising consultants apply to their business.

Newspapers of today are also known to have developed new techniques with the object of coming into closer contact with the public. One such device is Public opinion Poll which has assumed added importance in the context of the latest General Election, for instance. Such Polls are a more improved device than the older game of "Consequences" in the series "What the world said." The device of Opinion Polls is not like the 'Consequences', a post-mortem device.

It is, by nature, anticipatory. It is a sample survey aimed at ascertaining peoples' views on coming events. Apart from newspapers, Radio and Television adopt this strategy and spend fortunes on it, seeking to let the readers know the world's opinion on various subjects under the sun from the hydrogen bomb to breakfast cereals.

The targets are people of all sorts, or to be more precise, the ordinary people. This device, an enormously-expensive one, is sought to be justified on the ground that a modern democratic government should be interested in knowing what they think or how they react to important topics. One cannot rule out the possibility that the interviewers appointed to conduct these polls may put ideas into peoples' minds instead of discovering their real opinions. In other words, such polls may in the end reflect the opinion of the interviewers more than those of the interviewed. It is also possible that a poll verdict may misfire. One instance that comes to mind is the 1948 polls in the US Presidential Election. Although all the polls confidently predicted the victory of the Republican party candidate, Governor Dewey of New York, the actual results :showed the Democratic Party nominee, Harry S. Truman, winning by a comfortable margin.

DIFFERENT SURVEYS

Even then the fact remains that sample surveys have been a regular feature in the assessment of public opinion. Any topic under the sun may be chosen as the subject-matter of such polls. In U.K., for instance, polls have been held on such subjects as British holiday habits or Cross Channel Traffic as a guide to the prospect of a Channel Tunnel. Local authorities in different countries are known to have used them for guidance in planning amenities. Similarly, manufactures have resorted to them for estimating the prospect of marketing one or other of their new products-a tooth brush or a paste. It is on record that an interviewer sent out, say, by a toothpaste manufacturing firm, may ask their users to give them their opinion of the taste, colour and packing as well as the actual quality. In some instances, such a probe may be quite interesting. Here is an example. Sometimes an interviewer from a newspaper or an advertising agency arms himself with the previous day's papers. During his visit he asks which one the person usually takes, goes through it with him, noting which article he reads thoroughly, which he skims through, and which he skips altogether, and also which advertisements have caught his eye and as on.

Newspapers in India too are not averse to innovative programmes as referred to earlier. They are not concerned merely with reportage and dissemination of information about events. They also provide for recording of views and comments by experts and competent critics and observers on current trends and incidents, apart from those expressed in the leading articles as Editorials. This is a welcome move but it has some limitations in practice. The columnists, generally speaking, are persons who hold certain ideas or values to which their writings naturally confirm. And the discerning readers known what to expect from a columnist attached to a particular paper. They divide themselves into two broad categories-pro-and anti establishment. Their views are not consistently or strictly objective.

Challenge to Press

An additional threat to impartial assessment and effective remedy arises from the affiliation of a number of newspapers and periodicals, especially party organs, to one or other political party. This often results in partisan accounts, if not distortions. The evil of vested interest cannot possibly be eliminated from the presentation of news both in western countries and in India. In case of the former, it is however possible to cite instances in recent years when they have fought, valiantly acts of injustice as vigilant watch-dogs of the peoples' rights and even compelled mighty offenders to submit to public opinion, I wish I could make a similar claim on behalf of our newspapers.

In a large number of cases they are yet to develop an investigating wing. They are yet not in a mood to report on academic dereliction, corruption at the administrative and other levels, instances or gross lapses involving palpable social injustice, economic exploitation and even huge loss to the Exchequer and non-functioning of essential service-units. The powers that be practise an ostrich-like strategy and are reluctant to institute probes into all cases of alleged assaults on human right and dignity. Even when inquiry is ordered, the findings are not made known. The character of a crime is of well determined by the political affiliations of its perpetrator.

Certain basic factors relating to the weakness of the working of our democratic norms also deserve to be considered in this context. We extol democracy, but we remain blind to its lapses and contradictions in practice. This is due to a variety of reasons. I need cite only two main ones. Our literacy rate fails face short of the demands of a democratic state. Thus is a positive hindrance to the interests of a free and impartial press. Secondly, our press today is largely an industry run on predominantly professional lines by a group of individuals forming themselves into a sort of close corporation, primarily interested in profit making like any other investors in industry.

Or again, in a number of cases, they are committed to some ideologies which often make them imprevious to the other view. Not unoften when their self-interest demand, they do sacrifice truth and indulge in deliberate distortions. A recent assessment of the journalistic trends of today reads as follows:

Press and Practices

The general trend in newspapers whose proprietors in a number of cases have appropriated for themselves the role of Editors, has been disturbing enough. In regard to newspapers owned by industrial houses or business groups, truthful or honest reporting is none of their strong points. This offers a striking contrast to the code of journalism such as generally found favour with newspapers in pre-independence days. Excessive loyalties to owners, families or groups, as the case may be, have brought down individual or group-owned newspapers to a deplorable state in which they are no longer, as they formerly used to be, the zealous guardians of public morality, ethics and justice.

It is not my intention to single out the newspapers as solely responsible for the deficiencies referred to above. The versions of news or events announced over the Radio or presented in the news bulletins of T. V. are not unoften at variance with one another. Press communiques emanating from official sources are in most cases deliberately worded in oracular language and are accordingly difficult to comprehend. Not infrequently one is at a less to know where there truth lies, making confusion more confounded. This brings us to the question often asked-Can Radios, TVs and electronic media with all their sophisticated gadgets act as a substitute for newspapers? A TV set, for instance, provides no doubt feast for the eyes and the ears and serves out news all around the globe. It does not ordinarily offer comments for those who would like to be told about their import and implications.

A newspaper on the country give not only information on happenings here and abroad but also offers comments and observations on the same. The appeal is more deep-rooted, affecting our thinking process-the mind and the intellect, not merely the sense organs. Newspapers in such circumstances have little chance of suffering in importance. A TV. set cannot be a substitute for newspaper any more than for a book. Newspapers and books will continue to survive.

Significance of Letters

A review of the newspapers service would, however, remain inconclusive if a mention is not made of one of its essential sections which unfortunately has not received the attention it deserves. I mean the correspondence addressed to the Editor. To me, these are better vehicles of contemporary public thinking than even Special Representative's Reports. They not only give expression to feelings entertained by the writers, who in more cases represent the average section of the readers, but also place proper focus on the problem or problems on which the correspondents either seek clarification or express their own reactions, contrary to those expressed in the medium itself. The correspondents are obviously not ordinary newspaper readers.

They are communicators as well. It has been rightly claimed

that they are a separate category who use a newspaper as another medium to communicate their messages. They are essentially not in the business of communication, that is educated men and women, who feel impelled to respond to developments and to a newspaper's reports or comment, on them, though they affect them as much or as little that those do millions of others. They are public spirited though they are not public men.

They practise a kind of journalism, though they are not journalists. They can be interested and partisan; or they can be disinterested and nonpartisan; in either case they give life to a newspaper. It would not be an exaggeration to say that a newspaper is best judged by the quality of its readers 'views' columns.

The Times of India with a record of nearly two centuries of service behind it did an excellent job when it brought out to mark its Sequencial, the volume-Feed Back-Letters to the Editor of the Times of India, 1938-1988. In doing so they have provided us with a source-material on the nature and growth of public opinion over a period of a century and a half, whose importance cannot be underestimated. They have brought out the invisible but essential constituent of a news paper organisation. The newspaper world of India has expanded its scope of interest and activities over the year. In 1946 Jawaharlal Nehru advised the All India Newspaper Editors' Conference to think of starting their own foreign news service of a number of newspapers which could combine, he said, for the purpose and appoint their agents. I quote :

> I would particularly like them to go to places which are not sufficiently covered by other agencies on South East Asia, the Middle East and the rest of the world.

That deficiency does not exist today. To me the deficiency in present-day urban-based newspaper relates to news from the districts which find a negligible coverage in our dailies. This perhaps accounts for the steady rise in the number of District newspapers, especially periodicals. Their circulation is obviously limited and they are yet to find markets in urban centres. While international and global news demand their legitimate quota in a newspaper worth its name, is it not possible to devise some ways and means for lifting the virtual black-out of muffassil news in urban-based dailies.

I have been trying to share with you my hopes as well as fears in regard to the Press which, in spite of the electronic media, continues to be the most powerful single medium of public opinion. I have been emboldened to place the theme before you. The editor and the corps of journalistic variants merely do not constitute the newspaper personality. The readers are also an essential element who alone can assure its credibility. But the picture remains incomplete even then, Public Relations men are a vital part of the newspaper world.

The combination of all those constituents alone can impart to a newspaper the strength to resist pressures and be independent in the true sense of the term. If the Press in India in colonial days, played an effective role of which we feel proud, it can reasonably be expected that the Press would fight the battle with the same vigour and tenacity against the evils which, surround us-arrogance of power, challenge of casteism and communalism, growing social and economic disparities, the proneness to prefer parties to the country and the lack of cohesion in working together in areas of common accord.

If for reasons which are of a diverse nature it is not immediately possible for the Press and other media of opinion to revive the old tradition, Public Relations may be expected to give more thought to the problems and come up with a plan and programme so that public opinion is effectively reflected in the conduct of the government. A look around the present is enough to make one cynical, as I know the task ahead of us is pretty difficult. As I conclude, I am only reminded of the cynical comments of Samuel Butler. The public buys its opinion as it bags its meat, or takes in its milk on the principle that it is cheaper to do this than to keep a cow. So it is, but the milk is more likely to be watered

Middle Time

There has always been a practice of maintaining some kind of communication between the government and the people in the past. It was held more obligatory on the part of the reigning monarch to develop media of communication between his government and the masses during the Muslim rule in medieval India. There were several means of mass communication in medieval India, some independent and some other under the royal patronage. The independent means of mass communication were folklores, folk—tales, lyrics, songs, poetry, stories etc. those under the royal patronage included reading of khutabah, issue and broadcast of orders, issue of new coins, grants, reliefs, release of prisoners, open costs and public punishments, and the Dak system.

Here, it will be relevant to begin with a discussion of the media under the royal patronage. The accession of a new Emperor has always been one of the most important event of all times and required quick and wide publicity. Let us take an example of accession of a new Emperor and see as to how was it communicated to the people living in different parts of the empire. During the Muslim rule, when a new Emperor ascended the throne he took a new title as a mark of departure from his non-royal past "a Salim would blossom forth into a Jahangir, a Khurram into a Shahjahan." His title, along with his name, was popularised by issue of an order, coins, rants and reliefs, and sometimes, by release of prisoners. But the popular proclamation would come on Friday following the accession. Friday prayer of Muslims has a special significance, because, on Fridays all the Muslim of a locality assemble in the local mosque to offer their mid-day prayer. This prayer starts with the reading of Khutbah by the Imam of the mosque.

The Khutbah is a form of praise and prayer of God, the prophet, his 12 descendants, royalty and the sovereign. It included the praise of, and prayer for the sovereign. The mention of the

Emperor's name in the Khutbah constituted a legal proclamation of his accession to the throne. Since Khutbah was read before a large assembly of Muslims it served as a means of mass communication. It was so significant that if a provincial governor ever rebelled against the Emperor, he communicated his rebellion by taking a new title, ascending the throne as an independent monarch and getting the Khutbah read in his name.

A change of a regime of a successful crop was usually communicated to the masses in the same manner. Sometimes it included a very crude way of displaying the head of the slain ruler. Allauddin Khilji did it when he attempted a successful coup against his uncle and father-in-law, Jalaluddin in Karrah (Allahabad). Rulers have always been a source of inspiration to the people, who aspired, in the medieval times too, to have a glimpse of their rulers. Whenever, during his regime, Akbar, happened to travel through the countryside, people living in distant places used to gather in thousands to have a glimpse of the Emperor. But those, living in the capital and in the vicinity thereof, had the opportunity of face-to-face communication with the Emperor in Jharokha Darshan. Jharokha Darshan was personal appearance of the Emperor on the Jharokha (window) with the intention of freely meeting the people and receiving their petitions.

It was introduced by Akbar and became an established tradition during the region of his Successors. Even Aurangzeb continued it for a few years. It was a revival of an ancient Hindu custom, the object of which was to enable the common people to have direct access to the king. It was like an open and informal court (Darbar).

All kinds of people, high and low, men and women, were permitted to meet the emperor and present their petitions. People from distant places also came in Jharokha Darshan to meet the Emperor and seek his blessings. Badauni, a contemporary of Akbar, complains about the 'low people' assembling in Jharokha Darshan in Akbar's time suggests that the institution worked effectively under Akbar who spent about four and a half hours regularly in Jharokha Darshan. Though it was always a crowded affair and full of bustle, all important details and every word uttered by the Emperor was recorded in writing for further action. Thus the institution of Jharokha Darshan served as a means of mass communication during the regime of great Mughals.

Similarly, the open courts were also meant to communicate with the people. In certain cases the convicts were punished in public before a large assembly of people. The purpose was to communicate to the people about the gravity of the crime and its evil consequences. Punishment in the form of public degradation was inflicted throughout the medieval period. This punishment took the form of sometimes shaving the head of the criminal and parading him on as with his face turned towards its back and sometimes blackening the face of the culprit and parading him through the streets. In certain cases the criminals were punished in more torturous ways. The purpose was same as to create an awareness.

Crime and punishment have always been important material for the news. All such cases of crime and punishment were popularised soon in the form of stories. Not only crime and punishment but every instance of strange event, bravery, warfare, craft and cheating, sex scandals and adultery or a simple love story were communicated to the people in the form of some narrative. This means of transmission of these narratives was oratory. Oratory was an excellent means for diffusion of ideas. There were many learned and eloquent speakers known as 'Muzakkirs'. Their narratives, known as 'Tazkirs' were attentively listened to by scholars, artists, poets and others. Thetoric art was so gifted that it moved the audience into loud wailing and bursting of tears. Many such, stories and narratives are recorded in the historical works of medieval India. Thus, in the form of a book these narratives reached the educated and learned classes at different places and served as a media. Sometimes myths were also included among these narratives. The purpose was same as to create an atmosphere of awareness, to make people fearless and to develop in them more faith about the Emperor and his regime.

Apart from the above-mentioned media, there was a regular bilateral communication of information between the centre and the provinces and smaller units of the empire. There were official news writers (Waqainawis) posted at the court, provinces, districts and parganas. In fact news and espionage systems were so associated with each other that they were usually treated as twins. The intelligence officers (Barids) were the actual source of all kind of information to the Emperor.

Besides, the officers of different department, the provincial officers also gathered and sent information to the Emperor. Each and every matter concerning the state, wealth, land, revenue, crime and punishment, etc., was communicated to the Emperor. On the part of the Emperor all important matters relating to orders, reliefs, war and peace, administration, etc., were communicated to the people through their local officers.

The collection and dissemination of information was conducted by the superintendent of intelligence and posts (daroga-i-dak-chauki) who worked under the Prime Minister (Wazir) of the Empire. On the basis of his recommendations news writers were appointed in every province, district and parganas.. They were called Waqainawis or Waqainigar and.were directed to report all important occurrences in the province, district, or pargana where they happened to have been posted. They were posted in large towns, important markets were also attached to every field army. During the regimes of the Sultans like Balban and Allauddin Khilji, spies did this work and reported everything to the Sultan.

But in the Mughal period the system was much more organised. During the regime of Akbar, "fourteen zealous, experienced and impartial clerks" were appointed by the Emperor himself. Two of them were always on duty with the Emperor and their duties were so arranged that turn of each came after a fortnight. Abul Fazal gives a detailed account of their duties.

He writes, "Their duty is to write down the orders and doings of his Majesty and whatever the heads of the departments report; what his Majesty eats and drinks, when he sleeps, and when he rises; the etiquette in the state hall; the time his majesty spends in the Harem, when he goes to the, general and private assemblies the nature of hunting parties, the slaying of animals; when he marches, and when he halts; etc. They also maintained records of all appointments increase or decrease of taxes, despatch, the issue of order, the arrival of reports etc., All these records in the form a diary were corrected by one of the Emperor's servants, and then laid before the Emperor for approval. Copies of all such reports and records were made available to those who required them. The same records, after they were signed by the officers and the Emperor became the memorandum (Yadasht). It is evident that all such records were sources of information and served as media. It is also evident that these were made available to the official historians who, incorporated them into their historical accounts.

During the Sultanate period (1206-1526 AD) the local chiefs (Hakims) gathered all the relevant information and sent to the Emperor. But during the Mughal period (1526-1707) there was a separate post of Waqainawis in the provinces and he was required to work independently and honestly. Usually the post of the provincial Waqainawis was held by the Bakshi (the officer in-charge of military establishment) in addition to his duties. As Bakshi he was subordinate to the Government of the province but as Waqainawis he was independent of the Governor and was in direct contact with the central Government. In fact, he was required to report about the Governor's administration and conduct.

Thus, he exercised some kind of check on his immediate chief i.e., the provincial Governor. The independent and honest functioning of the Waqainawis was held very high and if someone caused any hindrance in the discharge of their duties he was not spared. During the regime of Emperor Jahangir the Governor of Gujarat was dismissed for manhandling the Waqainawis of

Ahmedabad who had recorded among (current) events certain affairs that implicated the Governor.

It must not be held that the Waqainawis were always very sincere and discharged their duties honestly. Some times -they entered into collusion with the local officers and failed to discharge their duties satisfactorily. Therefore, another category of news writers called the Sawanihgars or Kufianawis were appointed to reside secretly in the provinces and act as a spy and a check on the Waqainawis. They were posted at special places and on important occasion also. There was another class of News-writers known as harkaras. It was most secret class of news writers. They were posted in provinces and sent their reports along with the provincial posts to the capital.

On their part the provincial Waqainawis appointed their assistants to the districts and parganas and received information through them regularly. Sometimes news-writers were appointed to the districts and parganas directly from the Imperial Court. Thus there was a complete chain of transmission of information. All the news-writers were required to send information regularly. The Waqainawis sent his report once a week. Sawanihnigar or Khufia nawis sent twice a week, and the harkras once a month.

All the information was sent through an organised regular postal system. During the Sultanate period the post was of two kinds. The horse-post called litage and the foot-post known as dawa. The horse-post was run by the royal horses stationed at every mile. The foot-post had three stations per mile. At every station there was a pavilion in which sat the orders, always ready to carry the dark. Ibn Batuta, who was in Delhi Sultanate the regime of Muhammad Bin Tughlaq account of the dak system of the Sultanate period. He writes, "Each (courier) carried a rod, two cubits in the length with copper belts at the top. When the courier starts from the city he holds the letter in one hand and the rod in the other, and he runs as fast as he can. When the men in the pavilion hear the ringing of the bells they get ready. As soon as the courier reaches them one of them takes the letter from his hands and runs at the top speed shaking the rod all the while until he reaches the next dawa. And the same process continues till the letter reaches its destination.

This speedy postal system was controlled by a postal superintendent (malik-ul-barid) who acted as news-writer also.

When Shershah came to power, he improved this postal system to a considerable extent by construction of several roads with sarai's or rest houses along with them at interval of four miles. These sarais not only served as rest-houses for travellers but also as stations of dak chauki. This definitely improved the postal efficiency and the Shershah could get prompt information of every important matter through this relay postal system even from the remotest part of the empire. The office-in-charge of this postal system was Daroga-i-Dak-Chauki. His agents brought news in all ways, on foot and on horse, by rivers or over the mountains. This system continued during the Mughal regime. The horsemen and despatch-runners (couriers) were posted at a distance of one or two miles on the roads. They carried the information from one station to the other.

The promptness of this system depended upon the running of the couriers. During the Mughal regime Mewras were employed as despatch runners. They were basically soldiers and were famous as fast-runners. Emperor Akbar inducted them into the postal service. They are specially mentioned, in Ain-i-Akbari, as fast-runners and postmen. Among them there were certain runners who in one day could run on foot as fast as a horseman could ride at full speed.

2

The Backdrop

In the modern context, newspapers cannot compete with radio or TV in being first and fast with news. They can, however, serve independently and as supplementary to these media by giving more balanced account of news alongwith backgrounds, better interpretative, investigated and thorough reporting and coverage, wider variety of reading material and shades of opinions in their columns.

Magazines deal more with opinion interpretation, incisiveness and colour. Noticed or read by the elite and policy makers, leaders of parties and professions, as also by workers, farmers, students and housewives, they can influence public opinion and more so the policy makers.

Today, the press is not merely observing and reporting but asking, pursuing, investigating, doubting, demanding and sometimes even biting. It is far more vigilant and rancorous about fundamental and civil rights, corruption, economic exploitation and social abuses. Modern newspapers illuminate the mind through their cartoons, illustrations, graphics, features and human interest writings. They highlight or underline particular events by their headlines, leads, cutlines and column boxes. Their searching interviews, columnist writings and editorials furnish better comprehension of complicated events and affairs.

Reader columns in newspapers tie in readers and provide noticeable columns of public grievances. There are also engagement columns, notices, fitting advertisements, etc. for those who need them. Notwithstanding occasional bias and slants in reporting and writing, their concentrated urban approach and obsession with political and sensational news, professionally competent and disciplined dailies and magazines command comparatively better respect, credibility and acceptability than any other media. Even grassroots media, community papers and other small professional or specialised periodicals are dear to readers, though for different reasons. Thus, newspapers today occupy a prestigious position in the galaxy of media with their roles varying from the 4th Estate to the 5th Estate, from an informer to a critic, from a narrator to a commentator, from an investigator to an analyst, from a mentor to a teaser, from a peace preacher to violence or racialism baiter.

In developing countries the press has a special role to play as a social monitor, a constructive critic, the stimulator of debates on public issues and a medium of feedback while balancing the wheel of the Governmental structure. A great social vitaliser and the right arm of liberty, it is also a big enemy of tyrants and an exposer of public corruption. The media is also an interpreter of public events and a professional forum for investigative and interpretative journalism. It acts as a watchdog of a sleeping democracy and a public university for the masses. "A people without reliable newspapers," said Harold Laski, "is sooner or later a people without the basis for freedom."

History in View

In India, Independence constituted a turning point in the history of the Indian Press. It brought to a close the era of journalism as a mission and the media was left free to become a business or an industry. Refashioning the Press was part of the larger enterprise of refashioning society. The partition of the country made the Muslim League-dominated newspapers to quit or lapse. Consequently the Urdu and Bengali press suffered the most. Some of the important Urdu papers from Lahore sought to find a new home in Delhi, Amritsar and Jalandhar. The Anglo-Saxon group of papers lost their punch, homogeneity and *raison d'etre* as a group.

Comparing the Indian press then with the contemporary press in the West, there was no national newspaper in India which could play the role of an activist or act as the voice of the nation. There was not a single daily in the country with a circulation of even one lakh. The Times of India printed 94748 copies, the Hindu 69748, the Statesman 65032 and the Hindustan Times 48141 copies. The circulation of these big papers was in fact a pittance of the circulation of some foreign newspapers of the time: Le Petit journal selling more than a million copies per issue since 1886; in 1900 the daily Mail, London crossed the seven figure mark; in 1979, the Japanese Yomiuri Shimbun sold over 13 million copies per day in a nation of about 110 million. In Britain with a population of about 55 million the Sun sold four million copies a day.

The position of Indian language dailies was still lower. *Swadesamitran* with 39509 copies was considered a top-notch language daily; then followed *Sakal* (27262), *Mathrubhumi* (25736) and *Andhra Patrika* (23086). There were no worthwhile dailies in several states and languages. The capacity of newspapers, therefore, to influence public opinion for good or bad was of a limited nature.

Another feature of the Indian press was its concentration. Our of a total of 330 dailies, five owners controlled 29 papers and 31.2 per cent of circulation, while 15 owners controlled 54 newspapers and 50.1 per cent of the circulation. The Telugu daily Andhra Patrika, selling 23086 copies accounted for more than 50 per cent of the circulation in its language area. The diffusion rate which is an index of media growth was 7 per thousand.

The circumstances after the partition were alarmingly unsettling, but despite handicaps the Press in general increasingly turned its attention to the numerous constructive tasks ahead. The news started being presented and interpreted from that angle. Gradually newspapers strove for improved professional techniques and conveniences. Important or big newspapers began to enlist the services of special correspondents and seek more facilities of various kinds. Feature writings got impetus. Some eminent journalists like M. V. Kamath, Khushwant Singh, Kuldip Nayar, Dom Moraes, Arun Shourie, B. G. Verghese, A. G. Noorani, Shoba Kilachand, Abu Abraham, etc., achieved distinction by writing their sparkling by-lined columns in big English newspapers and magazines. The language newspapers too inducted equally famous personalities. In fact, some newspapers became popular because of these columns.

Most papers also followed the technique of writing behind-the-scene stories based on current affairs. That made newspapers more readable and in turn attracted more readers. Starting from R. K. Karanjia and Baburao Patel and passing on to Khushwant Singh, M J. Akbar, Ashwini Sarin, Neeraj Chaudhary, Pritish Nandy, Aroon Purie, Chaitanya Kelbag and Vikram Vohra emerged enterprising people journalism, which talked about not only political shenanigans and scoops but also focussed on prominent personalities, their life-styles, fads and habits. Couched in chatty, masala style, these writings made newspapers readable and provocative.

Journalists like Khushwant Singh gave a package of religion, sex and politics including jokes and made-up stories, which made some magazines and newspapers more poplar and caused an increase in their sale. M. J. Akbar's redressing of the Telegraph and Pritish Nandy's revamping of The Illustrated Weekly of India as a feature magazine, are other promotional devices to give a new look to publications and boost their circulation.

Journalistic ranks have expanded and management has shown signs of improvements. The result of these developments was a rise in circulation. As for the various language press, the increase in circulation was a cumulative result of the increase in formal education, rise in purchasing power caused by growing industrialisation, trade and commerce, the information explosion caused by the spurt of new planned programmes, acrimonious politics and class, caste and communal clashes, expansion of communications and transport facilities, the awakening caused by general elections, mass media and advertising expansion. Consequently the circulation of some dailies and weeklies touched record levels.

Quantitatively the press grew enormously both in terms of dailies and periodicals and their circulation (average number of copies sold or distributed free per publishing day). The number of all newspapers-covering any printed or cyclostyled periodical publication like dailies, weeklies and other periodicals-rose from 4769 and 1952 to 19937 in 1982, with a few periods of steep ascents like in 1970, 1979 and 1981 when there was a rise both in terms of number and circulation. Since the sixties the number of dailies quadrupled from a modest 330 to 1334 and periodicals of all categories and periodicity also expanded four times from 4439 to 18603. The circulation of all reporting newspapers depicts the same scale of having rocketed from over 1052000 to 50094000-more than five times, and of dailies from 2.5 millions in 1947 to 14.84 millions in 1982, indicating a six-fold expansion. The spurt in the circulation of periodicals during the last three decades was more pronounced and rose from 8 million to over 35 million-nearly four and a half times. This phenomenal expansion in number and circulation of periodicals is popularly known as the periodical or magazine explosion.

This quantitative stride has some important implications. The first is that now newspapers and periodicals are published by more States and Union Territories than in the sixties. Blanks where no newspaper is published are only Arunachal Pradesh and

Lakshadweep and thin areas are Nagaland, Andaman and Nicobar, Goa, Daman and Diu, Mizoram, Pondicherry, Meghalaya, Tripura, Manipur and Himachal Pradesh. So even today, at one end of Press development are heavyweight States and Union Territories like Maharashtra, West Bengal, Uttar Pradesh, Kerala, Delhi and Tamil Nadu where a large number of newspapers with sizable circulation originate; at the other end are blank or thin areas in this respect. Similarly there is a wide variation yet in the circulation of dailies per thousand population (an important criteria to judge whether a place is below or above UNESCO's minimum norm of 100 copies per thousand or population).

The range among the States differs from 44.14 copies in Kerala and 24.71 in Maharashtra to 3.62 copies in Nagaland, 2.72 copies in Sikkim and 1.95 copies in Assam. Among Union Territories the scale moves from 116.22 in Chandigarh and 48.36 in Delhi to 0.95 in Mizoram and 0.01 in Dadra and Nagar Haveli.

The second important feature of this growth pattern is a revelation of much faster rate of development in languages than in English. In fact a silent revolution has been taking place in the course of which the two century old dominance of the Press in English has been overcome by the Indian language Press in terms of both number and circulation. And it is not merely that the total circulation of all Hindi Newspapers including dailies has surpassed that of English newspapers, but the number and circulation of language newspapers as a whole has gone up. Also, in areas outside metropolitan cities, language newspapers have generally eclipsed every other English newspaper issued from these areas. The rate of growth of newspapers in Malayalam, Bengali, Kannada, Punjabi and Telugu is conspicuously high. In comparison, however, the share of Tamil, Urdu, Marathi and Gujarati in the total circulation chart has recorded a downward trend.

It is interesting to note that the circulation of some Indian language newspapers has reached spectacular proportions. The Anand Bazar Patrika in Bengali with a circulation of 416514 copies retains the pride of place as the largest circulated single daily in 1981 followed by another Bengali daily, Jugantar with a circulation of 314018 copies. Among periodicals Malayala Manorama, a Malayalam weekly from Kottayam, has the largest circulation.

Modern View

Another notable trend in the Indian press is towards localism. Purely local interest newspapers appear to be gaining ground at the expense of regional or national dailies. Pune affords a significant example. Three local Marathi dailies Sakat, Kesari, and Tarun Bharat not only compete with two big dailies originating from Bombay but command around 90 per cent of the total circulation of the five dailies in Pune. Similarly the dominance of the English daily Tribune of Chandigarh has not been surpassed by prestigious national English dailies coming in from Delhi.

Newspapers in India continue to be largely an urban phenomenon. Even in that respect there is a concentration inter se. Over 30 per cent of the newspapers are located in the four metropolitan cities. State capitals account for nearly 17 per cent. Other big cities with a population of over one lakh contain 30 per cent of the total. There are eighteen cities which account for 50 per cent of the total number of newspapers in the country. Only a handful of rural newspapers exist (which devote 40 per cent of their contents for rural areas).

Dailies are completely urban. But the analysis of publication of newspapers bring out one significant point that more newspapers are published from cities and towns other than metropolitan cities and state capitals. The reason is that except English papers which are largely concentrated in the four metropolitan cities, Hindi papers are published mainly from medium towns (with a population of one lakh and more) while the press in Assamese, Bengali, Kannada and Tamil are mostly concentrated in the State capital towns.

Location may be a matter of convenience or the question of availability of printing facilities. But circulation pattern is a better norm of judging how far medium serves the rural people. Dailies coming from big cities claim more than nineteenths of the total circulation of dailies in the country. The Press Commission's study of 11 dailies (4 big, 5 medium and 2 small) reveals that rural circulation of these papers varied from 9.75 to 21.96 per cent in the case of nine papers and in the case of Dinamani of Madras and Yugadharma of Jaipur, Nagpur and Jabalpur it stood at 63.56 per cent and 57.45 per cent respectively. The average rural circulation of these papers was 22.28 per cent.

In 1981, the number of newspapers stood at 19144. A sample of the reporting newspapers to the RNI shows that while the circulation of 453 newspapers owned by joint stock companies was more than 19.6 million (that is nearly 38.4 per cent), nearly 65 per cent of the newspapers are owned by individuals, but their share in the total circulation is only 36.2 per cent.

The way a press actually functions is influenced largely by the news values which prevail among journalists. And that is reflected in the gate-keeping function of the practitioners, including various forms of information or knowledge control or the selection and highlighting of news stories and their projection, headlining, backgrounding and interpretation.

Joseph Pulitzer, publisher of the St. Louis Post-Despatch and the New York World once instructed his staff to look for news stories that are original, distinctive, dramatic, romantic, thrilling, unique, curious, quaint, humorous, odd and apt-to-be talked about. To these may be added newness, the prominence of persons or places concerned, the proximity of the event to the place of publication, the human interest involved and timeliness. These constitute some of the attributes of good newscasting according to Western standards. The Second Press Commission of India finds that most of the commercial newspapers in India do not pursue these guidelines. Rather they imitate the cheap, though currently known as popular journalism of the West by highlighting news about petty politics, politicians and their pourings, flooding their news holes with stories of crimes, violence and aberrations and displaying creaking headlines and sensuous illustrations and ads. Equally questionable is the sense of "human interest" which often find reflection in the reporting of foreign news and photographs, foreign serials or syndicated features. The desi (local) contents are hardly flattering. These comments seem to be rather harsh, but it is very much our journalism today.

The Commission maintains that objection is not against reporting dirty politics, sensational events or crime and tension which in any way form a part of news flow. Rather it is to the preoccupation with them to such an extent that the readers are not supplied the information and discussion they need to discharge their responsibility to society, or to make judicious decisions or exercise wisely their franchise right.

The disproportionate picture of coverage in the Indian press is revealed by another study of the Second Press Commission. According to this study, Assamese dailies devoted the maximum of edited space-37 per cent-to political items and news regarding conflicts and tension, perhaps because of the controversy in the State on the issue of foreign nationals. Tamil, Punjabi, Hindi, Oriya and Telugu , dailies also devoted a large amount of space ranging from 41.6 to 31.6 to such items. These items occupied 23.7 per cent of the space in English dailies, the least for any daily.

Items devoted to economic development and , Government matters occupied 40.5 per cent space in Oriya dailies which was the maximum for any language. Hindi dailies devoted 29.0 per cent and English dailies 36.5 per cent space to such items. Assamese dailies devoted the least-19.6 per cent-space to such news.

In Sindhi dailies, news items on unrest, law and order and courts occupied 21.2 per cent of the space. Hindi dailies gave 1735 per cent and English dailies English dailies devoted the maximum 9.9 per cent space to sports, while Hindi dailies gave 6.0 per cent. Sindhi newspapers had the least amount-1.00 per cent of space given to such items.

Gujarati dailies had the maximum 22.5 per cent-space devoted to items on entertainment and culture. The percentage was 18.4 for Hindi and 6.4 for English dailies. The least space 5.8 per cent given to such items was in Oriya dailies.

Items of interest to woman and on social and human interest matters occupied 13.4 per cent of the space in Sindhi dailies. Hindi dailies gave 5.6 per cent and English dailies 4.1 per cent space to such items. The least space-3.0 per cent-give to such items was in Assamese dailies.

According to a random survey conducted by PR unit of the Council of Scientific and Industrial Research (CSIR) the space devoted to science news in Indian newspapers varies from .63 to 10.65 per cent of the total news content. The Hindu, Economic Times and Financial Express were found to be leading in the coverage of science news.

These analyses depict the need of a serious attempt on the part of the reader and professionally oriented newspapers to give deeper thought to the problem of giving a balanced coverage and adoption of healthier professional norms in selecting and projecting news in their columns.

Perhaps more distressing is the coverage of human interest stories culled out from western newspapers. That only shows the trend and mentality even of our best gate-keepers of newscasting. The Press Commission has quoted the selection of the following news stories and photographs by five leading English newspapers published in Delhi as illustrations of this unedifying trend, "(i) a 22-cm story of 2nd December 1980 (AP report from Leeds, U.K.) under the headline "Girl escapes attack by "ripper"'; (ii) 3-column photograph of 3rd December, 1980, showing two policemen on their night patrol talking to a young woman out alone on a Leeds Street near where the mass murderer, known as the Yorkshire Ripper, claimed his 13th victim; (iii) whole of the first page of the weekly section of a newspaper of 14th June, 1981 devoted to the first instalment of "The Yorkshire Ripper Story'; (iv) a 16-cm story (AP report from Los Angeles) on 25th June, 1981 under the headline 'Rapist on parole held again'; and (v) front-page 9-cm story (UNI report from Nairobi) on 6th November, 1981 about a Kenyan African who had 40 wives and wanted more."

This perversity is at its worst in film magazines in India and elsewhere in the Third World, continued the Commission's report. How morbidly these magazines pack their pages with rumours, gossips and speculative and unseemly exposures of the private lives of film stars, instead of dilating on professional aspects of the media or carrying critical articles of film appreciation.

Newscasting or reporting about development or rural affairs is no better. There too the trend is in giving more importance to what is wrong than what is right, to conflicts rather than to resolving them, to airing grievances than to getting redressals. It is no wonder then that the maximum output of the press in development or rural reporting consists of a miscellaneous succession of stories and images which have no relation to the actual lives of rural people or even to poor and weaker sections in urban areas. And what happens in such situations is that generally simple science, relevant technology, activating success and human interest stories or field based reports, which are the heart of development reporting, go by default.

Apart from this low rating of proper news values even techniques and quality of development reporting, except in a few newspapers and magazines, is poor, says the Commission, Readers hardly get a feeling of participation in the reported events, programmes or social change. Again, interpretative or in-depth journalism is as a low ebb yet.

According to the Commission, all investigative reporting is no development reporting, but the latter is essentially investigative. Apart from it one may add that it should also be interpretative, educative, expository and promotional in nature. It has also to be venturesome and innovating-professional qualities born out of commitment to public interest, fundamental duties and regard for the public weal. The actual news values displayed by professional gate-keepers or reporters in the bulk of newspapers today is however wide off these marks. According to a Magsaysay Award winner, India's editors or reporters even don't read public documents properly. Some of them plagiarize, add a few words of their own to it and call it a scoop. Even if they read a newspaper file, they call themselves investigative journalists. Most editors have competent staff, but they don't use it to good account.

There is need, therefore, to give news values a different orientation in the interest of higher professionalism, social health and national development, argues the Press Commission. It urges the organisations of publishers, editors and journalists to evaluate, on a continuing basis, the concept and contents of healthy news culture in the light of changing socio-political ethos. It reinforces Hutchins Commission's observation that journalists today should not regard only events as news, but also social and economic processes. Many activities of utmost social consequences lie below the surface of what are conventionally regarded as reportable incidents. In the Indian context these could be: Induction of new farming technology or participatory management in factories, adoption of new sources of energy like solar or gobar (cow dung) gas, introduction of new designs of low-cost housing, etc.

The Press Commission further holds that if conflict is news but not resolution of conflict, if the unusual and the bizarre is news rather than the normal, if news is what happened just a while ago (even if the event was not significant) and not a significant happening of a week or a month earlier which has only now come to light, the portrayal or reality in the press is bound to be distorted. Added to this aberration is often the slanting or hoisting of news done on the dictates of the personal or business interests of owners and pressure groups.

The former Prime Minister, Mrs. Indira Gandhi, in her theme address at Namedia in December 1983 also adverted to this unhealthy news sense displayed by our newspapers. She said that many journalists consider it smart to initiate the popular Western definition of bad news being good news and are bored by constructive and developmental activity. In this connection she cited a recent survey by the Press Council which showed that only two per cent newspaper space was devoted to social issues. Is this what really interests readers? she asked. Are they content to remain ignorant of what is happening in various spheres, of what deepens their understanding, what helps them discharge their duty as well-informed citizens? she added.

To rectify this aberration, what is actually required is the sharpening of news sense and social sensitiveness among media practitioners. They should also develop the ability to interpret events and trends in the context of various disciplines and cultural milieu of the region.

Should journalists alone be the gate-keepers of news? Should the desk personnel or reporters be allowed to have a free hand in selecting, interpreting, shaping, displaying, timing, withholding or repeating news, or should be consumers of news also be permitted to have a say in the matter? The Press Commission has preferred to follow the existing practice of leaving the discretion in these matters to journalists, government information officials and media managers. The commission also wants editors to have the final say in the acceptance or rejection of advertisements especially those which border on or cross the line between decency and obscenity or those which promote the notion of women as sex objects and run contrary to the social or news value of their newspapers.

The practice in the West however varies. In free marketing democracies like Japan, USA, West Germany and France, newspaper publishers seek to follow the 'serve and sell' policy of giving the bulk of news and editorial matter according to the ascertained demands, tastes, needs and feedbacks of readers. In some countries like Japan even incentives are offered to make housewives buy a particular brand of paper. On the other hand, in socialist countries or authoritarian states, the party guardians or autocratic rulers and their agents act as the censors of reading material, determining what will go and what will not.

As mentioned earlier, freedom of the press is not merely a professional right that is inherent in journalists or publishers. Ideally these interests have to be reconciled: those of the publishers, readers and society. Feedback surveys or ballots, readers' columns, opinion polls, interviews and direct contacts with readers, policy makers and public representatives can bridge the gap partly. Suggestion and public opinion columns, panel discussions, direct mail ballots and coupons, publisher's letters, professional seminars and magazines as also the ombudsmanship of the Press Council can further fill in the void.

In the absence of regular readership and public feedback mechanism or other safeguards, however, the claim of journalists to be sole censors or arbiters appears to be presumptuous. When newspapers are controlled by big business or are influenced by vested interests or pressures, they run the risk, says the Commission, of becoming vehicles of expression of these internal and external influences.

It is not, however, difficult as research and comparative studies bear out, to remove the dichotomy and gulf by delinking and diffusing ownership and control and by adopting a package of readership feedback mechanism and research, public representative consultation process and norms, codes and guidelines for gate-keeping evolved by the professional bodies. Some of these suggestions have been recommended by the commission itself. What one may conclude is that by taking some of these measures newspapers can become people's universities and development activists without compromising their professional standards, social responsibilities and communication role as free public informers, educators and custodians of public interest. And perhaps in this direction lies the future development of journalism in India.

As described earlier there has been an increase in the number and circulation of periodicals since 1970. Today we see glossy and attractively produced Magazines which can compete with any of their Western counterparts in excellence. The gross circulation of any one of these periodicals, however, has not yet touched a seven figure-a phenomenon common among many advanced countries. Nor have any of these magazines come anywhere near even a; single multi-editioned magazine like the Reader's Digest which publishes over 31 million copies in 17 languages.

In the group of Indian periodicals which appeared in 1981, monthlies constituted the largest ingredient followed by weeklies, fortnightlies, quarterlies and annuals. In terms of circulation also monthlies had an edge over others.

Growing Interest

The maximum number of periodicals are brought out in Hindi followed by English, Bengali and Urdu. In terms of circulation too Hindi periodicals maintain the top position (27.6 per cent). Then come English periodicals (20.6 per cent) and Tamil (10.9 per cent). Among the Indian languages Malayalam has the maximum circulation of weeklies as well as of other periodicals per 1000 of the linguistic population (1979 figures). Kashmiri comes at the bottom with hardly any circulation. Fifty-seven periodicals have a circulation of one lakh or more copies (1980). Five of them have a circulation exceeding 3 lakhs. The two top have circulation exceeding 5.5 lakhs.

The Registrar of Newspapers Report categorises, the journals into 21 groups according to the contents. The Second Planning Commission Report however, divides them into ten categories : (1) News and current affairs journals: (2) opinion journals; (3) farm journals; (4) economic and financial journals; (5) science journals; (6) literary and cultural magazines; (7) women journals; (8) children journals; (9) sports journals; and (10) film journals.

According to the Commission's calculation, news and current affairs journals constitute the largest group. The Illustrated Weekly of India, India Today and Link are the mast bearers of this group. A feature of the growth of such periodicals in recent years has been the emergence of investigative reporting in some of these journals and also a marked increase in circulation of such journals since 1977. Some top journalists, however, consider this type of investigative reporting, at least in a few of these journals as muck raking or gutter reporting; but a few better reports have proved to be earth shaking or stunning revelations. Qualitatively the coverage in India Today, Gentleman, the Illustrated Weekly of India, Sunday, Probe, Celebrity, Imprint, Sunday Observer, etc. is commendably supported by interpretative graphics and illustrations.

Literary and cultural magazines constitute the second largest group. The bulk of these magazines particularly those with a large circulation, however, follow a formula of mixed contents in order to appeal to different tastes and thereby attract more readers. Kumudam, a Tamil weekly, is a leading illustration of this group.

Opinion journals are distinct from news magazines as also from journals of entertainment for leisure time reading. They are generally imbued with social concern and a sense of purpose. Seminar and Mainstream are illustrations of this category.

Covering nearly three-fourths of the country's rural population there are only 345 farm journals (1979 figures). Shetkari and Gramsevak belong to this group. The number of copies of farm journals per 1000 rural literate population is only 1.5 per cent, a discouragingly low figure. Some weaknesses of these journals are that they use heavy terminologies in explaining technical information and they do not engage experts to write or report for them. It is probably because they cannot afford it.

Hindu Survey of Indian Industry, Business World, Business India and Udyog represent the economic and financial category of journals. The number of these journals is not sizable in the aggregate, though some of them are fast sellers. Their number, however, had taken an upward trend since 1952 and so also their circulation.

The growth of science journals to which belongs also a better seller like Science Today was evidently noticeable during the eighties but not significantly or adequately enough. Although the number rose from almost scratch and so also the circulation of these journals, their development is not as much as it should be according to its need. To popularise science and technology and inculcate scientific temper among the people is an imperative need. But the existing journals in this category cannot perform this task satisfactorily. This misgiving was also expressed by the Press Commission.

The number of women journals is still small despite an increase during the eighties. *Vanitha,* a Malayalam monthly from Kottayam has the highest circulation in this group. One dimension which distinguishes these journals from their Western counterparts is what a Press Commission Study points out that these journals consistently seek to direct women's energies into a narrow channel and to define their concerns, preoccupations and aspirations within an arbitrarily imposed feminine framework. The covers of these magazines generally feature a brightly dressed woman, baring some parts of her body. Apart from these aspects, these journals depict women's mental faculties and behaviour in a way as if they can fit only into a male-dominated social relationship. The study says that readers get an impression that the outside world belongs to men and that the issues which arise there do not affect woman except indirectly through the men related to them. The trend, however, is now changing for the better.

Despite some increase in the number of children's journals, their position in the market is very thin. The position of Indrajal

Comics in this group is the highest. Most magazines in this section only provide entertainment in the for of light reading. Some also carry informative articles including those on current and sports events, but the number of such articles in an issue is not more than two or three. One regrettable trend noticed by the Press Commission in children's magazines is an effort to depict sex and violence in a bid to increase circulation. Instead of resorting to originality and creativity, which can help to sell the magazines also, their sponsors are trying to lean on cheap circulation gimmicks.

Sports journals had a low rate of expansion of circulation upto 1975, but thereafter they started showing progress. Sports World today crosses five figures. Qualitatively they do not reflect the latest trends in sports journalism.

Film journals indicated an increase in number since the sixties, but professionally and circulation-wise their record does not show much improvement. Only Filmfare an English fortnightly from Bombay, touches a respectable figure. A study for the Press Commission says that the bane of many film journals is the lack of professional standards. Many of these journals resort to gossip and scandal about alleged peccadillos of film stars. It is an interesting finding that many articles in such magazines are written by PR men in the pay of film producers of staff and therefore attacks on some film stars are deliberate or -tendentious.

As an activist in the all round development of Indian society, development journalism can be a faithful ally of the whole process. This brand of journalism is, however, not merely economic or financial journalism. Neither is it a government mouthpiece. It doesn't imply polishing up press releases issued by the PR Departments. It is a positive, forward looking, field based, two way participatory and development promotional reporting and writing. It is pragmatic, result and action oriented and barefoot type of journalism. To this end, it has to be bold and venturesome investigative or expository reporting involving issues, problems and exercises of social significance or public interest.

But the perspective is not to write merely what is wrong, but also what can be the right thing and how it can be brought about. It should probe into the reasons for success or failures at different places under different conditions of various development programmes. Development Agency's National Adult Education or National Rural Employment programmes, Marginal Farmers and Agricultural labours Project, etc. affect the lives of common people such as small farmers. It is indeed a sad reflection that newspapers in India have not adequately taken up this type of dynamic journalism or reporting. It has not undertaken initiative in reviewing or reporting in depth development activities nor reporting incisively about socio-economic programmes or about the green and white revolutions that are taking place in rural or remote areas.

The Press Commission draws attention particularly to one defect in this area of development reporting. It finds that many newspapers today depend heavily on official hand-outs or briefings and not on field work or direct observation preferably participant observation. Instead of venturesome reporting in so far as it is oriented to social and economic issues like the exploitation of Harijans, tribals or contract labour the trading in human flesh or delays and corruption in public administration, they feel contended in loading their stories with big and small statistics. They fail to help the readers know how the beneficiaries feel or react about the claims and achievements of different development programmes.

The Commission points out yet another omission in development reporting. This relates to the praiseworthy performance of non-official agencies and workers in fields like education, leprosy relief, etc. Indeed it is a poor reflection on the professional standards of newspapers that they do not take initiative in India in reviewing such activities. Rather they themselves become aware of them after some non-officials have been honoured with international or national awards. Surely, the free press in developing countries should be more socially conscious and enterprising than what our press actually is. Also, there is a need for the big and small media to operate as change agents, watch-dogs or gate-keepers in the process of socio-economic development taking place in various parts of the country.

At the moment only a few language newspapers especially in Oriya, Telugu, Marathi, Malayalam, Bengali and Hindi are devoting an increasing proportion of space to development coverage like that of health, family welfare, industry, science and technology, agriculture, education and public utilities.

This conclusion is based on a study entitled "Percentage of front page space devoted to different themes in daily newspapers." Another study of the Commission reveals yet another healthy trend among some language newspapers (Bengali, Kannada and Malayalam dailies) besides English which were reporting regularly on development topics and socio-economic issues. Topics covered in such reports include the condition of tea garden labourers, problems of drought and irrigation, dowry deaths, ill-treatment of women, plight of under trial prisoners, living conditions of slum dwellers, and the like. This is a welcome development which needs to be emulated and encouraged also in other newspapers which have set their heart on serving rural people. This task, however, will warrant social aptitude and barefoot qualities on the part of reporters and communicators and their ability to understand, interpret and report on socio-economic issues in terms of the problems, needs, experience and language frameworks of rural readers.

3

Social Orientation

JOURNALISM VS DEMOCRACY

Press freedom provides the oxygen in a climate of a healthy democracy. It is a matter of common experience that the press can do well and perform its professional work smoothly if it operates in the open and competitive information market and does not itself throttle or vitiate the process of collecting, selecting and presenting the news objectively and truthfully. The Press commission had therefore underscored that it is only on this type of free press that people can largely depend for the primary data of their political thinking. It is because of the freedom both from black laws or menacing pressures from without and the irresponsible journalism from within that the Fourth Estate can function as a watch-dog, ombudsman, constructive critic, public investigator and expositor, philosopher, guide and even an entertainer of the society.

Press freedom is conceded by the constitution, but not as a separate entity or a special privilege. It is included in the individuals' right to freedom of speech and expression. The government, however, has resented the licentiousness shown by a few newspapers in always criticising the ruling party and only harping upon what is wrong about things. All our governments have preferred press freedom to be linked with social and fundamental responsibilities and the obligation to report objectively.

Taking into consideration the constraints of the Indian model of democracy and socialism and the objectives laid in the Preamble of the Constitution or its Directive Principles of the State Policy, the second Press Commission has advocated that the Press should be neither an adversary nor an ally of the Government, but a constructive critic. To be a mindless adversary or an unquestioning ally would be to abdicate judgement, states the report of the Press Commission. It further stresses that journalism is a public utility service and not merely an industry.

Whereas a doctor may cause harm only to a few dozen or at the most a few score patients during the full span of his career, a dishonest or unprofessional journalist can poison the minds of hundreds of thousands or millions of his fellowmen. It is true that journalism has to be a viable business if it is to be free from want and patronage, but a special plea for its fundamental duty and its responsibility to the society and readers is not far stretched. The Press Commission has therefore urged that in the changed circumstances today, the protection of the freedom of the issuer of news alone is not enough; the freedom of the consumer (readers and public) must also be protected.

The press is a great social asset, for it has to serve the entire community of varying minds with its raw material for thought, as also to act as a watch-dog by exercising its role to warn and curb forces of repression, corruption and divisiveness.

It is possible to have a free but responsible press and good, responsive and democratic government at the same time. In fact, the freedom of the press is the mother of all other freedoms. This freedom can be used to create a brave new world or to bring about universal catastrophe. It is imperative for the society and government to protect journalists and assure them conditions for working unhindered or undertake unrestrictedly investigative reporting strictly for professional purposes.

'More journalists are killed or kidnapped, victimised or persecuted than members of any other profession,' says Sean MacBride, Chairman of the International Commission for the Study of Communication Problems. They certainly need protection and perhaps a special status,' he adds. In India these suggestions need special consideration for instances abound when journalists were murdered or manhandled by terrorists, agents of politicians or infuriated mobs or were sacked by their proprietors at the instance of political barons or some other wire-pullers.

Press freedom is very fragile. It can be weighed from two sides :

(1) the external and internal pressures, and

(2) draconian or vexatious laws. The press has to be protected both ways.

The pressures could be six-fold:

(1) physical attacks on the editor or the offices of the newspaper or its employees by the aggrieved or angry mobs,

(2) obstructions posed in the expression of political opinions not to the liking of trade unions and newspaper employees,

(3) interference in the editorial autonomy by proprietors with a view to protecting their own business interests,

(4) pressures from advertisers

(5) interference by the functionaries of the government through selective and politically motivated exercise of powers under the law and through extra legal action, and

(6) inducements or favours sought by the journalists themselves. To give protection to the press in these respects the Press Commission and many other authorities have advocated the expansion of the jurisdiction of the Press

Council to be able to look into these complaints. The legal areas in which press freedom is sought to be augmented comprise immunity regarding disclosure of sources of information, defamation, contempt of legislatures and courts and regarding a few limitations ordained by the Press and Registration of Books Act 1867, Post and Telegraph Act, Industries (Development and Regulation Act) 1951, etc. To this end, the second Press Commission has suggested certain amendments in the existing press laws to expand reasonably the scope of press freedom and at the same time underscored the need to protect the right to privacy of the individual and prevent newspapers from indulgence in free style of character assassination.

Beside the promotion of products and services, advertising has a great role in sustaining the newspaper industry and free press.

Press advertising as a factor of newspaper economy is therefore taken very seriously by newspaper managements of modern times. Any restrictions imposed on advertising space or expenditure or newsprint supply would naturally evoke resentment among big and medium papers.

Till the second half of the sixties the advertisers and big advertising agencies in India depended primarily on dailies for extensive advertising. Thereafter a clear cut differentiation began to emerge that while daily newspapers should be used primarily for advertising capital goods, employment and trade notices and for institutional campaigns and periodicals should be employed for sustained advertising of consumer goods.

In fact the sudden increase in advertisement revenue after the sixties enabled leading Indian periodicals to improve their production standards and editorial content, thereby attracting a wider readership. Even for the bulk of other periodicals, income from advertisements became the mainstay of their economy.

Role of Advertisement

Today advertisements occupy a substantial proportion of space in newspapers. It is, however, only the big general interest magazines, and comparatively the English dailies attached to newspaper chains, and combines of large business houses who usurp the lion's share in the cake of advertising revenue. A trend to rectify this imbalance has been sought by the government by pursuing a liberal policy of giving special rates of government advertisements to language news papers besides augmenting their newsprint supply and granting them rebate from excise duties, etc. But still the big and medium dailies and periodicals, not withstanding competition from radio TV commercials, continue to have edge.

Notwithstanding the maximum of 40:60 space allotment suggested for advertisements by the first Press Commission, the space given to advertising has been actually increasing in big newspapers. According to data given in the annual reports of the Press Register there was no paper in 1965 which gave 60 per cent or more space to advertisements and there were only 10 papers which devoted 50 to 59 per cent space to advertisements. In 1981, three big and medium and 37 small papers started devoting 75 per cent or more space to advertisements.

And 5 big 25 medium and 112 small papers used between 50 and 74 per cent of their space for advertisements. The percentage of space devoted to advertisements was generally more in the case of dailies that periodicals.

However, the average space devoted to advertisements was found to be 39 per cent in the case of dailies 27 per cent in the case of weeklies and 31 per cent in the case of monthlies. According to ORG survey, 77 per cent of the total advertising revenue income and 51.8 per cent of the space was accounted for by big newspapers with a circulation of 50,000 and above.

This, a small chunk of big newspapers have an economic or competitive edge over the bulk of small and medium newspapers in the country. On an average the share of advertising revenue to the total income was merely 52 per cent in the case of big papers and a little over 26 per cent in the case of medium papers. The bigger dailies, particularly the big English dailies were usurping a disproportionately larger chunk of advertisement revenue in 1981 and therefore were in a position to offer more pages on the same selling price. Even from the point of view of the resale price, the big papers provided a benefit to the customers.

The second press Commission therefore felt that the prescription of a price-page schedule with fixed news to advertising ratio is absolutely necessary for the existing newspapers. In view of the need to help small and medium newspapers overcome disadvantage of lower advertisement incomes and smaller number of pages the Press Commission recommended a specific ratio of 60 per cent for big papers. A bold and fair suggestion, but its validity is a matter of speculation.

Quality Production

In India as has been already seen, good production did not brother the pioneer journalist in the past. Photo journalism and colour reproduction were at their embryonic stage. The opinion advocacy or adversary Journalism of those days with low print orders did not lend themselves to competitive or marketing urges in terms of variety or innovativeness in design or production. Things, however, started changing for the better during the 1950s and 1960s.

The vocation became a business of industry and subjected to: marketing and advertising pressures for better looks and attractive layouts and typography. The challenge of utilising resources optimally, effective economies in costs and ensuring speedier delivery schedules, motivated the owners to resort to modern printing technology for their papers. By this time the Indian printing scene was also exposed to the new trends in the West where two types of technological revolutions were sweeping the scene. Web offset and electronic printing technologies involving photo composition or computer controlled teletype setting or electronic typewriters were replacing the conventional hot metal linotype and monotype composing processes. For a' multilingual developing country like India these two technologies suited immensely, though they were costly. Among the obvious advantages of these technologies to Indian publishing in languages are the superior and consistent quality of letter image, elimination of the use of scarce material such as lead and the unlocking of capital invested in lead type faces.

During the last two decades, the big chain English newspaper publishers or language newspapers bringing out multi-editions and affected by competition have been gradually reeling towards sophisticated and modern technologies of various shades. So is the trend with some of the class A and class B printing houses where big magazines and medium newspapers are being printed as job work.

For instance, three giants among the Malayalam press Malayala Manorama, Mathrubhumi and Kerals Kaumudi are in competition to get into the faster and the latest printing processes. Of these three big Malayalam papers Kerala Kaumudi was the first to install the transmission link, a process by which composed matter can be sent column by column within two transmission points, thus enabling the resident editor to choose matter of local importance in his edition. This is an improvement on the facsimile transmission method employed by the Hindu which results in a comparatively more rigid similarity between all editions of the paper. Another high technology gadget that distinguishes Kaumudi is the tele-photo by which any major event occurring anywhere in the world can be splashed within a few hours in this paper.

There are today many language newspapers especially in Urdu, Hindi, Gujarati, Marathi and Telugu which have resorted to one or the other of the modern technologies. This is enabling them to offer colour printing as also modern layout and typographical designs to their advertising clients and readers-a significant landmark in language journalism.

The Hindu, was the first newspaper in India to install the latest computer technology both for printing and type setting processes. Instead of hot metal composing on stereo plates, a feature common to most of the other big dailies, typesetting in this paper is done by a typesetter working on one of the 24 video display units in an air-conditioned office. The type text is stored in one of the two computers and on editorial command, a laser camp photo typesetter produces bromides of the text and advertisement copies which are set and designed into complete pages, according to layout plans. Each page is then photographed by an automatic computerised camera to obtain a negative.

This is then printed by contact on to a thin polymer plate under high intensity lights. After etching, which takes only minutes, the plate is ready for printing the headquarter's edition. The images of these of these pages are then sent at the rate of seven minuted a page by facsimile transmission to Bangalore, Hyderabad, Coimbatore and Madurai for simultaneous printing of regional editions. Recently the Indian Express, telegraph and Aaj installed computerised photo typesetting systems.

The Illustrated weekly of India an allied magazine of the Bennett Coleman and Co. now uses electronic technology in colour separation and automatic processing of film negatives as also adopts a sophisticated printing process of in-depth colour printing known as photogravure.

The Weekly's photogravure machine has nine units and it can print an 80-page at the rate of 90000 copies per hour. It can also control paper tension and colour alignment. Folding and stitching is done automatically.

Another illustration of the latest technology-based printing press was the opening of a new unit called Mayar printers at Okhla Industrial estate where the new electronic dot generating colour scanner, the process camera, film and plate processors and photo typesetting units have been installed. This plant is fully computerised.

Apart from these sophisticated presses, according to the Press Registrar's Report of 1981. 366 dailies have their own publishing arrangements. Also 398 dailies have their own composing arrangements. In these units however the printing technologies used are predominantly relief, stereo plate flat-bed, lithography and offset and for composing mono, lino, inter type and hand composition systems with a sprinkling of photo composition. To help modernise the printing industry the government has assured all possible help. In the existing situation, there seems to be three options open for must of the newspaper publishers:

(1) to continue with the old technology,

(2) to obtain secondhand reconditioned equipment or to resort to the manufacture of such machines locally, or

(3) to take a leap into the new technology. At the 21st All India printers Conference, eminent overseas speakers advised Indian Printers not to hesitate in making up their minds in favour of adopting the new technology for it is like a moving train. The longer one takes to make up his mind, the harder it is to jump in later on.

The old technologies, however, cannot be discarded like the village cart. Some experts have suggested that India should continue to have an appropriate mix of old and new processes in such a manner that the adoption of the new technology by existing processes may allow them to survive initially for such period as they would choose to replace the old technology altogether. The Press Commission has left it to each publisher to decide what technology would suit its requirements best. Newspapers, particularly those which want to grow, should have an open mind and a progressive outlook while selecting proper technology. It has further recommended that the proposed newspaper development Commission should special attention to the development of printing and other technologies suitable for the Indian press, especially for

Indian language and small and medium newspapers. The Press Commission own preference was how ever for new electronics technology which has a clear advantage so far as composition in Indian script is considered. To meet the immediate requirement of small and medium newspapers it suggested that these units should be allowed to important, rebuild or recondition machines available abroad.

Till the time new production technologies sweep printing scene in the country, the well produced Hindu, Malayala Manorama, Times of India, India Today, Gentleman and Illustrated Weekly of India will coexist with hundreds of shabbily produced small papers, though liable to serve useful function at the grassroots level.

The Indian media scene presents a picture of congested basti with an overcrowding of small newspapers. In a total number of 1914 units, only 17$ belong to the category of big newspapers and the rest to the category of small papers. Although small newspapers have increased in number their share the total circulation has declined markedly during the last quarter century. In the daily press, the big paper have a share of 54.3 and medium 25.4 per cent of the circulation. In a country like India where three quarters of the people live in small towns and villages, mofussil newspapers, invariably small ones with circulation ranging from a few hundreds to 15000, have distinct role to play in the process democratizing communication than big newspaper.

Their functioning is however handicapped, their circulation in the rural areas is circumscribed, their economy is depressed and the their impact is reduced. People who have experience of publishing large and small daily newspapers testify that small newspapers can still grow more if they make themselves useful the local community by conveying information of local relevance and interest and seek to bag rural advertisements, rather than compete with the state capital or metropolitan newspapers ineffectively. Eve at the present stage of development in our country newspaper serving one or more districts with common cultural and economic features likely to be successful.

The reassuring examples of community newspapers the USA and critical newspapers in the UK are appropriate. The development of such newspapers will reduce the disparity between India's large rural population as compared to the small circulation and readership of newspapers in rural areas. Even if it is conceded that newspaper readership per copy is higher in rural papers, the rural reach of the Indian press is so limited that it should call for concern and attention, says the Press Commission. In this connection, extension of educational opportunities for children and illiterate adults and gainful employment for the youth, women and rural people is very necessary.

4

Basic Principles

'Media effects' mean different things to different people. A psychologist, for example, has 'psychological' effects in mind when talking about media effects; the sociologist, the 'social' effects, the anthropologist, the 'cultural' effects, the political scientist the 'political' effects, the economist the 'economic' effects, the preacher, the 'moral' effects, the advertiser, the 'market' effects... and so on.

Parents too are concerned about the amount of time their children spend with television, music, comics, and films, and the effects this might have on their children's behaviour and attitudes. Then there are school teachers who worry about their students' exposure to adult material, and the police who scapegoat the media for social violence and delinquency. So, any attempt to understand 'effects' must necessarily take into account from whose perspective the 'effects' are being investigated.

'Effects' are of various types and various gradations too. They may be short-term, medium-term or long-term; they may be deep or profound, or transient or superficial as in the case of fashions, mannerisms, and life-styles. Then there are influences of a passing nature or a more permanent nature.

Can influences be termed as 'effects?' How are 'influences', 'effects' distinct from 'impacts', or are they mere synonyms for the same social phenomena? Few media sociologists have subjected the inadequacy of everyday language to fathom the complexity of media effects to any kind of critical scrutiny.

But what precisely are 'the media?' Are they the technologies (printing presses, the telegraph, telephones, radio and TV sets, audio and video recorders, video and movie cameras, satellites, computers, etc.) or the 'genres', the 'programmes' (the software) or the contents of individual media? Or, are they the cultural and entertainment industries which are today one of the fastest growing businesses owned by large media conglomerates? Or, are they the many media organisations involved in the production, distribution and exhibition of media materials? The sheer imprecision in all talk about 'the media' and 'effects' seems to be characteristic of the social sciences. But then, it must be conceded, the social sciences are not 'exact' sciences like the physical and natural sciences. For, while the social sciences study human beings and their behaviour in different situations, the natural sciences study minerals, plants, and animals.

Moreover, social scientists and media professionals rarely consider the infinite variety of 'uses' the different media and the different programmes are put to, in different contexts. In most cases, the use of the term 'effects' is misleading because it suggests that the media "do something" to people, as though people are inorganic creatures, who do not bring their own personalities to play in the communication process. It also implies that the media are actors, and that the people are acted upon. So while the media are active, audiences are unresponsive if not passive. These assumptions about media and audiences have their origin in Aristotelian linear models of communication where persuasion is seen as the primary goal of all communication.

The truth is that we have little precise knowledge or proven data about media effects since they invariably take place in combination with a whole lot of social, economic and cultural variables. Do effects relate to change, however slight, in attitude and behaviour (both elusive terms and comprehensive in meaning)? Perhaps. The extent of change (if any) depends on the variations in the desires and inclinations of individual members of an audience, and in the way they as individuals and as members of different social and cultural groups respond to various types of stimuli from the mass media. It has to be noted, moreover, that people can be influenced without paying attention and without changing at all, that there is often no relationship between what a person learned, knew or recalled on the one hand and what he did or how he felt on the other. It follows therefore that one can learn things without believing them, believe things without doing them, and do things without learning or believing them.

How to Correlate? : The 'interaction' (a much more accurate term than 'effects') between media and human beings is an extremely complex phenomenon. It becomes even more complex when we realize that there are a great variety of media offering numerous programme genres, and also the fact that there are a whole variety of people and groups listening, viewing, reading in a countless number of socio-cultural environments. Perhaps, the only safe conclusion on 'effects' (or 'interactions') of the media is that arrived at by Bernard Berelson several years ago: 'Some kinds of communication on some kinds of issues, brought to the attention of some kinds of people under some kinds of conditions have some kinds of effects."

Various Concepts

Several theories related to the effects or changes brought about by the media (largely television) on individuals and society have been propounded by both 'functionalist' and 'critical' schools of communication. The 'functionalist' theorists begin with the assumption that the media have a role and a function in society: to stabilise, reinforce and maintain the consensus in society. They do not see the question of power and conflict as a major driving force in society; they assume that the competition among the various groups in society allows for free and fair play, and all groups have an equal chance to dominate and to control.

The 'critical' theorists, on the other hand, place the struggle for power among social classes/groups at the centre of society; the mass media are invariably employed by the dominant class to propagate its ideology. Further, while the 'functionalists' research media effects using empirical quantitative methods, the 'critical' theorists are so not much concerned with effects as the cultural and political context in which media experiences take place, the ownership and economics of the media, and the various ways in which audiences 'read' the media.

These theories range from one extreme position of all-powerful wide-ranging effects of the media, to the opposing extreme position where the media have no effects at all. At the one extreme are writers and researchers like Marie Winn who take the media, especially television, to be a 'plug-in drug'; at the other extreme is Joseph Klapper who concluded from his longitudinal research that media succeed only in 'reinforcing' old attitudes, habits, and beliefs. In between, are the 'negotiation' or interaction theorists who suggest that effects, like meanings of media texts, are ultimately 'negotiated' by audiences. This is sometimes termed the 'mediation perspective'.

Most media theories deal directly with the 'effects' of the contents of programmes on opinions, attitudes, perceptions, beliefs and social behaviour. The theories have their basis largely in research on television and film, though some in speculation or personal experience. The largest number of studies have been on the effects of violence in television programmes on the behaviour of children and adolescents; others on the effects of propaganda on personal opinion and on voting behaviour. Since early effects research was based on the 'persuasion' model of communication (the Lasswell model and the Shanon-Weaver model, for instance) and carried out by social psychologists, the results often pointed to strong effects, for that is what they were looking for in the first place. The social contexts in which the media were experienced (say the family, the home, the theatre, the school or the peer group) were rarely taken into account. The stimulus-response experiments to measure effects were frequently carried out in laboratories using mechanical pre-test and post-test methods of research. Thus the results they obtained turned out to be along expected lines.

Reinforcement : Limited Effects Theory : Joseph Klapper and others, for example, believed that media reinforce existing values and attitudes. Only then, after all, can programmes of the media be popular with a majority of social groups which have an interest in the perpetuation of their own traditions and statuses. Lazarsfeld and Merton held that the mass media 'cannot be relied upon to work for changes, even minor changes, in the social structure.'

Some mass communication theorists (Lazarsfeld, Merton, and Winn for instance) argue that media have a 'narcotizing dysfunction' that distracts audiences from real problems and in fact prevents their doing anything about them. In other words, the mass media, have a drug-like addictive effect, lulling audiences into passivity and a sense of elation. Exposure to a flood of information, say Lazarsfeld and Merton, may serve to narcotize rather than energize the average reader or listener. As an increasing amount of time is devoted to reading and listening, a decreasing share is available for organized action. The interested and informed citizen can congratulate himself on his lofty state of interest and information and fail to see that he has abstained from decision and action. He comes to mistake knowing about problems of the day for doing something about them.

First proposed in 1948, the theory appears dated particularly after the galvanizing impact together with a combination of many other factors the mass media had in bringing the Vietnam war to an end, and in throwing Nixon out as a result of Watergate. In

India, the press publicity given to excesses of the emergency, particularly through underground literature, did contribute to bringing about an end to the emergency.

Closely related to the 'narcosis' theory, is the 'cartharsis' theory of media effects. Seymour Feshbach, the main exponent of the theory, argued that the media may have a 'cathartic' effect on people that somehow purges them of many anti-social and unfulfilled desires, frustrations and feelings of hostility.

In one of his laboratory studies, Feshbach-subjected college students to savage insults and criticism at the hands of experimenters; the experimental group was then shown an aggressive film of a brutal boxing-match, while the 'control group' was shown a dull film. When they were later questioned about their opinions of the experimenters, those students who had seen the film on boxing felt less hostile to their experimenters than those students who were shown the 'control' film.

However, in an almost identical laboratory experiment by Leonard Berkowitz, the experimenters were introduced to the students as either a boxer or a rhetoric student. The students were then exposed to either a violent boxing film or a neutral non-violent film. Later, they had the chance to give electrical shocks (under the pretext of a separate experiment) to the 'boxer' or the rhetoric student.

It was found that those students who had seen the boxing film gave the largest number of shocks to the 'boxer.' Berkowitz concluded that the boxing film was responsible for the aggressive response of the students. Other experiments have revealed that children in particular are likely to imitate violence in films if the violent actions in the film are rewarded.

Laboratory experiments are by their nature artificial for they cannot re-create the different conditions, environments, and states of mind in which violent films are seen. The reactions to violence in films can be very varied as is well demonstrated in Philip Schlesinger's work on 'Women viewing Violence.'

The 'narcosis' and 'catharsis' theories represent extreme views. So does Ernest Van den Hag's view that 'mass communications, taken together are demeaning, debasing and de-personalizing instruments of manipulation at worst; middle-class hedonism at best.' Yet another extreme theory is that of Frederic Wertham which says that the content of the media is 'corruptive in general and specifically teaches materialism, brutality, antisocial behaviour and callousness towards other humans.'

It is a Matter of Chance : In contrast, Aldous Huxley took the stand that media indeed do teach people things, but most of them are of no consequence; they also have effects, but mostly in unimportant and trivial facets of our lives although we may think that they are important.

These trivial facets are fashions, mannerisms, mating habits, and food habits. As Schramm, Lyle and Parker found in their study of children and television, 'television could be an especially effective agent of incidental learning while the child is still young. This is because at that time it seems so real.'

By the 1950s and sixties, communication researchers began to fine tune their methods and their theories. Elihu Katz, Denis McQuail and Michael Gurevitch introduced what they termed the 'uses and gratifications' theory of media effects.

They turned their attention to how audiences used the media to live out their fantasy lives and to seek out other gratifications, or even to inform and educate themselves about the world and its people. Thus media 'effects' were related to the needs and activities of audiences.

The theory was largely concerned with the selection, reception and nature of response of audiences to the media, the assumption being that individual members in an audience made conscious and motivated selection of channels and programmes. It was also assumed that audiences made supplementary and compensatory uses of the mass media.

Factors Concerning Culture

George Gerbner's dissatisfaction with effects research led him to evolve a sophisticated theory grounded on his longitudinal research on American television. He and his team undertook a content analysis of television programmes, looking at portrayals of gender, violence, the family, portrayal of minorities, and then matched these with actual situations, behaviours and attitudes in American society. Take the portrayal of crime, for instance. Gerbner concluded that there was a 'cultivation' effect or enculturation effect on audiences highly exposed to television. Audiences 'adopted' the perceptions and values which were consistently portrayed in different programme genres.

Gerbner and his team attempted 'to move beyond the analysis of effects on individual behaviour and to analyse communication systems at a social structural level.' Television was seen as the arm of the industrial and military establishment, an agent of social control.

Technology at Work

"The medium is the message", wrote Marshall McLuhan, setting the controversy over media effects on its head. No matter what the contents of programmes, he argued, people will watch television; it commands their attention as no other medium has. He warned like a doomsday prophet that "the electronic media are transforming every aspect of man's life and re-structuring civilization, not so much by the content of their messages, as by the nature itself of television, movies, computers and other media." Mass communications, therefore, are neither good nor bad, but rather mystical devices that possess powers to change the way mankind lives and thinks. For instance, Indian cities are already witness to some changes in eating, sleeping and socialising habits as a result of the introduction of television.

A rather different kind of effect on which no theory has yet been built is the impact of media among and within themselves.

Mass communicators are known to review each other's work, and reporters carefully go through rival papers, and switch on to news programmes on the air. It is no surprise, therefore, that 'copycatting' in content and form has become a common phenomenon. Let a topic be introduced in one paper, and the others take it up with a vengeance. So when a 'health' programme proves popular on TV, every newspaper introduces a 'health' column.

Then there are the effects of new media upon the old, and vice versa. The formats of Doordarshan's newscasts and features have in fact been copied from All India Radio and magazines are all profusely illustrated because of the impact of television. Again, short stories first published in the papers or magazines, are turned into radio, TV and cinema scripts. All these inter-media and intramedia effects may be called "reflex effects" or "bandwagon effects."

Use of Education

Right from pre-Independence days, attempts have been made by both government and private groups to use the media for educational purposes. Dadasaheb Phalke, the pioneer of Indian cinema, made educational documentaries such as 'The growth of a Pea plant' and 'How to Make a Film' besides fictional films. Radio experiments in the use of radio for promoting literacy and education were conducted as early as the 1930s. Television was introduced into India by the Nehru Government with the primary aim of exploiting the medium for distance education. B.G. Verghese's Chattera experiment attempted to use the daily newspaper to educate urban Delhites about rural people and their problems. The most ambitious attempt to exploit the mass media for education was of course, SITE (Satellite Instructional Television Experiment). It sought to educate rural people in six states of India about the need for family planning, improved agriculture, hygiene, nutrition and health care. Classroom-type instructions were also provided to school children.

Today, Doordarshan devotes at least ten per cent of its telecast time to educational or enrichment programmes for farmers, school children, youth and other groups. It has taken to promoting literacy on a nationwide scale. UGC's 'Countrywide classroom' and IGNOU's early morning transmissions are ambitious post-SITE attempts to use television for higher education.

Do media educate? How effective are the mass media in educating the people of our country? What are the 'effects' of media on 'education?' These are all loaded and difficult questions to which there can be no straight cut-and-dry answers. Literate and educated people benefit much more from educational media than the less literate and educated, unless the education-oriented programmes are specifically geared to the needs, interests and levels of specific groups. This is an essential condition of any educational programme on any medium to have some kind of 'effect.' Even before groups and regions can benefit from education through the print or the electronic media, they will need to become 'media literate.' Media literacy precedes or is simultaneous with the skill to learn from the media.

The folk media are perhaps much more effective in promoting the message of literacy than any of the mass media. In Kerala, Maharashtra, Andhra Pradesh and other states, folk forms of the local regions have been utilised both by voluntary social action groups and by government-supported literacy campaigns. For example, in Maharashtra, literacy campaigns have used folk musical forms such as lavani, powada, gondhal, jagar and others. During the campaign, cultural teams went out to the different villages on Kalajathas. The main thrust of the messages conveyed through song, dance and discussions was literacy. However, it was reported that other issues such as mother and child care, family planning, watershed management, the problem of alcoholism and dowry, small savings and agricultural development were also conveyed. In some campaigns, the message of literacy was spread by relating the folk forms to local festivals: akshar kandlis and akshar rangoli at the time of Diwali and Akshar Ganpathi at the time of the popular festivals of Maharashtra.

In the campaign at Sindhdurg, haldi-kumkum celebrations were widely used to mobilise women and to bring them together to discuss issues related to their everyday lives. However, in all these campaigns, there were few attempts to place literacy in the context of political, social and economic structures in the rural and urban areas. (for further details Cf. D. Saldanha: 'Cultural Communication in Literacy. Economic and Political Weekly, May 15, 1993, pp. 981-989).

It appears then that the media by themselves (whether modern or folk) do not promote literacy. Nor is commitment enough. The social structures obtaining at the grass-root need to be taken into account, as well as the infrastructure in the form of schools, teachers, volunteers, post-literacy facilities, and the caste and communal divides. A factor often overlooked is the time available to agricultural and industrial workers to respond in any meaningful way to literacy drives in the media.

Familial Factors

The TV, cable and satellite 'invasion' of urban India is of great concern to parents and teachers. With so much time given to watching the small screen, parents are worried that little or no time will remain for conversation in the family, for family get-togethers and for family visits. However, parents must acknowledge that they too spend a lot of time with television, and that frequently they exercise no control on what their children watch and when. Further, parents frequently use television as a baby-sister or as an excuse for staying at home. Except for Andal Narayanan's pioneering study on the Impact of Television on Viewers, and Neena Behl's close look at what happens to one Indian village when television is introduced in it, there are hardly any studies that take a hard critical look at what happens in the family when television enters the home and how it becomes part of the furniture after a few years.

Multi-channel television often creates friction among siblings, or between parents and children, or even between parents themselves. But then TV also helps to bring a family closer especially when all members enjoy a popular programme together. It provides topics for conversation, for expressing opinions and for family discussions. A lot depends upon what the members of the family do with television. Since few Indian families can afford more than one TV set, gathering around the TV set is similar to the earlier practice of gathering round a fireplace. The family, like any other social institution, is a power structure. The exercise of power in the home, in earlier times, was through the breadwinner, generally the man of the house. The remote control device now puts power in the hands that hold it.

Ethnographic and focus group studies of the place of television in the lives of families clearly point to the remote control in most families being held by male rather than female members. However, in many Indian homes where the female is dominant, the remote control is invariably in the hands of the mother. In some families though, the remote control is in the hands of the children.

Without communication an individual could never become a human being; without mass communication an individual could never become part of modern society. Socialisation is a life-long active process, beginning on the day of one's birth. The child learns to socialise from the parents and the social groups he or she belongs to. As children grow up they come into contact with other social groups, but their basic loyalties are to their own primary and secondary groups which provide them their sets of attitudes, beliefs, and norms of behaviour.

Children come under three kinds of social control : (1) tradition orientation-social control based on tradition; (2) inner orientation-social control achieved through standards, guidelines or values existing in each individual; and (3) external or other orientation-social control achieved by conformity to standards existing in other persons and groups.

The child of today comes into contact with groups other than those in school; for instance, through the mass media, which give him/her access to remote groups and their cultures. Besides, the mass media provide models of behaviour, and norms of living. The child begins to imitate them, particularly in cases where he or she is least integrated into the family or the peer group. Such children rely heavily on media advice and models; while others do not since their activities outside the home provide them greater stimuli and other role models.

But the socialisation effects of mass media cannot match the power of the home, the neighbourhood and the school where interpersonal relationships exist. In contrast, socialisation through the mass media is depersonalised and hence effective mainly in the peripheral areas of life. One would expect a national outlook to follow from a wide exposure to national news and social advertisements in the mass media.

But communalism continues to hold out against all attempts at national integration through the media-so deep-rooted are our attitudes and beliefs. So also social evils like the dowry system, child marriages, caste conflicts and the like persist. The mass media are not a panacea for social or economic under-development as some governments are prone to believe.

In any study of media influence on children, or on the influence of children's interests and needs on the media, the age-group is an important variable. Other equally important variables are social class, religious and cultural background, linguistic background and community. It has been found from research in the West that the pre-operational child (aged 5 years and below), responds differently from the child belonging to the concrete operations stage (6 to 11 years) or to the formal operations stage (11 to 12 years). To illustrate, young children aged five and below see a series of separate and fragmentary incidents rather than the story of a film. They do not invariably recognise the identities of the principal character throughout the film, and they tend to believe implicitly what they see on TV to be real. And, interestingly, they sometimes read incidents into the plot from their own imaginations, or add incidents and events that they think should have occurred.

The 6 to 11 year old child, however, understands the story of a film, but still understands only the concrete physical behaviour of film performers. Only at the age of 10 or 11, does he usually understand the feelings and motivations and put himself in the shoes of a character. The 11 to 12 year old comprehends films as efficiently as adults, and comes to realize the make-believe fantasy world of films. He also gradually begins to understand the emotional relationships in films, and to appreciate some and dislike other aspects of films. Besides, he can imagine hypothetically the sorts of relationships which may exist between film characters even if the relationships are not presented on the screen. Recent ethnographic and semiotic studies of children's interaction with television suggests that children make for a 'lively audience' and are highly discriminating and critical viewers.

Impact on Children

Children below the age of 16 comprise almost 40 per cent of the population of India. Yet barely five per cent of total telecast time is directly aimed at children; this is equally true of radio, fiction and documentary cinema, and the press. On television, programmes for children devote a lot of time to animation films and puppet shows. Several American animation series like 'Spiderman', 'Heman', and 'Mickey and Donald', have featured on Indian television. The advertisements that usually accompany them relate to toys and dolls. Interestingly, terrorist-related toys like 'G I Joe', 'Barbie' dolls, sold by India toy manufacturers like Funskool, an MRF-controlled company based in Goa, and Leo Toys of Blowplast company, are advertised regularly on children's programmes. Funskool is a collaborator of a subsidiary of Hasbro, the world's largest toy manufacturer, and the makers of 'G I Joe'; Leo Toys collaborates with Mattels, the second largest toy manufacturer in the United States. Mattel produced the TV series on 'He-man' to promote the sale of their toys. It has set up a Barbie Friends Club, 'an interactive club where children could emulate the role model' The members of the club-over 12,000 of them between the ages of 6 and 12 years at a subscription fee of Rs. 95 each-write letters to Barbie and she writes back to them. It is claimed that Barbie receives over a hundred letters every day.

Should Doordarshan allow itself to become a commercial medium for the peddling of transnational manufacturers and their toys? The Joshi Committee warned against this 'cultural invasion', but Doordarshan has not heeded the warning. The Joshi Committee Report also observed that 'reviews of children's reaction to film and television in India have indicated that animation is not always successful with Indian child audiences.

Unfamiliarity with the technique sometimes makes it difficult for Indian children to identify the characters and objects.' For Indian children to comprehend them it is necessary to keep the drawings in animation films simple and realistic and the message needs to be conveyed in a direct manner. It therefore urged that research-based software be produced so that programmes are appropriate in terms of the child's level of development as well as his or her life situation.

The comic strips that daily newspapers, Sunday newspapers, and magazines publish regularly for young readers are mostly 'syndicated' comics from the United States. Columns for children frequently include quizzes, contests and stories. Children's magazines like Chandamama (in different languages), Target, Quest, and Heights carry similar fare.

While there is a National Film Foundation for Children and Young People, and children's film festivals are organized sporadically, very little attention is in fact paid to the production of films for children on a regular basis. The Films Division, on the other hand, is the foremost producer of short animation films, either directly educational in nature, or telling popular stories from the Panchatantra or the wealth of Indian folk-tale tradition.

The Joshi Committee Report (1984) learned from its extensive analysis of television software that 'most of our children's programmes seem to have been designed for the upper-class child. This is somewhat paradoxical: the ultimate objective is to use television for education purposes, and it is the urban child who least needs additional educational inputs. Instead, television programmes should be directed primarily towards disadvantaged children in rural and urban areas.' The irony is that 'disadvantaged children' do not possess or have access to television receivers.

The Joshi Report also noted that children's programmes are among the most substandard of all programmes produced. Indeed, children's programmes are considered child's play; producers who are under-utilized at other work are allocated the children's programme section.

Further, the time slotted for telecasting children's programmes is generally at the beginning of the evening's transmission, when most children should be playing outdoors.

Since children do not have any purchasing power, market researchers do not study children as television or radio audiences, or as readers. Except for SITE studies of children's response to educational programmes, and a few other studies, we have little significant research on children's use of, or interaction with, the mass media.

Importance of Women

The Joshi Committee Report observed in 1984 that Doordarshan is 'dominated by feature films and film-based programmes that exploit the female form to titillate and/or, through their socially insensitive approach, simply trivialize and debase the image of womanhood.' It therefore urged not only a reduction of the number of future films and film-based programmes on television but, more positively, "the incorporation of the 'women's dimension' in all programmes and "the need for a separate focus on and for women."

Other recommendations of the Joshi Committee Report included the following :

(1) The improvement of women's condition, status and image be defined as a major objective of Doordarshan.

(2) The formulation of clear guidelines regarding the positive portrayal of women on television, and a system of monitoring the implementation of these guidelines.

(3) The redefinition of the image and the promotion of the male 'ideal' as one who is carrying and willing to share in household, childcare and contraceptive responsibilities.

(4) The need for orientation courses for all Doordarshan policy makers, programming and production staff so that they are sensitised to social issues with particular reference to women's issues and their implications in society.

(5) The careful scrutiny (by a special committee) of all advertisements shown on television, to ensure that they do not portray women in derogatory and stereotyped ways.

(6) The need for a weekly programme on viewers' views, in which the audience, critics, commentators, women's organizations are called upon to analyse and evaluate the week's programmes.

(7) The involvement of Mahila Mandalas in the installation of community television sets, and in community viewing arrangements in rural areas.

Women's organizations across the country (such as AWAG in Ahmedabad, Vimochana in Bangalore, and the Committees on Portrayal of Women in the Media, in New Delhi and Mumbai), periodicals like Manushi and Stree, and Departments of Women's Studies in universities, have been active for a decade now in carrying out research on representations of women in the various mass media. Over a dozen serious studies, involving both quantitative and qualitative methodologies, have been conducted; the majority of them are available, however, only in mimeo.

Doordarshan's portrayal of women in its various programmes has been subjected to close critical analysis by a number of researchers.

Two major studies are: Affirmation and Denial: Construction of Femininity on Indian Television by Prabha Krishnan and Anita Dighe (1990), and Vision Unveiled by Nandini Prasad (1994). The first study was conducted by Krishnan, Dighe and Rao in 1986. Programmes over a period of 15 days a sample of 30 news programmes, 30 special interest group programmes, 55 general enrichment programmes, 33 art and entertainment programmes, 27 fiction-oriented and cinema programmes, 186 commercials and two audience-contact programmes-a total sample of 363 items were scrutinized for women-related references. The largely quantitative analysis indicated certain definite trends:

In the first place, news related to women did not exceed 2.5 minutes out of the total 20 minutes. Women were news makers in less than ten per cent of the 30 news programmes telecast, mostly in the foreign news items that related to Margaret Thatcher and Corazon Aquino. Further, women invariably figured in the political news as wives, mothers, daughters of well-known men. They also appeared frequently as members of audiences and as victims of some calamity or accident.

A significant number of women appeared as shoppers. In development-oriented news items, women featured as workers in tea plantations, sericulture poultry farming, etc., and as beneficiaries of welfare schemes. In women's programmes the focus was on the woman at home. The 'experts' in these programmes were men; in farmers' programmes all the experts were men; women, however, compared most children's programmes.

Where commercials were concerned, the life-styles promoted were largely elitist; the models in the commercials were overwhelmingly light-skinned. In voice-overs, male voices were presented as 'authoritative'; female voices as informative and 'seductive.' Women featured in all categories of commercials, but they were dominant in ads for foods, grooming and household items.

Prasad's content analysis of Doordarshan programmes was carried out in 1992, using a large sample of two and a half months of national news bulletins. The sample extended from October 1 to December 15, 1992, with every second day's bulletin comprising the sample, i.e. a total of 38 news bulletins. Prasad found that a mere 20 news items during the entire period related to women. Of the 20 news items, 5 related to social issues, 3 to mobilising public opinion on women's issues, and 11 to other women-related issues.

Prasad's examination of the portrayal of women in Doordarshan's advertisements reveals that out of a total sample of 210 ads, 63 showed women in 'traditional' roles, 35 in a 'non-traditional' role, and 117 in a 'neutral manner.' Descriptive analyses of the portrayal of women in popular television serials include those by Leela Rao, Jyoti Punwani and others.

Less than two per cent of broadcasting time on radio is devoted to programmes on or for women, yet over 25 per cent of radio advertising is directed at women, in the form of advertisements on cosmetics, food products, beverages and fabrics. The songs selected for broadcast on All India Radio and Vividh Bharati are 'by and large on religious themes or depicting themes of coy young women waiting to be married.' The plays convey the message of the ideal woman who is a housewife and mother. If she is employed, then surely she must be neğlecting her home and children. Stereotypes of women are reinforced in songs, plays and commercial jingles.

An exhaustive study of the portrayal of women in Hindi and Gujarati films was conducted in 1976 by Ila Pathak and her colleagues at AWAG. Their analysis of 12 Hindi and six Gujarati films showed that the films emphasised young, beautiful and sexually attractive women; portrayed women in terms of their relationship to men; depicted women in traditional female occupations; and as overwhelmingly emotional, dependent, superstitious, and irrational beings. Besides, they stressed marriage as a goal for women, and offered a double standard of morality.

Dasgupta and Hedge did a quantitative analysis of 30 Hindi films available on video in a mid-Western city in the United States, with the objective of investigating how they dealt with 'mistreatment' of women. The analysis led them to conclude that mistreatment was not a central concern of any film; that mis-treatments (such as physical battering, assault, rape, homicide) occurred regularly when women step out of their traditional roles; and that mistreatment served the common function of returning straying women to their stereotypical and socially approved behaviour patterns.

The recurrence of mis-treatments on the Hindi screen was, therefore, an established mechanism to monitor and perpetuate the patriarchal order. Another study by Vijaya Mulay revealed that women continue to be portrayed in traditional ways, and that in a few films, women beatings were popularized as a form of tanung and romancing. Madhu Kishwar, editor of Manushi, found that Films Division documentaries on family planning contained a strong sexist bias: they underscored the importance of sons over daughters, the responsibility of family planning as a woman's duty, and the general passive nature of women.

Studies of the print media have focused on the reporting of rape cases in the press ('as merely spicy news stories'), the presentation of women in women's sections of newspapers, general interest magazines and women's magazines. Ammu Joseph and Kalpana Sharma critiqued the news media's presentation of women's issues in their study, Whose News?

Ila Pathak's study of women's sections in the Gujarati dailies of Ahmedabad, for instance, found that there were hardly any articles devoted to a serious discussion of women's problems at home or in society. Dasgupta's look at the Sunday editions of four

English dailies found that articles on women were middle-class and urban-biased, and were restricted to a limited range of themes which did not take into account the political and economic realities of Indian women.

An analysis of fiction in three women's magazines and two general interest magazines concluded that they contained 'images and norms which should discourage female employment, particularly in higher-status occupations.'

Women's magazines have come in for a lot of criticism. Often, they are no more than a mixed bag of recipes, tips on beauty aids, romantic stories, features on women's issues, and discussions on gender problems, and of course women-oriented advertisements. Butalia found that, the advertisements, even in women's magazines, were sexist.

Aminu Amin's 1982 study of 'Commercial Ads and the Great Health Robbery of Women and Children' showed how advertisers and manufacturers play on the susceptibility and vulnerability of women consumers and cheat them into buying food products, cosmetics, sanitary napkins, soaps and detergents that are positively harmful to the health of their families. The study also revealed that 'men in advertisements are fully clothed, appear confident and dignified' while the women are presented as glamorous but in traditional roles.

Further, 'wares for men were sold for durability and economy; those for women for beauty and glamour.' Kalia's analysis of the language used in Indian school textbooks also concluded that it was clearly 'sexist.' Another analysis of the textbook series called Let's Learn English concluded that women were few in number when it come to central characters, and they were shown as either mothers or teachers.

Besides the question of 'representations', the focus of research has been the job opportunities for women, especially at decision-making levels, in the production, administration and technical departments of the various media. The most widely discussed is S.R. Joshi's study for UNESCO entitled Invisible Barriers: Women at Senior Levels. It analyses the status of women's employment at senior levels in Doordarshan. It found that women headed three out of 18 stations; that at the Delhi station 40 per cent of producers are women.

Another important finding was that 'although overall employment figures were not available, 28 per cent of the producers at two other stations are women, with responsibility for determining the content of programmes'. Besides, one-third of the women at these levels are unmarried, compared to only one-tenth of the men. The women have fewer children, and are better educated though mostly in the arts, compared to the men, half of whom had gone for courses in science, engineering and commerce. According to the study, a large proportion of the women thought that there would be a change in programme content with an increase in the proportion of female employees programme quality would improve and a more balanced perspective would emerge.

But there are more women in senior positions in the government-owned radio and television than in the press which continues to be male-dominated. A 1987 study by the Women and Media Group, Bombay, discovered that women journalists are mainly on the staff of women's magazines; the women journalists in the daily newspapers and the news magazines also confine themselves to women-related issues and 'soft' news stories. Gita Aravamudan's study of the status of women journalists in Kerala, the state with the highest literacy in the land, found that most are employed by women's magazines, or hold desk jobs; dailies such as Malayala Manorama and Kerala Koumadi however, did not employ women as a matter of policy.

Recognizing Audience

A largely neglected area in women-and-the-media studies has been audience research. Most of the audience research available has been conducted by market researchers where women are taken to be 'consumers'

The kind of research questions that need to be looked at are: How do women from different social classes 'read' the stereotypes in the various mass media and their genres? Do they, for instance, swallow the stereotypical representations hook, line and sinker, or reject or even 're-read' them? Again, how are programmes for women on radio and television produced? Who takes the vital decisions on programme content? Does the very fact that women are producers necessarily add a women's dimension to the programme? Women film directors like Aparna Sen and Sai Paranjpe have sensitized us to women's issues, but so have Satyajit Ray, Kumar Shahani, Mani Kaul, Basu Chatterjee, and Shyam Benegal.

Further, women-centred serials on Doordarshan (Rajani; It's A Woman's World, Kashmakesh. Chehre, Poornima, Rathachakra, Rathen Au Bhai Hain, Swayamsiddha, Basanti, Shanti, and several others) have attempted, some with greater success than others, to probe the woman/gender question through interesting narratives.

Further, several women have entered print and electronic journalism, but one wonders whether this alone has made any difference to professional values and news values which have been evolved and moulded by patriarchy, politics and the market. The core of professional journalism is still 'hard news'; 'soft news' which women reporters and feature-writers are generally asked to cover, is considered less important.

Factors Responsible for Consumerism : To most advertisers, people are not customers or even people but mere 'consumers.' Advertisers seek to entice target consumers to consume as much as possible, as frequently as possible, and with as much relish and envy or vanity as possible. It is not without significance that we are urged to buy and to consume wherever we are and whenever we switch on the radio, TV, cable or satellite TV, or read newspapers and magazines.

Day in and day out we are bombarded with print and electronic messages promising us fun, frolic and happiness if we 'consume.' It does not matter whether we have the purchasing power to try out 'impulse products' like ice-creams, chocolates, candies, or soft drinks, but if we do not consume like the rest of the world we are likely to be left behind in the rat-race.

It is not only advertising that directly promotes consumption beyond one's means, but also 'sponsored' programmes and columns and supplements. The subtle messages of soap-operas, quiz and game shows (where expensive prizes are gifted by business and industrial houses), elite-oriented news and current affairs programmes, sports programmes, fashion shows, children's magazines and programmes, cartoon shows, 'advertorials' and almost every programme-all tell one persuasive story: consume or be damned. Advertisers like to believe that the consumer enjoys the freedom of choice. He is, after all, not compelled to buy. He must learn to live within his means. What is more, the consumer is not a moron; she is your wife!

The question that needs to be raised is: Do the mass media which thrive on advertising lead to excessive consumption in society, or is the other way around: Does an affluent and economically developed society or community persuade the mass media to turn consumerist? It is true that both manufacturing and service industries in developed economies spend more on advertising and media relations than those in developing economies. However, it is equally true that the world's biggest markets for consumer product as well as for consumer durable are in the less developed countries. Further, during the past decade or so, growth in advertising expenditure in Asian countries has been steadily rising, while it has been reduced in the United States and other western countries.

In sum, consumerism is a fall-out of an industrial society, especially a society that swears by the economic laws of the free market and a liberal democracy. The assumption of such a society is that an 'invisible hand' controls the forces that compete freely with one another, and that justice and equity is promoted by such competition. The reality is that in a so-called open and free market the law of the jungle prevails, and only the most aggressive survive. Public welfare and concern fall by the wayside. The Indian experience of 'privatization' and 'liberalization' during the post-Rajiv Gandhi years suggests that some 'regulation' is imperative if the public will is to be maintained.

FACTORS RELATED TO SOCIETY

Over three thousand studies have been conducted during the past forty years in the United States alone that suggest that there is a 'correlation' between social aggression and the viewing of violence on the big and small screens. According to the American Psychological Association, by the time an average American child is ten or eleven years old, he/she would have seen 8,000 murders and 10,000 acts of violence on television.

Few studies on the subject have been conducted in India, and Indian children are not yet exposed to the excessive violence that American children are, at least on television. However, with the arrival of satellite television which is dominated by American films and television programmes, the Indian child is no doubt likely to be exposed to more and more violent fare.

Of course, popular Indian films too have a surfeit of violence, much of it stylised, but some of it vivid and realistic, often bordering on the pornographic. There have been cases of children and adults imitating on-screen violence and the modus operandi of gangsters, robbers and murderers. Such cases get prominent coverage in the press and other media. But all this does not lead one to the conclusion that cinema or television violence is the primary or even the secondary cause of violence in our society. At the most, screen violence may be one of the many contributory factors. More influential factors are poverty, frustration, unemployment, revenge, family clashes, urban decay, loss of self-esteem, a sense of failure in other words, a combination of sociological, psychological, economic and cultural factors.

In any case, the 'correlations' that the American studies have found between screen violence and individual acts of violence do not mean that screen violence has 'caused' the violent behaviour. Statistical correlations, however significant, may point to an 'association' but hardly ever to a cause-and-effect relationship. What is of greater concern is the effect of 'desensitization' which could result from repeated exposure to scenes of violence in programmes, news and cartoons.

Exposure to violence constantly and on a daily basis can desensitize us to violence in real life: violence against women and children, for instance, will shock or move us much less than we ought to as human beings. Further, we might be convinced that violence is a part of society, and that it is normal, even glamorous to be aggressive and 'macho' in one's behaviour. It might lead us to believe that some groups (for instance, tribals, dalits and leftists) are naturally violent, and such stereotypes might endure.

Violence in the news and in comic strips is rarely talked about. While the portrayal of violence in the press and broadcast media is condoned because it is 'factual' and deals with real-life incidents, the caricatures of violent fights and clashes between heroes and villains are condoned because they are presented in a light and humorous manner. There has been hardly any study in India or elsewhere in Asia about the influence of such violent portrayals on society.

A recent study sponsored by AMIC, Singapore, of television violence in six Asian countries concluded that where American origin fare dominated, as in the Philippines and Thailand, the violent scenes were more numerous than in indigenous programmes, though this was not the case in Japanese television. The violence on the Indian television screen was found to be mostly in the popular Hindi and regional language films. The

Indian Institute of Mass Communication, New-Delhi, undertook a study of television violence in 1996, using the Gerbner model of 'cultivation analysis.'

But violence is not related to crime alone. It must take into account state violence, like that of the police and the armed forces, or the violence of the law which does not bring the guilty to book, or which delays justice, or worse, punishes the innocent. Such violence too is sometimes the subject of cinema and television. The portrayal of such violence could help raise consciousness and thus lead to social reform (e.g. the film Ardh Satya, and the television serial, Tamas). Violence in the mass media is frequently associated with sex.

Indeed, rape or forced sex is the most violent crime that is often depicted graphically on the big and small screen. In recent years, a rape sequence has almost become obligatory in the popular film. Rape sequences are sometimes followed by scenes of blood and gore, since scores have to be settled and the rape avenged. Further, villains need to frequent night clubs where titillating cabarets are put on for their entertainment. The censors come down heavily on a few films, but the majority of popular films are 'passed' as okay for the entire family. Foreign television soap-operas, sitcoms, detective serials, music videos, and even talk shows and sports relays (especially those from the United States, Australia and Britain) have dollops of sex and violence, often verging on soft-core pornography. Doordarshan and Zee TV, in order to compete with STAR-TV, have begun imitating the fare on the satellite channels uplinked from Hong Kong, and other Asian cities.

5

Practical Aspects

After it assumed power in 1989, the National Front government came out first with a Cabinet Paper and then introduced the Prasar Bharati Bill in December 1989. According to P. Upendra, the Minister for Information and Broadcasting, the Bill borrowed from the Prasar Bharati Bill of 1979 and took into account the changed circumstances and the present ethos. Many, however, felt that the bill was put before the nation in a hurry. A national debate was initiated, in many cases with the active encouragement of the government to arrive at a consensus on the framework and the modalities of media autonomy.

The Bill, after incorporating some amendments, was unanimously passed in both Houses of Parliament. But following a change of government in October 1990, the lack of political good will to translate the concept into a working proposition was apparent. While there was no official pronouncement, the interim government headed by Chandrashekhar continued to maintain the status quo. The dissolution of the Lok Sabha in April 1991 signed the death warrant of the Prasar Bharati Bill, which then had needed only the Presidential assent for becoming Law. The death of Rajiv Gandhi and the advent of Congress rule in June

1991, under P.V. Narasimha Rao, put an end to any hopes about the issue. Meanwhile, the question of broadcasting autonomy has become irrelevant as other sources of information and entertainment viz., STAR TV, CNN and BBC have burst into view in the wake of the Gulf War. The invasion from the skies has begun.

Today, the rapid expansion of television in India in terms of availability (7 channels) and sheer expansion (545 TV stations) speaks of unqualified success by any standards. TV has often reached a high degree of professional excellence in its news coverage. The 32-hour continuous election telecast in May-June 1991 involving on-the-spot reporting from the counting booths even in the remote corners of the country and the swift shuttling between the national network and the local centres was a refreshingly dramatic experience for the viewers. But barring occasional and isolated instances, it has steadily developed an urban bias and an elitist approach, popularising, in the process, an alien life style and culture far removed from the realities of Indian life.

The Doordarshan has always suffered from the dichotomy between policy pronounce-ments (which emphasize the use of the mass media for social progress) and the continuous drift and departure from them in actual practice. In a developing and democratic country like India, access to television and the social benefit accruing from it, is a crucial test of the social relevance of such an expensive medium. The reason to the establishment of the Doordarshan in India, according to official statements, is to create a sense of participation in our efforts to usher in a new social order. As early as February 1973, a seminar on software objectives sponsored by the government recommended that, "Television must be used in the development process as an instrument of social change and national cohesion by unhesitatingly upholding progressive values and involving the community in a free dialogue. Indian TV has to shun an elitist approach and consumer value system and evolve a truly national model."

Officially the task assigned to the electronic media is three-fold. First, "the AIR and Doordarshan should inform people about happenings in India and the world, objectively, fairly and without any bias, as adequately and quickly as possible." Second, "the electronic media should get across to the people the policies and programmes that the government has framed for accelerating the process of socio-economic transformation." And finally, the broadcast media should pursue "an open policy and a policy that does not shirk issues and the responsibilities connected to these issues in order to develop an informed and participative citizenry; so that people know and think for themselves what is good for them and for the country." There can be no serious difference of opinion on these objectives. The reach of the electronic media together with the high percentage of the illiterate population make the broadcast media the most appropriate vehicles of national communication.

Mrs. Indira Gandhi, who played a leading role in the growth of TV in India, saw its role primarily as a promoter of development and education in a backward country. She repeatedly affirmed the national importance of utilising TV not just for the idle entertainment of the elite but for the uplift of the poor, especially in the inaccessible rural areas. But in effect and in actual practice, the purchase of a TV set is seen as wholesale investment in entertainment which obviates the bother and expense of going to an auditorium or a stadium. Even a cursory examination of its programmes during any week makes it clear that the order in which Doordarshan fulfils the three functions of the medium are entertainment first, information second and education third. This is true even after the introduction of the five Metro channels.

Even a casual viewer cannot but notice that the Doordarshan does not practice what it preaches and evidently such guidelines are honoured more in the breach then in the observance. The official media, despite occasional airs of openness, are generally identified as the propaganda wing of the party in power. These media do not present a balanced and non-partisan view of the events and happenings, which an average citizen so badly requires in order to arrive at an informed judgement. India may demand free and balanced flow of information at the international level. But at home, the distinction between the ruling party and the government, between the party interest and the national interest often gets blurred. In addition to the lack of objectivity and frankness, the news on Doordarshan also suffers from an overdose of elite and urban values.

From inception, broadcasting in India has been looked upon as a public service for the promotion of social objectives. The concept of advertisements for the promotion of consumer's goods was also considered incompatible with the prevailing philosophy of the "socialistic pattern of society." What causes alarm today is the proliferation in the mass media of these very advertisements for consumer goods.

In a developing country like India, radio and TV should be viewed as a national resource for the uplift of the masses. It is only through a strong media network that the right kind of information and education can be imparted to the people. But the media in our country, like elsewhere in the world, have buckled under the pressure of commercial interests. As a result, besides discrimination of information or the 'haves' from the 'have-nots', there is erosion of regional and cultural identities and ethics. Mindless entertainment with little or no educative value defeats the very purpose of building up a strong media network. For one, it is definitely not in the interest of the people to provide them with unproductive media fare. For another, it is nothing but unjustifiable use of invaluable resources.

The question that inevitably arises is whether we should use TV for promoting a humane social order or to create synthetic needs.

Under the existing system Doordarshan has become a tool for the promotion of crass consumerism. It is a strange paradox that this public investment, which facilitated the rapid expansion of the TV network in a poor country, is now being exploited by the big businesses for building their own corporate images. While it is conceded that ad revenue makes a network viable and independent, the same advertising also dictates the nature, form and content of the media software. Every noble intention to arouse social consciousness through the media gets traded for unhealthy programming. Here is an example.

Advertisers would always prefer to sponsor those programmes which create the proper mood in the viewers to buy their products. Their choice, invariably, falls on entertainment programmes. On rare occasions when serious programmes on topics like environment preservation, public hygiene or any significant social issues like land reforms or minimum wages are telecast, no sponsor is usually available. This is in stark contrast to the situation when advertisers lined up to spend a total of Rs. 35 crore on the serial 'Mahabharat' alone. To play the role of communicator-cum-educator in developing countries, broadcasting media have to provide software that would enrich the lives of the people. A communication policy would have to specify some guidelines to our communicators regarding balanced programming. Here, 'balanced' would mean the right mix of entertainment, information and education.

Role of Press

The press in a democratic country plays a vital role in creating, moulding, and reflecting public opinion. It is a fundamental institution of our society.

Though the press in India is free, it suffers from many ills. It has yet to identify its true post-independence role so as to ensure against haphazard growth and directionless expansion.

There are a few in-built handicaps such as vast geographical area, illiteracy, poverty, multiplicity of languages, and absence of adequate communication facilities. Some other bottlenecks exist, like the linking of ownership of newspapers with other industrial or commercial enterprises; limited newspaper ownership with closely held 'share interest'; urban-oriented expansion of newspapers leaving the vast country side population untouched, inadequate and expensive newsprint, and the lack of local advertisement support.

Eminent journalists have pointed out several drawbacks which stand in the way of making the press in India an independent and impartial instrument of communication of news and views. Some of these drawbacks are: the present system of accreditation of journalists; the government's allocation of newsprint; fixation of advertisement rates; favours to journalists in the form of perquisites such as subsidized housing, medical facilities, etc., heavy dependence of the press on official releases.

For a comprehensive and an in-depth examination of the state of the Indian press and the steps that need to be taken for its development on sound and healthy lines, the Government of India appointed the second Press Commission on 18 May, 1978, headed by Justice K. M. Mathew.

The appointment of the Second Press Commission had become necessary as the Indian Press had undergone several changes, had taken new strides, and acquired an added significance with an ever-expanding readership.

One of the recommendations of the Second Press Commission was to include both positive and negative aspects of an event in development reports. This implied that these reports should investigate the reasons for success as well as failure at different places and under different conditions of various development programmes affecting the lives of the common people. But most of our newspapers merely carry official handouts giving statistics of man-days of employment provided, persons made literate or area brought under irrigation.

The reporting of non-official initiatives in rural development, education reform, struggle against superstitious beliefs. Evil practices like dowry and Sati or other areas of social campaign, is even less extensive than in-depth reporting of the implementation of official development programmes. The Commission says: "our newspapers usually become aware of such non-official activities only after they have been honoured by a Jamnalal Bajaj Foundation award or Magsaysay award."

Another long standing criticism of the press is that it carries too much bad news at the expense of the good. To gain maximum readership, the press emphasizes the exceptional rather than the representative; the sensational rather than the significant. Many activities of the utmost social consequence are not considered reportable incidents.

But, as Indira Gandhi never tired of pointing out, "the meek may one day inherit the earth, but never the headlines." This brings us inevitably to the question of social responsibility. Certainly, the press has travelled a long way from the arrogant attitude of the newspaper owners who said, "A newspaper is a private enterprise owing nothing whatsoever to the public, which grants it no franchise. After all, responsible journalism is journalism with a conscience." Nikhil Chakravarthy, an eminent journalist, had said that, "Even if you don't like someone or disagree with him ideologically, you must be fair."

A journalist is confronted with ethical decisions almost daily. Should a news source go unnamed? Should a "leak" possibly affecting national security be used? Does the public interest override individual privacy? Should a rape victim's identity be disclosed? Should communities be identified in a communal clash or gory details of violence reported? General professional codes call for truth, accuracy, impartiality and fair play. Unlike most countries where a free press exists, there is no universally accepted code of conduct in enforcement in India. Even the professional bodies have not been unanimous in developing any. Nor has any serious effort been made by the press to find out what the society thinks of it let alone identify the possible areas of disagreement.

The Indian press had always been known for its sanity over sensitive issues like communal disturbances. But on the threshold of the nineties, it appeared that a large section of the press lost its sense of balance and fairness while reporting such highly explosive issues and events. Barring a few glorious exceptions, most of the newspapers betrayed a distinct and dangerous slant in reporting the Ram Janmabhoomi-Babri Masjid controversy.

For all this, the absence of a code of professional conduct in our country is more or less made up for by the adherence of the press to the social responsibility theory. And the performance of the press can be evaluated on the basis of this single criterion. Such accountability to the public serves as a self-regulatory mechanism in place of an explicit policy.

New Ways

What is the role of the government in making the mass media truly effective vehicles of culture, creativity and expression? Whatever the nature of media ownership-whether government, public corporation, or private enterprise-it is the government which is ultimately responsible for ensuring the use of broadcasting frequencies in the public interest.

Programme content is based on the objectives of the medium, these objectives form the basis for media policies. In our country, the Ministry of Information and Broadcasting monitors the content of the print and electronic media to ensure that all the mass media serve their noble purpose; to be tolls in the process of development and change. The improvement and expansion of the media network is directly linked to this goal.

From time to time various Committees and Commissions have been set up for the purpose of evaluating the working of the communication network. Attempts have been made to formulate a mass media policy based on their recommendations, whether or not these suggestions will be incorporated to the working of the media system depends on the authorities. In response to some of the policy considerations the government may decide to make resources available through direct budgets, or grants or provided fiscal advantages to quality productions, or offer preferential customs duties when importing hardware or software, etc. Alternatively, the media policy itself may be the outcome of such decisions and regulations.

Public participation in the formulation of national mass media policies may be achieved by setting up Mass Media Policy Council, with representatives from among media professionals and others concerned with the role of communication in society.

To implement policy initiatives, institutions may be started or existing ones improved for training and research in the media of film, radio and television broadcasting, printing and book production, etc. It is of utmost importance to chalk out a detailed communication policy to guide the growth of the communication networks. Piecemeal initiatives only harm the functioning of the media system. A comprehensive policy would help bring about more effective and purposeful communication.

For effective mass communication it is essential that mass communications have as much information as possible about the audiences or receivers. Although mass audience for each medium is seen as a large group of unknown people, there are also specific audience for particular contents.

Information technology has advanced so much in the years that it is now possible for people, while sitting in their drawing rooms, to witness the events taking place in any part of the world or even in space. We can watch the live coverage of sports events or music concerts taking place thousands of miles away. Indira Gandhi was able to talk to Rakesh Sharma in the space shuttle and the whole of the world could watch them in conversation. The war in Iraq was shown live by CNN. Teleconferencing makes it possible not only to watch events far away but also to participate in the action.

Technology has expanded the audiences manifold. Today we think in terms of audiences spread over the whole world, a phenomenon which Marshall McLuhan called global village. National boundaries hold no barriers for mass communication.

Still communication cannot be without targets. Mass communication is effective if it is produced for specific groups people. Thus, on the one hand, audiences of mass communication are spread across the national boundaries; on the other hand media content has to be target oriented.

We have seen that each of these media has certain advantages over the others. We have also seen that different people exhibit different preferences for media use.

The term mass in used to denote different things. In physics, the word mass refers to the quality of matter or material contained in an object. It may also mean a quantity of matter of indefinite shape and size—a lump.

Sometimes the word mass is used to refer to common people, specially the lower classes. Mass also has both negative and positive meanings. In the negative sense, it refers to the ignorant and unruly mass. Mass implies a lack of culture, intelligence and even of rationality. In socialist tradition, mass has a positive meaning. It connotes the strength and solidarity of ordinary working people when organised together for political ends.

In general usage, the word mass refers to people in a large number. If we say masses are ignorant, we mean that a very large proportion of the population ignorant. Similarly, when we say mass destruction means destruction on a very large scale. Mass awareness programme refers to a programme that aims to create awareness amongst a very large number of people. In fact, the important feature of mass is its very large size in terms of the number of individuals. It will be appropriate if we say that mass refers to an infinite number of individuals. The size of mass is very large and unknown.

Secondly, masses are geographically distributed. Very large number of large of people may be attending a public meeting. They are physically present anywhere and everywhere. When we say masses in developing countries are poor we refer to the people living in Africa, Asian, Latin America and perhaps some other and perhaps some other parts of the world as well.

Since the masses are very large in size and in physical terms the people are distributed all over, they are anonymous to each other. They are not even conscious of the presence of one another. There may be a vague feeling of others like us but it is not well defined. Since the people are anonymous to one another, the masses are unorganised. Unlike the people in a public meeting, there is not organisation and therefore no leadership or hierarchy in mass. Further, the masses are not capable of behaving as one unit. We can conclude that for our purpose that mass to an infinitely large number of people who are physically located at different places and are not organised at all as a group. In fact scholars like Roymard Williams have summarised that masses actually do not exist, it is only a way of conceiving large groups of people as masses.

Society is a large and complex system. With modernisation the complexity of the society further increase. The traditional society has a well defined social system in which individuals are closely tied to each other, mainly through kinship ties. But industrialisation and urbanisation lead to the formation of society where interdependence of numbers in economic terms increase manifold but kinship ties gradually fade away. The individuals become more self-centred. The socially, economically and politically isolated. The modernising societies experience an increase in individuality. The individuals develop a strong alienation with the community as a whole. There is an increased growth of segmental and contractual relationships. Such a society which is very large in size but where members are isolated and relationships are contractual is called a mass society.

However, the concept of mass society is not to be equated with of massive society. It is more than the massive society. There are many traditional society that are very large in a numbers but are not necessarily mass societies. The individuals in a traditional and Selznick have explained the concept of mass society as follows.

"Modern society is made up of masses in the sense that there has emerged a vast mass of segregated, isolated individuals interdependent in all sorts of specialised ways. Yet lacking in any central unifying value or purpose. The weakening of traditional bonds, the growth of rationality and the division of labour, have created societies made up of individuals who are only loosely bound together. In this sense, the mass society is something closer to an aggregate than to a tightly knit group. In fact, as stated earlier, mass society has no continuous existence, except in the minds of those who want to reach as many people as possible. It will be useful to further understand the concept of mass society using a set of contrasts with other kinds of units in social life, like group, crowd and public.

In a small all members know each other. They are aware of their common membership, share the same value, have a certain structure of relationship which are relatively stable. The members of a group interact other for a purpose.

The crowd is a spontaneous collection of individuals. It is temporary and never reappears with the same composition. Members of a crowd may strongly identify with each other. More important, they share the same mood. But there exists no order or structure in the crowd. In many cases the actions of the crowd are emotional, sometimes irrational also. Crowd is physically present within observable boundaries, that is, at a particular place.

Unlike crowd, public is widely dispersed. Its size may be small or large. Generally public is identified with some cause, purpose or activity. Public may be quite heterogeneous and members may not be aware of each other. Usually public is identified by the people who want to perceive a large of people as targets.

Let us illustrate each of the above discussed concept with example from our day to day life. Each one of us belongs to many groups simultaneously. Family is the primary unit and basis for all social life. We are all members of our families. Along with this we are also members of class, team, peer group, club etc. On a railway platform we are a part of the crowd. A crowd is also formed when we together to protest against the non-availability of goods.

Political parties treat us as public when they tell us about their policies and plans. We are public for public for police when it informs us about the imposition of curfew. We move in small group of friends or families in a mela. In the mela, we become a part of the crowd but for those displaying their items we are a public.

The Audience

The commonly used meaning of the term media audience is the aggregate of persons forming readers, listeners, viewers of different media, that is, the content of different media. In other words, audience is a group if individuals with a common pattern of media consumption. Such individuals share common access or exposure to the same mass communication products. There are four different ways of looking at media audiences. These are media reach, media access, media exposure and media exposure and media effects. We shall discuss these approaches one by one.

Approach of a Journalist

The owners and producers of the mass media conceive the total population whom their communications can reach. The signals of All India Radio are available to about 95 percent of the population living in about 85 percent of country's area. So the total population of India may be treated as audience for All India Radio. Similarly, Doordarshan can claim more than 80 percent of the population as its audience because its signals can reach that many people. For a newspaper, audience would be defined in terms of all individuals who are within the distribution range of the papers. For a cable TV system the audience reach will include all residents within the wired area.

Mass media may be available but the capacity or willingness to us the media may not be there. A large section of the population does not have the radio receivers or television sets. Thus, only those who own the radio sets may be treated as audiences of All India Radio. But access may not overlap ownership. In fact, there are many people who watch television programmes at the houses of neighbours or friends or in community centre. Groups watching a popular television at television shop is a common sight. Many families do not buy newspapers but their members may read newspapers at various places like teashop, barbershop, library or even at neighbours' or friends' house. This, those who have direct access by virtue of ownership along with those who are non-owners but get exposed in other ways accessible audience. Who are non-owners but get exposed in other ways constitute the accessible audience.

Everyone who has access to radio or television does not necessarily use them. In a family that subscribes to a actually expose themselves to the media audiences. Again, no one is exposed to the total content of any medium. No one listens to all the programmes broadcast by All India Radio. Similarly, it is impossible to watch all the programmes of Doordarshan. Many people do not even glace at the commerce page of the newspapers. There are many young people, specially students, who read only the sports page. So audiences can also be seen as programme specific or content specific, that is, populations actually exposed to specific media contents.

Another important aspect of media behaviour is that all users of media content are not uniformly exposed. There are people who listen to news everyday without fail. Others may listen to news, says on an average of five days a week. Still others may be people whose exposure to news or radio is nil.

Actual Impact

Another way to think about audiences is in terms of individuals who have been exposed to mass communication products and have undergone a change in their knowledge, opinions, attitude or behaviour. A person may not recall anything of the person, after watching an advertisement, may immediately rush to buy the advertised products. Voters generally do not change their voting preference after listening to election broadcasts by the representatives of political parties.

Actual Feedback

The most interesting feature of a mass communication audience is its dual nature. At one level media audience is a collectivity formed in response to media content and defined by attention to that content. When a new newspaper is launched, people gradually start reading it. MTV, STAR TV, and ZEE TV have created their own audiences.

Alternatively, audience may be conceived as collectivity that exists already in the systems and mass media may begin to cater to its information and entertainment needs. Krishi Darshan may aim to cater to the needs of the farmers. Yuvvani attempts to cater to needs of the youth. Femina is meant for the women whereas seminar is meant for the intellectuals. In the first case, media or its content is the cause of the creation of the audience, but in the second case, the audience become the cause of the creation of the media content. In many case, it is very difficult to determine whether audience is responsible for creation of the media content or the media content has created the audience. The fact is that the audiences are both, the cause as well as the response to the mass communication process. A new newspaper creates its own readership but at the same time it tries to the needs of the targeted readers.

The original audiences were the sets of spectators for games, stage plays or dispension of justice by the king. Such pre-media audiences existed in all cultures in one form or another. Audience for religious discourses have played a very significant role in the spread of social and political ethos.

Invention of printing revolutionised the whole character of audience. This was the beginning of mass audience. The most important change that the took place was that the audience participation as a private act became possible. People could now take the printed materials to secluded places and undergo a totally private experience. This led to another important change. The audiences become delocalised. It was no more necessary for all members of the audience to be present at one place. A book had readers spread all over the world.

The advent of newspapers created mass audiences in the real sense. Newspapers also converted mass audiences into potential receivers of commercial message or advertising. The advent of electronic media further delocalised the audiences. The information carried by electro-magnetic waves could cross the national boundaries. The audiences were now spread over the whole world. The members were separated from each other and their distance, physical and social, from the communicators also increased.

The audiences now not only took the form and character of masses but they also acquired the features of a mass society. The satellite communication, coupled with cable network on the ground, has brought a situation where the whole world population can be treated as one audience.

The types of audiences can be distinguished based on their demographics characteristics and mental make up.

Elite audience are composed of the people who are decision-makers and trend-setters in the society. They are economically well to do and are highly educated. They have high status in the society. Their numbers is very small but their influence is very strong. They may also be the owners or controllers of the mass media institutions. The members of the elite audience are the early adopters of communication technologies. Their actual media consumption is generally low.

General Audience : They are very large and highly divers groups that represent the broad cross-section of the society. Majority of the people to this category. The media content is generally targeted at them. Their participation determines the success or failure of content or medium.

Specialised Audiences : These audience are composed of individuals who possess similar characteristic. They are relatively small in number. Mass media generate special contents for these audience groups. Programmes for tribals, for housewives, for college students, etc. are example of programmes for specialised audiences. Similarly, journals like Mainstream, Femina and Economic and Political Weekly have limited but known readership.

The Clientele

Rise of consumerism has led to a situation where audiences are treated as markets. The media products is a commodity or service offered for sale to a given body of potential consumers, in competition with other media products. Their potential or actual consumers can be referred to as markets.

With the commercialisation of broadcasting and telecasting in our country, the audience are being treated more as markets. There is competition between Doordarshan, STAR TV, ZEE TV, MTV to capture as big an audience as possible. Drastic changes in the programme content of Doordarshan main and Metro channels is an indication of the fact that even the state controlled medium is forced to view audiences as markets. Audience, according to the market concept, can be defined as an aggregate of potential consumers with a known socio-economic profile at which medium or message is directed.

Audience has a dual significance for the media. Firstly, as set of potential or actual consumers of media content and secondly, as the audience for advertising message. Thus a market for media content is simultaneously a market for other products; media serve as advertising vehicles for delivering messages to the potential customers of other products. Advertising is the largest source of revenue for all media. In fact, no medium can survive if not supported by advertising or some other sources.

Till the time AIR and Doordarshan were not commercial, the government used to subsidies their services. The most popular programmes of radio and television attract the maximum advertising. Not only that, advertising rates are the highest for prime time programmes. The treatment of audiences as markets has social and moral implication as well. First, when the relationship between the media and audience is that of producer and consumer, the character if relationship become manipulative. The aim is torn sell as much as possible.

Secondly, the members of the audiences are markets and are treated as passive receivers. The audience are lured by cleverly designed message, Thirdly, the success of the media is measured not in terms of needs fulfilled but in terms of sales of the products. Lastly, the market view is that of the media owners and media producers. Audiences never see themselves as markets.

Audience is the single most important element in any conception of mass communication. The development of the relationship between the mass media and the audience can be seen in two contrasting ways. We may consider the availability of a large number of media units as media explosion. In this conception, the media occupy the central position and information from the various media is seen as acting upon the audience.

But if we observe the media audience relationship carefully, we find that the audiences actually exercise their choice as to which medium is to be used and also which content they would like to be exposed to. Marshall McLuhan saw the audiences at the centre of the numerous attacks by different media. He referred to this as media implosion as against the media explosion.

The efforts required for attending to mass communication may be considered in terms of the availability of the media and the ease with which we may use the media.

Expense involved and the time required are also important factors in "the effort required." Watching a film on television is less expensive, less time consuming and little efforts is required for it as compared to watching a film in a cinema hall.

The uses and gratification theory of the media effects proposes that basic human needs motivate individuals to attend to particular forms of mass media and to select and use messages in ways they find personally gratifying. Thus, audience members make a conscious and motivated selection amongst the various mass media and also amongst the various item of content.

The producers of mass communication keep a hand on the pulse of their audiences in order to make their products more and more acceptable. Audience feedback systems are the mechanisms through which information regarding audience reaction is taken back to the owners, controllers and producers of the media. There are two distinct feedback system; market-based feedback system and research based feed-back system.

Mass Communicators receive the following information through the market-based feedback system : (a) audience access to the media; (b) audience exposure to the media.

The above mentioned information is received by the communicators by three methods :

> Audiences decision to subscribe to newspapers or magazines is a direct feedback about the popularity of the publication. Rise and fall of circulation is a very important feedback that the market provides. More and more houses paying for cable TV connections indicate the increased popularity of the. satellite channels. At the same time, it may also indicate that the audiences are not very happy with the Doordarshan

programmes. Increased circulation of a news paper implies endorsement of the style and editorial policies of the new paper. Sales at box-office is a good feedback about the popularity of a film.

Sometimes, audience reactions to, mass communication are very actively solicited. Coupons, rebate offers, bring-this-and-get-a-discount and similar practices are used to measure the impact of particular promotional efforts.

For books, magazines, papers, video and audio cassettes, film and cable TV connections, the audience behavior has a direct bearing. More consumers mean more revenues. In case of radio and television and even news papers and magazines, the largest share of revenue comes from advertising. But again the advertising rates are determined by audience size, and thereby audiences exert their influence, through indirectly.

Direct Feedback : Mechanisms of direct feedback are provided in each media system. Newspapers and magazines have columns reserved for letters to the editor sent by the readers. Similarly, radio and television networks have programmes reserved for comments, reaction suggestion from the audiences. Unsolicited letters and telephones also provide important feedback. In some cases, casual conversation between employees of mass media and members of audience may provide important feedback.

A careful observation of the media in our country over the last two decades would reveal the felt needs for direct feedback from the audiences increasing. Space devoted to the letters to the editor column in newspapers and magazines has increased. Similarly, more and more air time is being given on radio and television for programmes where representative of the audience are allowed to give their reaction and suggestion.

Media Reviews : Media give the greatest importance to the feedback through the reviews. Every news paper and magazine has media review column written by a media critic. In these columns, the media critics examine the mass communication of radio and television. Similarly, there are regular review of films, audio and video cassettes published in newspapers and magazines.

The role these media reviews is two fold. One, the owners, controllers and specially the producers of radio and television programmes take the comments very seriously. Secondly, these reviews provide information to the audiences. They, in fact, provide expert opinion and influence audience to notice and use particular mass media content. A radio or television programmes or a film or book or a song sequence commented favourably becomes acceptable to the audiences. Many people buy or read a book after reading its review. In our country, there were no reviews of the print media except in academic journals till recently. Now, some newspapers have introduced these. For example, The Pioneer has a weekly column Blue Pencil by G S Bhargava. It appears on very Sunday and critically comments on the coverage in different newspapers.

Firstly, the critic acts as a link between the producers and the audience. At this point, the critic performs the role of calling attention to the availability of information and recommending responses. Secondly, the critic may provide his expert comments to the producers. At this point, the act is an interpretation of how and why the audiences reacted positively or negatively to the content. Various functions performed by the reviewers can be listed as follows :

(a) Informing audience what is new and interesting.

(b) Raising the cultural level of the community.

(c) Advising the audiences on how to use their time and money.

(d) Helping artists and performers to understand how their efforts are being received by the audiences.

(e) Recording the history of mass communication.

(f) Entertaining audiences with their articles and reports.

The market-based feed back and the reviews are more or less

passive systems. Feedback information gets generated without the producers making efforts for it.

They leave many questions unanswered. A newspaper will get information that its circulation is decreasing but it is not known as to who are the people who have stopped subscribing and why have they done so. Similarly, media critics may not comments at all on a programme or their comments may be considered subjective. Research based feedback systems are created to provide systematic information about audience response to a particular mass communication products of services.

Many media organisations have their own audience systems. For example, there are Audience Research in All Radio and Doordarshan. These units keep on collecting audiences responses to various programmes. Based on the research finding, the producers may improve their programme; some programmes may be discontinued or their timings may be changed.

Reliable and systematic information collected about the listenership or viewership leads to ratings of different programmes. The use of the media by advertisers and made to reach the desired audiences in a more cost effective manner. In our country, programmes regularly. It is hoped that soon it will evolve into an authentic and reliable system. Mass communication does not mean communication for everyone. The media and their audiences come together through a process or natural selection. Media tend to select their audiences by means of content. The audiences also tend to select among and within the media primarily on the basis of content.

Different media may different audiences but there is a considerable overlap between the audiences of one medium with those of the other. Researchers have shown that persons who are above average in exposure to one medium to other media as well. A person who reads a news paper is likely also to read magazines, listen to radio and watch television. Lazarsfeld and Merton called this phenomenon as all-or-non principle. A person interested in escapist entertainment will find it in books, magazines, films and televisions. Anyone who has little opportunity to use one medium because of poverty, illiteracy, ignorance or lack of time or interest-will probably have little opportunity to use any medium.

Newspapers attract very heterogeneous audiences. Children and young people generally do not read newspapers. Most of the readers read only the headlines or at the most read the introductory paragraphs. The finance page has a special readership composed of businessmen and those involved in economic and commercial activities. Sports page has an audience of predominantly young people. Editorial and edit page contents have a very small readership.

Magazines are generally read by people with more education and those belonging to higher economic strata, in general, young people are likely to use newspapers and magazines for entertainment, older people for information and views on matters of public life. Adults do more news reading than young people; the latter pay more attention to photographs and visuals like cartoons and comic strips.

More males read newspaper and also at greater length than females. Higher economic status is generally accompanied by increase in the reading of public news, sports news and society news. People belongs to low and very low socio-economic strata generally read local newspapers or they more attention to local news in regional or national news papers. Middle-class readers to read national news papers. Highly educated and rich people tend to read international newspapers and magazines or the newspapers and publications of other countries.

Before the advent of television, radio was the medium for all classes. However, many people neither owned radio sets nor did they have access to radio in any other way. Transistor revolution spread the ownership of radio receiving sets very widely. But in our country at no time more than 60 percent of the families owned radio sets.

Not-so-poor people and belonging to lower middle classes generally owned single band or two band radio sets. As a consequence, their exposure was mostly confined to local radio station or medium wave stations. People with efficient receiving systems listened not only to AIR but also to foreign systems like BBC, Voice of America, Radio, Moscow.

After the advent of television, radio listening in television owning households has fallen drastically. Many television owning households do not use the radio sets at all. The predominant use of radio today is for music in the background while people are engaged in other works. Many people use radio as an announcer or time. Unlike in U.S and other western countries, radio is not much used in motor vehicles in our country. Audio-tape players have become more popular in cars, buses and trucks.

Young persons use radio to listen to film and non-film music. Adults also listen to music but they tend to use radio as a source of news and information. Housewives may use radio as a companion during the day when they are alone. Young men and women appearing in competitive tests use radio as an important source of information, specially news and current affairs programme. Spotlight and Samayaki are very popular among those sitting in civil services examinations.

The tremendous popularity of television is at the expense of radio. With the advent of television, total time devoted to the media has increased. All sections of the population wish to watch television. Many have their own sets. Others watch television at neighbours or friends houses or at community centres.

News and current affairs programmes of Doordarshan are seen by more educated section of the society. Common people tend to watch entertaining serials. Ramayana on Doordarshan had the largest ever largest ever audience. DD Metro is more popular than the main channel of Doordarshan. Generally, people now subscribe to cable network systems. ZEE TV has a wide audience in Hindi-speaking middle and lower classes. The audience of STAR TV is restricted to middle and upper middle classes. MTV has an audience of young and rich who are relatively more exposed to western culture and values.

Research has shown that programmes like Krishi Darshan have very small audiences even among the farmers. It is important to note that the viewers of television also become the audience of the films. A number of films are shown on various channels of television. Besides there are many programmes that the based on films. The television and films industries have become closely related and there are films now produced only for television.

Till television spread its networks, films were the most widely used mass media. All sections of the population, very poor to very rich, went to cinema theatres to watch films.

With the advent of television, VCR, VCP, satellite transmission and cable networks, the films watching in cinema halls has decreased considerably. But the total exposure to films has perhaps increased.

Different types of films have different audiences. Common people generally like to watch masala-films that have an adequate mixture of emotions, comedy, violence, dance, music, sex etc. The new-wave films, the art films and low cost films have an audience that is composed of more educated, socially conscious and intellectual section. Religious films based on epics have an audience composed mainly of rural people, women, illiterate poor etc. Similarly, informative films or films with social messages have different audiences.

Books attract people who are above average in education and also in their use of the serious contents of other media. Books are more likely to attract young adults than older ones, people living in urban rather than in rural areas, people or high income rather than low income. Readers of English books attract audiences more from highly educated, well-off people. Books in Hindi languages are read mostly by the people belonging to these language groups. Generally, book-readers have a high exposure to other media.

Communication is one of those human activities that everyone recognise but few can define satisfactorily. Communication is talking to one another, it is television, it is spreading information, it is our hair style, it is literary criticism: the list is endless. This is one of problems facing academics: can we properly apply the term 'a subject of study' to something as diverse and multi-faceted as human communication actually is? Is there any hope of linking the study of, say, facial expression with literary criticism? Is it even an exercise worth attempting?

The doubts that lie behind questions like these may give rise to the view that communication is not a subject, in the normal academic sense of the world, but is a multi-disciplinary area of study. This view would propose that what the psychologists have to tell us about human communicative behaviour has very little to do with what the literary critic has.

This lack of agreement about the nature of communication studies is necessarily reflected in this book. What we have tried to do is to give some coherence to the confusion by basing the book upon the following assumptions.

— assume that communication is amenable to study, but that we need a number of disciplinary approaches to be able to study it comprehensively.

— assume that all communication involves signs and codes. Signs are artefacts or acts that refer to something other than themselves, that is they are signifying constructs. Codes are the systems into which signs are organised and which determines how signs may be related to each other.

— assume, too, that these signs and codes are transmitted or made available to others: and that transmitting or receiving signs/codes/communication is the practice of social relationships.

— assume that communication is central to the life of our culture: without it culture of any kind must die. Consequently the study of communication involves the study of the culture with which it is integrated.

Underlying these assumptions is a general definition of communication as 'social interaction through messages.'

The structure of this book reflects the fact that there are two main schools in the study of communication. The first sees communication as the transmission of messages. It is concerned with how senders and receivers encode and decode, with how transmitters use the channels and media of communication. It is concerned with matters like efficiency and accuracy. It sees communication as a process by which one person affects the behaviour or state of mind of another. If the effect is different from or smaller than that which was intended, this school tends to talk in terms of communication failure, and to look to the stages in the process to find out where the failure occurred. For the sake of convenience we shall refer to this as the 'process' school.

The second school sees communication as the production and exchange of meanings. It is concerned with how messages, or texts, interact with people in order to produce meanings; that is, it is concerned with the role of texts in our culture. It uses terms like signification, and does not consider misunderstandings to be necessarily evidence of communication failure—they may result from cultural differences between sender and receiver. For this school, the study of communication is the study of text and culture. The main method of study is semiotics (the science of signs and meanings), and that is the label we shall use to identify this approach.

The process school tends to draw upon the social sciences, psychology and sociology in particular, and tends to address itself to acts of communication. The semiotic school tends to draw upon linguistics and the arts subjects, and tends to address itself to work of communication.

Each school interprets our definition of communication as social interaction through messages in its own way. The first defines social interaction as the process by which one person relates himself to others, or affects the behaviour, state of mind or emotional response of another, and, of course, vice versa. This is close to the common-sense, everyday use of the phrase. Sometimes, however, defines social interaction as that which constitutes the individual as a member of his culture or society.

The two schools also differ in their understanding of what constitutes a message. The process school sees a message as that which is transmitted by the communication process. Many of its followers believe that intention is a crucial factor in deciding what constitutes a message. The sender's intention may be stated or unstated, conscious or unconscious, but must be retrievable by analysis. The message is what the sender puts into it by whatever means.

For sometimes, on the other hand, the message is a construction of signs which, defined as transmitter of the message, declines in importance. The emphasis shifts to the text and how it is 'read.' And reading is the process of discovering meanings that occurs when the reader interacts or negotiates with the text. This negotiation takes place as the reader, brings aspects of his cultural experience to bear upon the codes and signs which make up the text. It also involves some shared understanding of what the next the text is about. We have only to see how different papers report the same event differently to realise how important is this understanding, this view of the world, which each paper shares with its readers. So readers with different social experiences or from different cultures may find different meanings in the same text. This is not, as we have said, necessarily of communication failure.

The message, then, is not something sent from A to B, but an element in a structured relationships whose other elements include external reality and the producer/reader. Processes is that they occupy the same place in this structured relationship.

We might model this structure as a triangle in which the arrows represent constant interaction, the structure is not but a dynamic practice.

At one time or another almost everyone has responded to the question "How did this [disaster] happen?" with a statement like "Don't ask me. I just work here." In some cases the excuses is a legitimate one. Someone other than the person making the statement made a decision or took a step which created a problem, but far too often it is a decision, action, or lack of action by the person offering the excuse that led to the inefficiency or failure. Although the performance of every member of an organisation is in many ways influenced by the activities of other members, in the final analysis it is the individuals' choices which decide their destiny in the organisation.

It concentrates on communication in organisations because it is through communication that individual employees gain the information on which they base choices and exercise the influence which translates their choices into action. The goal of this book is to give readers a sense of how organisational communication is used strategically, that is, how individual employees analyse the situations thy face at work and choose the appropriate communication strategies to use in those situations.

The book assumes that all employees are goal-oriented in some important ways and that if they understand how communication functions in their organisation they will be better able to use their communication skills to achieve their objectives and those of their organisations. The book explains when it is appropriate to use a variety of communication strategies, including the denial or responsibility and the claim of ignorance ("I don't know. I just work here"), and more important, when not to use them.

One of the most important recent developments in the way people look at organisations has been the increasing amount of attention paid to different aspects of communication. Managers and researchers alike have recognised that businesses must maintain at least an adequate level of communication in order to survive, that increasing the effectiveness of communication within a firm contributes to the efficiency of its operation, and that in some cases highly effective communication can increase productivity and eventually profitability.

Perhaps more important has been the realisation that people who understand how communication functions in a business, who have developed a wide repertory of written and oral communicative skills, and who have learned when and how to use those skills seem to advance more rapidly and contribute more fully to their organisations than people who have not done so. As a result the number of college courses and professional training programs concerned with organisational communication has mushroomed. Of course employees cannot function effectively unless they possess the technical skills that their positions require.

But more and more it appears that being also able to recognise, diagnose, and solve communication-related problems is vital to the success of people in even the most technical occupations. Accountants must be able to gain complete, accurate, and sometimes sensitive information from their clients, supervisors of production lines must be able to obtain adequate and timely information on which to base their decisions, managers of different divisions must be able to give their subordinates clear instructions, make sure those instructions are understood, create conditions in which their commands will be carried out, and obtain reliable feedback about the completion of the tasks that they have assigned. In a recent survey of 700 middle managers, almost 85 percent of the respondents reported that it was their subordinates' communication skills (or lack or them) which determined their success or failure in critical situations. Although these managers also noted that factors like their subordinates' job-related expertise and loyalty to their supervisor and organisation also had an important impact on their effectiveness, it was their ability to communicate effectively that was crucial in most cases.

However, being able to communicate effectively at work requires two kinds of knowledge. First, it requires an understanding of the relationships that exit between communication and the operation of organisations. Since communication processes influence the way an organisation operates and are simultaneously influenced by key characteristics of the organisation, neither organisations nor organisational communication can be understood adequately if they are examined in isolation of each other. Second, effective communication depends on employees' understanding how to choose appropriate communication strategies in different situations.

This book intends to provide readers with an understanding of strategic communication skills, the ability to analyse a situation, select an appropriate communication strategy from a number of available options, and employ that strategy in an optimal way.

However understanding strategic communication demands that an individual understand how communication functions in organisations, how it creates and solves problems, how it makes some situations occur and how it prevents others, how it makes some outcomes more probable and others improbable. This chapter will introduce these two most important concepts: the role of communication in organisations and the characteristics of strategic organisational communication. Subsequent chapters will expand each of these concepts and explain how they contribute to the success of complex organisations and their members.

Historically, formal organisations have been examined from two very different perspectives. One view has depicted them as the combination of a number of different components, each of which is linked to each other on the basis of some carefully planned and clearly articulated design. People who accept this perspective believe that organisations are designed in three distinct steps. Designing an organisation begins with an analysis of a potential market and a decision about what products-goods or services the organisation should produce.

Designers then decide which tasks must be performed in order to produce the desired output and determine how each of these tasks can be completed most efficiently. Finally, designers organise the various tasks into structures and sequences which are intended to maximise the efficiency of the total operation. Since many of the components of the organisation are people, someone must be assigned the job of seeing that all who are involved in each part of the production process understand the tasks they are to perform, how they are to accomplish those tasks, the fact that they must accomplish them in a timely and efficient manner if the organisation is to function properly. In this perspective, communication is important for instrumental reasons. It functions in ways which allow members to share the information necessary for the successful completion of a complex array of interdependent tasks.

Although the end products, task requirements, employee skills, or relationships among these components may change when market conditions or technologies change, this perspective assumes that the rational design of an organisation will stay relatively constant. At least, the organisation will stay stable enough so that the designers can draw a picture, usually in the form of an "organisational chart," which accurately reflects its operation.

Another viewpoint describes organisations as complex, interdependent matrices of ongoing process, not as a rational, carefully planned combination of interrelated static components. This distinction is important for two reasons. First, it leads to a view of the members of an organisation as actors, not as relatively inert components of the organisation. Employees constantly are making choices about how they will act in the variety of situations they face. Second, organisations are networks of interdependent human actors whose actions both create situations they face allow them to respond to those situations.

Although organisations can be designed by objective, outside planners, their designs constantly are in a state of change. Businesses are composed of large numbers of people who constantly are monitoring their own actions and the actions of others, processing that information, and choosing those courses of action that they think are appropriate. This description of organisations does not imply that their members are either manipulative or Machiavellian although it would admit that some of them are. Instead, it suggests that people are active agents who have their own reasons for acting as they do.

They are not mechanical components of the production process, doing only what they are designed to do in precisely that way in which they are designed to do it. They are choice-making members whose actions are part of a complicated array of ongoing processes.

Within this perspective, communication is important to an organisation for two reasons. First, communication is the means through which people acquire the information and develop the criteria by which they decide how to act. Second, communication is the process through which they put their choices into practice. That is, through communication members of organisations learn that there are precedents in their organisation which constrain their choices, and they learn what those precedents are. Through communication with others, they develop and express the purposes which guide their actions. They are able to consider the potential effects of different actions only because they are capable of communicating. In addition, it is through communication that members of an organisation are able to coordinate their actions with other members of the organisation. Because the complex array of tasks that must be performed in an organisation are independent, each member of the organisation can perform only if other members do also.

In almost situations, only a small proportion of the activities of any one employees will be necessary preconditions for the successful action of other employees. However, for each member of the organisation, there are some actions that must be taken if the organisation is to operate. And, because all members must depend on the actions of some other member(s) in order to do their jobs, they must be able to predict accurately what those other people will do in different situations. Being able to do so requires employees to understand why they act as they do and to recognise that they regularly respond to certain situations in predictable ways.

Communications is the process through which people make sense out of the actions of other people, it is the means by which they are able to understand how they can coordinate their actions with the actions of others. Human action is contextual, it is the result of the choices people make within the situations they perceive themselves to be.

Unfortunately, these two views of organisations and communication often are seen as being mutually exclusive. Scholars who focus their attention on the design or structure of organisations and the functions of communication in organisation that have been described in this chapter often overlook the complex processes through which people decide how to act at work. Conversely, when scholars concentrates on understanding the relationships between processes of communication and processes of organising, they often deemphasise the tasks people perform at work and the function communication plays in the completion of those tasks. Understanding strategic organisational communication requires an analysis of both the functions of communication in organisations and the processes through which communication guides the actions of members.

Working Method

In some important ways communication functions as a tool for members of organisations: It allows them to issue, receive, interpret, and act on commands; it allows them to create and maintain productive business and personal relationships with other members of the organisations; and it allows them to manage ambiguity and uncertainty.

Two types of communication make up the "command" function: direction and feedback. People perform necessary task effectively only when they choose both to initiate action and to limit their actions in clearly prescribed ways. Some members of organisations, usually those given the formal titles of supervisor or manager, issue messages which tell other members to take action and to limit that action to a particular series to be taken at a specified time and at a specified place. If the person to whom the message is directed does not act, or if the person acts inappropriately, the command function will not be wholly successful.

It is inevitable that people will resist commands to some degree. In order to function, organisations must influence people to act in ways in which they otherwise would not act. For instance, few humans would choose on their own to perform seemingly minor, repetitive tasks hour after hour, day after day. But a large proportion of production-oriented organisations could not exist if it was not possible for some people to persuade other people to perform these tasks at a predetermined rate for a predetermined period of time with a minimal amount of creativity.

Assembly lines operate successfully only because a complex array of very specific commands are communicated to a large number of people in a way that somehow persuade them to follow those commands exactly. If any worker a does a job in a new, varied, unanticipated or creative way, the productivity of the assembly line is reduced. When automobile workers respond to the boredom of their jobs by choosing to install parts backward, upside down, or not at all, the quality of the final product usually us reduced. When they respond by celebrating the end of monotonous week with a Thursday afternoon or Thursday through Sunday visit to a local bar, their ability to follow commands exactly on subsequent days usually is reduced. Although these deviations from expected behaviour often do little damage, they create enough problems that most Americans learn at an early age "not to buy a car which was built on Friday."

Other types of organisations involve even larger numbers of people whose actions must be initiated and controlled if the organisation is to function. Consequently, the command function of communication relies on process of persuasion and influence. Its effectiveness depends on the availability of some form of influence and some communication strategies through which some members organisations can persuade other members to act in specific and unnatural ways.

The command function also involves the production of adequate feedback about the actions that actually are taken by people who have been issued commands. Supervisors often assume that their subordinates will carry out their commands. This assumption is especially strong when the supervisor has issued a set of routine instructions. Comfortable in the knowledge that their commands will be carried out, supervisors instruct other people to take actions which, when completed, will allow the task that the unit has taken on to be accomplished. If any of the people who are involved in the command process fail to carry out the commands they were given properly or promptly, the supervisors will need to modify the commands that were given to the other people and accurate feedback about the extent to which each of their commands has been carried out.

Almost all people who have worked in organisations which produce tangible products can remember instances in which they found themselves surrounded by piles and piles of partially finished products because some person or group of people failed to receive, understand, or carry out commands. These situations usually strike the workers who are gazing at the piles as being terribly funny, both because they know that the error is someone else's headache and because they have been allowed to take a lengthy break while waiting for the bottleneck to be eliminated and the unfinished products to reach their stations. Rarely does the supervisor who issued the commands find the situation quite as humorous. The piles of unfinished products do, however, give this supervisor feedback about the effects of the commands. Organisations do seem to function more efficiently when supervisors have access to more timely and less tangible command-related feedback.

Command-related communication typically comes in one of two forms: publications and instructions. The differences between the two forms are important because employees' reactions to a command are related in part to the form in which it is issued. Organisations produce a variety of formal written policies and procedures. The published communications have three important characteristics. First, they create the impression that the commands is directed to a general audience. No one has been picked out as the recipient; the message seems to be addressed to anyone. Second, they create the impression that the command is official; that is, it is written by the organisation or by someone who represents the organisation rather than by any one individual. Finally, They suggest, both that the command is a relatively permanent injunction and, indirectly, that the problem it addresses is important and recurring.

In contrast, instructions are oral commands, generally given in a face-to-face encounter and addressed to a single person or clearly defined group of persons. Instructions are highly flexible commands which seem to be transient rather than permanent. They are viewed as being linked to a specific problem which is relatively new, rare, or unprecedented and are from an individual rather than from the "organisation." Because publications and instructions are different forms of commands, they are appropriate to different kinds of situations. The success of any command depends on part being issued in the proper form.

One function of communication in formal organisations is the command function. Because organisations are composed of large numbers of people who play interdependent roles, their actions must be coordinated effectively. Successful coordination is achieved when members initiate the actions they have been directed to undertake. It occurs when some members of the organisation communicate in ways that create the kind of situations in which other members of the organisation will choose to take the precise actions that are envisioned in the commands. Both the process of creating a appropriate situation and the creation of clear and influential command messages depend on the strategic competence and communication skills of the participants. The command function of organisational communication relies totally on complex processes of constructing, interpreting, and choosing actions in response to a particular type of communication.

Organisational communication also fulfils a relational function, businesses are composed of human beings who are involved in interpersonal relationships with other human beings. Unlike non-work relationships, in which people have a relatively wide degree of freedom in deciding who to form relationships with, the structure of formal organisations dictates that each employee must form relationships with a clearly defined group of people. Sometimes, perhaps most of the time, members of organisations are required to form effective "working relationships" with people with whom they never would choose to form personal relationships. For a number of reasons, imposed relationships are less stable and more prone to friction than are "natural" ones.

Like natural relationships, working relationships can succeed only if the parties involved can achieve at least a minimal degree of understanding and cooperation. To do so they must be able to comprehend the meaning of the messages they exchanges with each other, assess each others' motivations with some degree of accuracy, and negotiate some agreements about how they will act toward one another.

Unless these minimal requirements are met, the development of effective working relationships is impossible. Like all relationships, working relationships inevitably will involve some friction, misunderstanding, and conflict about the proper nature of the relationship. However, in non-working relationships the parties usually develop a degree of commitment to each other and to the continuation of the relationship. Typically they will have voluntary started relationship and will made a number of decisions to continue it in spite of conflicts and frictions because they continue to receive benefits from it. To some degree at least, their commitment is mutual and intrinsic to the relationship. In working relationships, the parties may have very little commitment to the relationship itself.

Someone or something else, a supervisor of the organisation-initiated the relationship, the parties stay in it because their roles in the organisation seem to demand that they continue to work together, and the benefits they receive from it are derived from their place in the organisation rather than from the relationship itself.

When people lack an intrinsic commitment to a relationship, it is more difficult to resolve their differences and the degree of communication skills necessary to maintain it is greater. Minor irritations are not overlooked, minor conflicts are not easily resolved, and major disagreements erupt into open confrontation because neither party is as concerned that an open conflict might threaten the continuation of the relationship.

Fortunately, and almost inevitably, people do form close personal relationships with some of those with whom they have effective working relationships. Although this means that their work situations will be more pleasant than otherwise would be the case, it also adds a number of complicating factors to the relationship. They must negotiate boundaries the two dimensions of their relationship, arriving at some mutual agreement that they will communicate differently with each other while at work than they will while in other contexts. In addition, they must cope with the fact that their personal relationship is being observed by a large number of people with whom they have working relationships and that the existence of the personal relationship may further complicate some of their working relationships. "Don't have an affair with your boss, or at least don't let anyone know you are" really is very good advice.

Through processes of communication, working 'relationships are formed, maintained, and in some cases, transformed into personal relationships. As these relationships begin and develop, the participants in them begin to perceive their jobs, their organisation, and their roles in that organisation differently. These perceptions combine to define the situations that each individual believes one faces at work. Perceptions provide the parameters and guidelines within which each individual makes decisions about how to act. These choices influence the character of the relationships with other members of the organisation, and these changed relationships influence other members' perceptions of their organisation and thus influence their actions.

Other members' actions in turn alter the character of their relationship and consequently influence the parameters and guidelines within which other members make their choices. In a complex matrix of processes, communication, relationships, perceptions, and choices, the "situations" in which people find themselves at work are created.

In addition, the relationships that people form at work influence their performance in complicated and important ways. Employees' perceptions of and satisfaction with the tasks they are asked to perform are affected by the quality of the relationships they form with the people around them. Similarly, their satisfaction with their jobs will influence their ability to form valued and stable relationships with their co-workers. The quality of employees' relationships with their co-workers influences their ability to gain the information and support they need in order to perform their job and influences their willingness to provide the information and support their co-workers need. The nature of supervisors' relationships with subordinates influences their ability to understand the messages they exchange and the probability that any particular command will be carried out. For all these reasons, the relational and command functions of organisational communication are interdependent and interactive. The success of one depends largely on the success of the other.

The third major function of communication in organisations is the management of ambiguity. Humans are essentially choice-making beings, and their activities at work are essentially choice-making activities. Each day they face a series of decision-making situations. In some of these situations they make choices for the organisation; in others their decisions are more personal. Their choice making is complicated by two factors. The first involves the multitude of motivations an individual generally incorporates into decision making. In each organisational choice-making situation, a person simultaneously must consider the effects selecting one of a number of available options will have on one, one's co-workers, and one's organisation. In some situations the personal concern will be more important than the relational or organisational ones; in others, the decision maker will be concerned primarily with the interests of the organisation and only indirectly concerned with one's own interests.

Some different situations will involve different combinations of self, relationship, and organisational interest, organisational choice-making is a complex and potentially confusing process. If the individual faces a situation which provides clear and explicit guidelines for determining how these interests should be balanced, it is relatively easy to make effective choices. However, choice making typically takes place in situations in which the guidelines for action are either unclear or contradictory. Communication then becomes the process through which an actor manages an ambiguous situation.

Second, organisational choice making is complicated by the ambiguity of the organisations themselves. The objectives of an organisation at a particular time often are not clear to its members. In addition, the objectives of a particular unit in the organisation or of particular members also may be ambiguous. In organisations which are undergoing rapid change or which exist in rapidly changing environments, these objectives may be particularly confused.

Also, the complex histories of modern organisations complicate the choice making of their individual members. Most situations are not completely unprecedented. The people involved have faced similar situations in the past and can draw on those experiences to help them make effective choices in the new situation. But precedents sometimes hurt choice making more than they help it. Individuals will recall that in similar situations in the past they made a certain choice. They also remember that their choice was followed by a certain good or bad result. They will tend to believe that it was their decision that led to the result. If the outcome was favourable, they will tend to repeat the decision.

If the outcome was negative, they will tend to avoid taking any similar course of action. But in most cases, choices made by a single individual are only one part of a complicated series of events and decisions which lead to an observed outcome. Not realising this, individual tend to make subsequent choices based on the mistaken belief that it was their choice that cause a particular outcome to occur in the past. In this way the availability of precedents can reduce the quality of the choices that are made.

Precedents complicate choice making in another way. When faced with a decision people tend to search their memories for similar situations. When they discover a precedent they feel a great sense of relief because the new situation suddenly becomes clearer and easier to manage. However, people often discover precedents which really are not precedents at all. They recall past situations that they were able to manage and then define the new situation in a way which makes it seems similar to the past, comfortable situation. Through this process they often overlook important differences between the two.

Organisational choice-making situations are inherently complex and almost always ambiguous. They are simplified and sometimes distorted by characteristically human thought processes. They also are simplified and sometimes distorted,by typical communication process. Members of organisations use communication in two primary ways in their attempts to manage ambiguity. First, they communicate to each other in order to structure, to make sense out of, new situations. They seek out information which will help them gain a perspective on the problem, and they seek out support from others which will confirm their interpretation, of the problem and strengthen their commitment to a particular course.

In addition, they use communication in favour of a particular way of looking at the problem and in support of a preferred option. Through communication with other members of the organisation they are able to create a shared mutual understanding of what a problem is and how it should be addressed. If the information they gain through communication has been sufficient, relevant, and accurate, and if the shared perspective that they have created has been appropriate to the problem, communication will have improved their decision making.

But if the information gained has been inadequate in any significant way, or if the perspective that has been adopted by the people who were involved in the communication is flawed in any important respect, the availability of communication will have reduced the quality of the decision and further complicated choice making in the future. In the latter case, organisational communication has been used to reduce ambiguity artificially; it has not been used to manage ambiguity successfully. Sometimes processes of communication allow members of organisations to make foolish decisions and become comfortable with and strongly committed to them. In other instances communication allows members to make choices which satisfy their needs and the needs of their organisations. In some cases organisational communication even may provide the basis for making the best possible decisions. A variety of processes inevitably influences the potential effectiveness of the ambiguity-management function of organisational communication.

Communication fulfils three major functions in formal organisations—a command function, a relational function, and an ambiguity—management function. For any organisation to succeed, each of these functions must operate at or above some minimal level of effectiveness. For any individual members of an organisation to perform their roles successfully, they must be capable of using a variety of communication skills to issue effective commands and respond adequately to commands issued by others, to develop and sustain efficient working relationships, and to manage ambiguity strategically.

However, some kinds of organisations are designed in ways which lead their members to rely most heavily on one of these three communication functions. Some organisations rely most heavily on the command function, others on the role of communication in the management of relationships, and others on the effective management of ambiguity.

Every organisation must have adequate command, relational and ambiguity managing communication. However, the relative importance of these three functions varies in the three different types of organisations. "Traditional" organisations, rely most heavily on the command function of communication and less heavily on the other two. Human relations and resources organisations depend on effective relational communication. Some versions of this type also rely heavily on the command function. In most versions the ambiguity-managing function has a limited role.

The final type, "systems-contingency" organisations, relies heavily on ambiguity-managing communication. In this type, relational and command functions, are important in some situations and less important to others. In fact, it is the assumption that command and relational communication must be combined in different proportions in different situations that distinguishes the systems-contingency type from the traditional and human relations and resources type. The ideas of the German sociologist Max Weber have been an important part of the study of organisations for decades. In America Weber is best known for his analysis of bureaucracy and bureaucratic organisations and for his discussion of the relationships between the characteristics of a culture and the uses of three different types of leadership-traditional, rational-legal, and charismatic authority.

An equally important but less well-known component of Weber's work is the overall perspective that he took in studying organisations, the theory of "ideal types." This perspective rests on a particular set of assumptions about the nature of organisations and the appropriate means of studying them. His ideas provide a method through which employees can understand their organisations and make effective decisions about how to act on them.

Weber's primary assumption was that organisations are composed of human actors who are enmeshed in independent activities and who continually are making decisions about how to act. Their choices are based on the meanings they attribute to the actions of others and on their interpretations of the organisational situations in which they are involved. When people enter formal organisations they bring with them a long history of monitoring their actions and the actions of others, of processing the information they obtain, and of choosing from among a number of options. People from a particular culture develop ways of monitoring perceiving, and acting which are very much like another.

These perceptual "filters" are not identical, of course, because every individual has had unique experiences and has been part of a particular group of relationships with others. To some extent all members of a culture will have developed their own beliefs about what actions are "normal" and proper and about what meanings can be attached to different messages.

However, within all this diversity and individuality lies a common core, a culture-bound framework for making sense out of people's actions and of deciding how to act in response. It is this common interpretive schema that defines a culture and distinguishes it from other cultures.

When employees from a particular culture come together within a formal organisation they bring with them a common way of interpreting and responding to one another. But once they come together, their interpretive frameworks begin to change in subtle but important ways. Human develop their interpretive frameworks through their experiences with other people. Relationships formed with people at work provide us with additional experience communicating with and making sense out of the communication of others.

As a result, people drawn together in a formal organisation begin to form new "mini-cultures" at work. These new ways of interpreting and acting both retain the basic frame-work of the employees' general culture and reflect the more specific frameworks that develop through working relationships. The complicated interrelationship that exists between the broad patterns of action that characterise a society and the patterns that develop within an organisational "culture" was the basis of Weber's theory of ideal types.

Weber argued that researchers can understand organisations if they can understand how actors (employees) in them interpret their surroundings and choose among the wide variety of different courses of action that are available to them. The study of organisations should begin with careful observations of the choices that employees make.

Eventually these observations will reveal that different groups of employees use different sense-making schemes. Researchers will begin to recognise that members of some organisations typically interpret and act in ways which are different from those in which people act in other organisations. At some point these observers will begin to construct mental images of organisations whose employees share the same basic interpretive frameworks.

For example, employees may perceive that their organisation is like an army—a formal structure with a clearly defined administrative staff which, for some as yet unexplained reasons, is obedient to commands issues by superiors.

This type of organisation would function properly if it exhibited a number of necessary characteristics: each member of the staff occupies a specific position in the organisation which has been clearly defined, written duties and a clear place in the hierarchy of the organisation: each person knows who the supervisor is? who the subordinates are? and how each of them fits into the hierarchy of the organisation: each employee is selected on the basis of qualifications for the job, determined by some "objective" measure like educational background or a score on an examination; works under a contract which can be terminated if performance is inadequate; and can be promoted to a more responsible or higher paying position only on the basis of performance or seniority.

Of course, there may be no "real" organisation anywhere which has all these characteristics. Because this type of organisation is an abstraction, which represents the perceptions of a number of different groups of employees, it exists only in the mind of the observer; it is an "idealised" example of a particular "type" of organisation. It is an image of how a certain type of organisation should be designed and how it ought to operate, note a summary of the characteristics and operations of a group of real organisations.

But these mental conceptions of ideal types can be useful for researchers. If researchers or managers or any other members of a real organisation understand how different types of organisations should be designed and operated, they can use that knowledge to detect and solve problems in their own organisation. To do so, they would examine their organisation, looking for features of its design or operation which do not correspond to the necessary features of the most relevant ideal type. Armed with perceptions of the essential features of a number of different types, the researcher or manager can discover cases in which the members of the organisation do not choose to act in the ways that are necessary for the organisation to function efficiently.

Once these discrepancies are discovered the observer can make careful decisions about how to alter the organisation or change the conditions under which the members make decisions about how to act. When these changes are implemented, the real organisation will begin to operate more like the ideal type to which it is most closely related.

Unfortunately, these are very abstract ideas. A summary of them might increase their clarity. Weber's approach to the study of organisations rests on his theory of ideal types. It suggest that an observer can begin to understand how an organisation operates by attempting to understand how its members interpret and respond to the situations they face in the organisation. The observer then can design the organisation to increase the probability that its members will choose to act in precisely those ways that are in its best interests.

Employees always will make their own decisions about how to act. They are human, and consequently they will continually be involved in observing, processing, and responding to their surroundings. But they make their choices based on their interpretations of the situations they face. Both their perceptions and many of the key characteristics of the situations they face can be created strategically through communication.

However, appropriate situations can be created only if the people who design organisations know the elements that must be included. The search for these necessary features begins with the construction of a group of ideal types of organisations. Observers ask "What kinds of organisations do employees' interpretive frameworks suggest are possible?" and construct a list of features necessary for each of these "mythical" organisations to operate most efficiently. The most important features will involve the conditions under which employees will choose to initiate and limit their actions in desired ways. Among these necessary features will be certain characteristics of organisational communication. After observers have delineated the features of each ideal type of organisation, they can begin to examine existing organisations, searching for points at which the real organisations differ from the ideal type. If they can detect important differences and determine the reasons for them, they can begin to isolate problems in the real organisation and develop strategies for reducing them.

Of course, Weber assumed that most of the "observers" would be scholars involved in academic research. But his perspective can just as readily be used by employees. The social psychologist Fritz Heider once argued that human beings think like researchers think, that the same analytical tools that theorists use to understand the world around them can be used by other people to understand their environment and to decide how to act in the situations they face.

Heider's notion that people are "naive theorists" suggest that all theoretical perspectives, of which Weber's of ideal types is one, are based on our interpretations of reality and can be used by us to understand the realities that surround us. This assumption underlies the ideas that will be presented throughout the book. If readers can understand how communication functions in different types of organisations, they can examine their own organisations, determine how communication functions there, and choose the best communicative strategies for responding to the situations they face.

Equipped with an understanding of how communication functions in different types of organisations and explanations of why communication functions differently in real organisations, readers can intelligently observe their own organisations and ask themselves these questions: how does communication operate in any organisation? How must people, including myself, act in order for this organisation to operate successfully? Why do they sometimes act in those ways and sometimes act differently? How can I act in order to make the organisation work more effectively and to make the greatest contribution to its success and to my advancement?

These are the kinds of questions. Weber suggested that researchers must ask; the questions provide the kind of information from organisational theory has made. More important, they are the kinds of questions that members of organisations must ask themselves before they can choose the best communication strategies to use in different organisational situations.

Through understanding how different types of organisations operate and why a particular organisation functions differently, the "naive theorists" who make up an organisation can adopt the best available communication strategies.

Factual Attempts

For more than two thousand years communication scholars have argued that people communicate most effectively if they adopt the communication strategies that are most appropriate to the situations they face. Plato's intellectual rival, Gorgias, argued that knowing how to adapt to different situations was the only kind of knowledge that was available to human beings and, consequently, should be the focus of education. Some equivalent to Gorgias' concept of adaptation, an idea he labelled Kairos, has been important to the study of human communication since his time.

Historically, training students in the art of adapting their communication to different situations has involved two steps : (1) teaching them to analyse the situations they face and choose the best strategies for those situations, and (2) equipping them with the repertoire of communication skills needed to implement those strategies.

This book will concentrate on providing readers with the first kind of knowledge. It will examine the myriad of features which make up organisational situations, plan the kinds of communication in which employees must be competent, they and their organisations are to function effectively, describe the strategic through which they can gain the information necessary for them to adapt intelligently to the situation they face at work, and provide guidelines for choosing the optional communication strategies to use in those situation.

Although it will discuss a variety of communication skills and suggest when and how those skills might be used by members of organisations, it will make no attempt to provide detailed training in the skills themselves.

6

Professional Aspects

A professional journalist is easily identified: he is on the payroll of a journal; he reports for his paper, or he may write features or editorials or edit copy.

He is known by different names : Reporter, Feature Writer, Special Correspondent, Sub-Editor, Assistant Editor, Sports Editor, City Editor, Commercial Editor, News Editor etc. The range of work he does is as wide as the world around him. He may report on crime, law and order, political developments, the courts, the Executive, the Legislature, people, fashions, art, music, drama, literature indeed, whatever makes news.

A journalist does more than that he edits what others write, he comments and criticizes and he puts together the news. Primarily, it is a profession for the man trained to do the particular job in the complex business of bringing out a journal. It is definitely not for amateurs.

Professional Reporting

Time was when it used to be said that a journalist is born, not made, that you could not push a man through a journalism school and he would emerge at the other end a journalist. Mahatma Gandhi never saw the inside of a journalism school. Neither did Bal Gangadhar Tilak. Nor did a score of distinguished editors since James August and Hicky brought out the first full-fledged printed newspaper in India, *The Bengal Gazette* on 29 January 1780. Yet, they were men who brought much honour to the profession.

But those were different times. It was sufficient, then, for any one with a sense of mission, to declare himself a journalist, buy or hire a printing press and bring out a journal. Today, however, things are quite different, more complicated. And while, no doubt, some are born journalists, they would be even better if they attended a course in journalism.

Beginning in India

This fact, indeed, was recognized as early as in 1920 by none other than Dr. Annie Besant, founder of the National University at Adyar, Madras. The University was launched under the auspices of the Theosophical Society and its first chancellor was Rabindranath Tagore. Dr. Besant was the Pro-Chancellor and Sir C. P. Ramaswamy Iyer, Vice-Chancellor. The University had courses in arts, science and commerce and the subject of journalism was added to the Arts Faculty and was part of the English Department. Dr. James H. Cousins was the Head of the Department of English and Journalism.

The subjects taught were: History of journalism, press laws, editorial practice and newspaper administration. Though the Degree Course was closed down at the end of five years it is interesting to note that the importance of adequate training had been recognised as long ago as 1920 and that among the first teachers of journalism were such men of note as N. S. Rama Rao, C. S. Trilokekar, Yadunath Sarkar, and Seshagiri Rao.

We may, therefore, concede for the moment that to be a good journalist it is important to receive adequate and obviously the right kind of training. But-and here we may enter a caveat-not everyone who aspires to be a journalist necessarily becomes one merely by receiving a diploma. Which makes us turn to the next question: What makes a journalist?

There are as many answers to the question as there are leaders of journalism. "Vitality" according to James Reston of the *New York Times.*

"Hustling" according to Paul Miller of the Gannett group of newspapers in the United States. "Ferreting out the truth" according to another distinguished editor, Herbert Brucker.

Of course, a journalist should be fun of energy, must be able to get at the truth, if necessary by hustling, but these are partial answers. More things go into the making of a journalist than mere energy or the drive to do a job. Yet, there is much sense in what Mr. Reston once said in a talk to the Columbia School of Journalism: I am a strong advocate of education and specialized training for newspapermen. Yet on the Washington staff of the *New York Times* we have men with multiple degrees from universities.and other men who did not complete their higher education for-one reason or other... Both do well. In going over their records, I am struck by the fact that all of them have this one great quality-vitality, drive, aliveness-call it what you will.

It occurs to me, therefore, that the most thorough education and the finest training in some speciality are of no avail to make a newspaper man outstanding unless he also had the necessary vitality to get on with the job.

S. Sadanand, founder editor of the *Free Press Journal* fits Reston's description to a T. Sadanand never went to college and yet-all those who knew him would concede that he was a great journalist. He was a man of tremendous vitality and what Reston called "aliveness" and "drive". And what he was, he sought in others. The point about such a man is that, while he may not have come to his profession with a university degree, he would have enough-energy and initiative to provide himself with the kind of education needed to be a good-and successful-journalist. In the old days men with the necessary drive got themselves jobs as journalists and educated themselves as they went along. They were largely self-taught men. Today, however, with competition being what it is for the few openings available to aspiring men and women, the wise among them would acquire the necessary pre-education before applying for a post.

The Needs

The student of journalism must have, to start with, a good degree whether it be in the arts, sciences or commerce. This presumes that he can write grammatically and is familiar with the structure of a sentence. It is advisable that a student who had graduated in a non-English medium take a special course in English to get the utmost benefit from studies in journalism imparted in that language.

This does not mean that a student not proficient in English cannot benefit from a course in journalism. The essentials of journalism hold good whether the future journalist works for an English or an Indian-language newspaper. Accuracy, honesty and sensitivity to news are universal assets. In the absence of journalism courses in the Indian languages there is only one way in which an aspirant can learn his trade: by attending courses in the English language.

What is essential is that whichever be the language in which the journalist intends to pursue his calling he be well versed in it. Journalists deal in facts; but facts are expressed in words, whether they are in English, Hindi, Marathi, Malayalam or Tamil. A journalist who is not proficient in the language of his choice cannot possibly hope to make an impact on his readers.

This leads to the issue of proficiency not just in one language, but several. The more languages one knows, the more one's chances of landing a job, especially these days when states vie with one another to conduct their business in the regional languages. Even in the thirties, forties and fifties, the reporter who understood and was conversant with Hindi, Urdu, Gujarati and Marathi, not to speak of Telugu and Tamil had a head start over others, especially while covering All India Congress Committee meetings. What was true of past years is even more true today.

As an addendum it may be stated that the journalist who is conversant with a foreign language such as French, German, Russian or Arabic stands a better chance of being selected for posts abroad than one who knows only English.

Is journalism a business, profession, craft or trade? It is fashionable to say that journalism is a profession like law or medicine or engineering. A profession it is, but, at the same time, it is a craft that has to be learnt. And woe to the publisher journalist who is ignorant of the principles of business management. Sadanand was a great journalist but a poor business manager and, in the end, was a sad failure. He would' have been a better journalist if he was a better business manager.

Successful journalism is not necessarily good journalism but good journalism needs to be successful journalism as well. The primary purpose of a journalist is to communicate and a journal that does not sell is a journal that fails of its primary purpose. To say, therefore, that journalism is a lofty profession and not a trade or a craft is a bit of snobbery that one can usefully do without.

Good writing is taught not only because excellence by itself is a desirable asset but also because it sells. And a sub-editor who is sound lay-out man is worth his weight in gold. To say that making a lay-out is a profession and not an art is not to understand the meaning of words. Journalism no doubt is a profession, but a journalist who limits himself to his profession is more likely to find that he has that most unenviable of talent un saleable Knowledge. The history of journalism is littered with the lives of men whose snobbery would not permit them to see themselves as businessmen and traders as well.

Journalist as a Professional

A professional is a man who has had training in his particular field. An individual is not allowed to practice medicine unless he is certified by a duly recognized medical school. Lawyers, chartered accountants and in some countries even barbers and "beauticians" have to acquire a certificate that recognizes their competence. It would be in the fitness of things, therefore, if news papermen too acquire adequate recognition of their professional talent from their competitors.

However, in the absence of institutional recognition a journalist in India acquires professional respectability by the very fact of being on a journal's payroll. The belief, obviously, is that if a person is on the payroll he must be-competent.

In the circumstances the only way to distinguish a professional from the amateur is to find out whether the person is actively employed on a full-time basis by a newspaper or journal. If he is, he literally qualifies himself to be known as a professional. The free-lance journalist-one who is not regularly employed but is a frequent contributor-is just that a free-lance journalist.

Free-lance Reporting

The Random House Dictionary of the English language defines a free-lance as a person who works as a writer, designer, performer etc., but not on a *regular* salary basis for anyone employer, organization or the like. The description or definition obviously stems from the fact that in the middle ages, military adventurers, often of knightly rank, offered their mercenary services to who ever paid them best. Their lances were, so to speak, available to the highest bidder. The term is now applicable to writers, designers and all who sell their work to whoever offers them the best terms. They may be amateurs or professionals who have retired but whose work is deemed worthy of acceptance. Among the best-known freelancers, surely, is Ruskin Bond, the short-story writer who contributes widely and is considered a success.

Free-lancing, however, is not an easy way to make a living, especially in India where magazines and journals are not known to be good paymasters. The free-lance writer with demonstrated ability to produce acceptable work, of course may eventually hope to reach the status of a contract writer, assured of a regular in come. Such a status assumes that the writer is on contract to write a set series of articles for editors. Should a writer be commissioned to do a piece, the editor would be morally bound to accept it, unless it is downright hopeless. An editor, however, is not bound to print the piece though he is bound to pay for it. Frequently editors accept articles "for possible use" or lay down their own conditions beforehand that give them freedom to reject a commissioned article.

Free-lancing for a beginner is a precarious way to make a living. A person willing to free-lance must either be willing to live on a subsistence level or have sufficient financial means to stay alive without having to depend on income from writing. Many free lancers have regular jobs that guarantee them their bread and butter Jagjit Singh, the distinguished science writer, was a railway administrator.

Few writers can expect to launch a successful full-time career in free-lancing until they are thoroughly competent and *well-known.* Too often competence is not enough; they must be recognised as competent. The recognition factor, in the case of freelancers is just as important as the competence factor. A. G. Noorani, the lawyer is frequently commissioned to write in-depth articles from as varied a lot as *The Illustrated Weekly of India* or *Sunday* because he is a regular writer for the *Indian Express.* N. J. Nanporia is, similarly, a frequent contributor to various magazines on the strength not only of his unquestioned competence but because he is recognised as an authority on international affairs.

Another free-lance writer of repute is Chanchal Sarkar who is a Director of the International Press Institute. *Science Today* has an entire stable of free-lance writers who write knowledgeably on science subjects.

Experts in Field

Unless he is very well known, a free-lancer is wise to specialize in a field where he has little or no competition. Noorani is a lawyer who can write competently on law-he has few competitors in his particular field. Many astrologers in India make a respectable earning by turning out astrology columns which are invariably popular. A free-lancer who is in great demand rapidly acquires status. Requests have gone to them from editors to produce quick copy when regular staff members are fully engaged or are not adjudged sufficiently competent to contribute on special subjects. On the roster of the *Illustrated Weekly of India's* contributors are such distinguished names as K. P. S. Menon, C. N. Vakil or Nikhil Chakravarthy.

There is one note of warning to the young man or woman who wants to be a journalist. You will not from your first week in office be writing stories which make politicians humble and governments shake. It will be a long time before you get a by-line. The only way up is hard work and merit will first have to be proved. Because you write good essays in school is no guarantee that you will make a good journalist.

7

Organisational Structure

To the outsider, journalism and ethics are about as incongruous a mixture as you can get. Even to put the two words in the same sentence is to risk reducing the listener to helpless laughter.

To the insider on a mass-market tabloid, ethics are largely an irrelevance. Editors, pressured by intense competition for readers, demand that staff cut ethical corners; and competition among staff encourages some to respond. Lecturing these journalists about ethics is as pointless as advocating celibacy to sailors arriving in port after six months at sea.

To the insider working on a quality paper, where there is virtually unanimous agreement about basic professional morality, ethics are a code of principles to which all journalists should adhere, or at least feel guilty about if they do not. They are rarely, if ever, required to step outside this code.

Ethics, more than any other aspect of the job, are where personal circumstance produces experiences so that the different ethics employed are barely recognisable as the same thing. The reason is that ethics, as actually practised, are conditioned less by morals than by what is rewarded or punished in any given newspaper. On a British mass market tabloid (or agency serving one) journalists may be regarded, paid and promoted according to how many dramatic, possibly invasive, stories they produce. Not too many questions are asked about how they obtained them or what degree of exaggeration is involved.

Indeed the news desk, or higher executives, often tell reporters what line they want, regardless of any reservations reporters have. Not much scope for Mr. or Ms. Proper here. At the other extreme-on a US paper enjoying a monopoly and sharing the same city as its sources and readers-reporters are judged and rewarded differently, with ethics playing a far greater part in their lives. Ultimately the main factor in deciding what ethics are actually practised is competition. In monopoly situations, papers know that there is no rival paper to scoop them, and readers have no alternative to turn to-save for giving up papers altogether. This lack of competition gives the journalists the moral luxury of generally being able to apply far more idealised standards of professional ethics.

In a mass market, highly competitive and with a macho culture, almost the only sanction on what papers will do to get a story, or publish once they have got it, is the prospect of upsetting readers, especially to the point where they will not buy the paper.

Only then will word go out to the staff, and the little news agencies that feed them, that it is time to call a halt (perhaps only temporarily) to stealing pictures from the bereaved, invading hospitals where sick celebrities are being treated, publishing pictures of royal children in private moments, condemning a community for violence without sufficient evidence, or whatever. On tabloids especially, the periodic little eruptions of ethics that are sometimes seen nearly always come from proprietors acutely aware that readers can always, and maybe are about to, buy another paper. Or that the government is about to legislate.

But journalists have a sanction, too. We do not have to be mere creatures of the papers we work for; we have a choice. Just as readers can stop buying, so journalists can change jobs. We can decide that there are some things we will not do and leave the paper—either discreetly after having found another post, or publicly, in a blaze of righteous indignation. If more of us did that, and made clear our reasons for doing so, journalism would be better for it.

This element of moral choice, the distinction between how papers acting under commercial pressures expect us to behave and how we can choose to behave, explains why ethics have a daily purpose—or rather, two purposes. The first is to provide some kind of moral compass, telling us how far we are diverging from a desired route.

So far as I know, the magnetic north in our trade is found in the clauses of an unwritten contract which should exist between all newspapers and their readers:

- Every story in the paper is a result of decisions made free of political, commercial or non-commercial pressure.
- None are there because of any favours or money exchanged.
- All stories are written and edited in a spirit of free enquiry, and chosen for publication entirely on their own merits, be they real or imagined.

Second, ethics provides a practical guide to the production of safe and credible journalism. Honestly, with plain dealing and with the removal of conflicts of interest are the best ways to do this job because they are the safest ways to do it. At the most base level, they keep you out of the courts and help you to sleep at nights. And, at the risk of shocking some of the more raunchy reporters, ethics are the most decent way to do the job, too, giving us attitudes to readers (and sources) that are based on some sensitivity, rather than mere sly commercial calculation.

Various Concepts and Suggestions

Viewed like this, ethics are not some optional extra but are integral to every aspect of the job. This book therefore deals with them as they occur - in handling sources, asking questions, writing, etc. and not in some moral parking lot tucked away from the main action. There are, however, some general principles and these have been gathered here. If you want to be a propagandist, then go and work in public relations, or politics. Journalists should owe no loyalty to anyone or anything else; not a political party, source, commercial interest, non-commercial interest or particular cause, however worthy. Balanced journalism is difficult enough to achieve without such conflicts of interest. The Washington Post newspaper has a rule that its journalists cannot take part in any political activity. That includes marching on demonstrations. So when several Post reporters were spotted on an abortion rights demonstration, they were told they would not be allowed to cover anything touching on the abortion issue.

The dangers of allowing a missionary zeal for some cause to infect reporting are even more obvious. One of the more notorious examples is Walter Duranty, the New York Times correspondent in Moscow in the 1920s and 1930s. So taken was he by the ideology of the new Soviet Union that his reporting was often little more than propaganda. At the height of the famine in the Ukraine, for instance, largely engineered by Stalin to break local resistance to Soviet control, Duranty wrote of 'village markets overflowing with eggs, fruit, poultry, vegetables, milk and butter' at prices far lower than in Moscow.

'Anyone can see this is not famine, but abundance', he added; and a Pulitzer committee, knowing no better, gave him a prize. In fact, millions died, and Duranty knew this full well, telling colleagues in private that he thought the death toll was around ten million. Malcolm Muggeridge, the Manchester Guardian's reporter in Moscow at the time, called him 'the biggest liar of any journalist I have ever met.'

Each story should be an open-minded attempt to find out what really happened, accompanied by a willingness to print that truth, however uncomfortable it may be to our own, or the paper's, cherished beliefs. Thus, journalists should not accept work which seeks to bolster a point of view in the face of evidence, or undertake reporting which aims to support a preconceived theory.

You would think this so self-evident that it would not need stating. But every day you can read reporting which stretches and strains the facts to fit a particular thesis. One of the worst examples in recent memory was committed by the Sun, Britain's biggest-selling daily. For reasons best known to himself, the then editor became convinced that Aids was a disease limited to drug addicts and homosexuals. On several occasions government statistics were wilfully manhandled to support this view. The most flagrant occasion was a story headlined 'Straight Sex Cannot Give You Aids —Official', which reported, among other absurdities, that the chances of getting Aids from heterosexual sex were 'statistically invisible. Anything else is homosexual propaganda.' Eventually, the volume of protests at this coverage produced an apology - which the paper ran at the bottom of page 28.

Here, and this is no isolated case, was reporting that deceived readers and possibly endangered them. Preconceived theories have no place in journalism. Newspapers should be at war with closed minds, not employing them.

This means not only money and free gifts, but also the promise of advantage or preferment. It specifically means two things. The first is hidden advertising, where journalists or their papers take money for writing public relations pieces about firms or people which then appear in the editorial columns parading as normal stories. In recent years this has become a widespread practice in countries like Russia, and the temptation to write hidden advertising in places where pay is very poor is understandable. But that does not make it journalism. It is advertising, PR, puffs, whatever you call it, dressed up to look like journalism. It is a deception, and a damaging one. First, it breaks the basic contract with readers, with stories, purporting to be a normal editorial in print only because money has changed hands. Second, such deceptions destroy any trust that should exist between readers and papers.

Third, the practice makes editors suspect their staff have taken bribes to write about a company when their story may be perfectly honest. Fourth, editors and publishers will, like hotel owners paying waiters low salaries because of tips, use hidden advertising as an excuse not to pay journalists properly. Fifth, it establishes that the journalists who do it have their pens and minds available for hire. What will they accept money for next? Writing favourable stories about criminal groups% Keeping stories about wrongdoing out of the paper: That is but a short step away from collecting information with a view to selling its destruction or suppression. In other words, blackmail.

Lest anyone think this a good original money-making scheme, an American publisher called Robert Harrison got there first in the 1950s with a magazine called Confidential. It specialised in Hollywood scandal and, by paying large sums for tips and information, he and his investigators obtained decidedly intimate details of the stars' private lives. Each story was well-researched and Harrison's staff were not fussy about their methods, hiring prostitutes to trap victims, secretly taping and filming encounters and confessions. Sales of Confidential soared and eventually hit four million. But soon the temptation to sell the negatives, tapes and other evidence to wealthy stars proved too strong. The inevitable court case happened, a staff member killed herself, the editor shot his wife and himself in a New York taxicab, Harrison sold the magazine and both he and it went into a richly-deserved oblivion.

Hidden advertising (which should be correctly labelled 'advertising' and typographically treated accordingly), is very rare in developed countries. Far more common is the acceptance by journalists of what they call 'freebies', that is, free trips with vacation companies, free meals from restaurants or free tickets from theatres, all given so that journalists can review them. The danger here is that the writer will feel obliged to write a favourable piece. This need not be so, and the dangers can be minimised and faith kept with the reader if it is made plain somewhere in the piece or in a footnote that the ticket/trip/meal or whatever was given free to the newspaper.

It is not unusual, especially on smaller, less profitable or local papers, for advertisers to try to use their commercial weight to bully the paper. This pressure should be resisted at all times. It normally comes from the paper's advertising department who will say to the editor that it would be helpful if this important client could have some 'good coverage'. A few years ago the Riverside Press-Enterprize, a paper in California, published a total of eleven news pieces and 22 photographs of a new department store called Nordstrom's in the six days before, during and immediately after its opening in the town. These 400 column inches appeared in the same week as 20 full pages of ads for the store. A coincidence? Unlikely.

More rarely, groups of advertisers act in concert to try to force the paper to change its coverage. When I took over as editor of a British provincial paper, one of the things I did was to stop the automatic reporting of all shop-lifting court cases because they were so common as to be boring. Within a week, all the department stores in the city approached the publisher and told him that unless reporting of all shop lifting cases was resumed they would withdraw their advertising, which was considerable. They said the coverage acted as a deterrent to would be thieves. Luckily the publisher supported me. The advertisers' threat was not carried out.

The danger of giving in to advertisers' pressure, whether individual or collective, is that your content ceases to be freely chosen. You would also find that what is granted to one advertiser would soon be demanded by many. Give in once, and you would never be free of the pressure.

A journalist has power. It should never be abused, either in the course of a story or in one's daily life. Prosecuting personal disputes with stores, neighbours, etc. by threatening exposure or reference to high-placed connections is bullying, and unsafe bullying at that. How could you ever write a future story about any person or organisation you have threatened in this way? How could you write about the connections you have used in your threat? You will be in their pocket for the favour you owe them. Neither should you use your newspaper's headed notepaper to write a letter demanding preferential treatment, compensation for some alleged negligence or faulty service. It implies to the recipient that your paper exists as a sort of private protection racket for its staff.

It sometimes happens that you are asked by someone to 'forget' a story, or part of it, in return for some favour, or even cash. It is clearly wrong to accept such an offer, for the same reasons as it is wrong to put in a story for favours. When friends are involved, refusal might be more delicately phrased, but just as swift and sure. So should it be with colleagues, as these two stories illustrate.

The first case comes from Oregon in the United States where a few years ago a local television station reported that the long-time chief of staff of the state's Republican senator had served for 25 years as director of a bank that collapsed and was bailed out at a cost to taxpayers of $100 million. It was suggested that the man's involvement with the bank may have influenced the senator's position on bank deregulation and the subsequent bailout. The story was picked up by the Associated Press and was the talk of the state, but the main newspaper in the state, the Oregonian, chose to ignore it. It also ignored allegations a week later that the chief of staff's official travel, at taxpayer's expense, had included 52 trips to New York, where he published an annual guidebook to the city that had earned him more than $1 million.

The paper's reluctance to write this story may have had something to do with the fact that the chief of staff wrote a weekly column for the paper. It eventually published parts of the story only after the Washington Post gave the revelations national exposure. Contrast this with a paper called the Daily Item in Sudbury, Pennsylvania. Among the daily stories from the police in one issue was an uncensored account of charges filed against a town resident for driving at an unsafe speed under the influence of alcohol. The item included the man's name, age, address and occupation - editor of the Daily Item. Which paper would you trust most, the Item or the Oregonian?

Inventing information is obviously wrong and dangerous. So, too, is even a light doctoring of the facts, embellishment of the truth or temporary amnesia about certain details that inconvenience the main thrust of the story. Your report will be a cheat. This applies with equal force to photographers and the dishonest 'set-up' picture, where an event or situation is staged to imitate some alleged reality.

Some news photographers in Western Europe also have been known to carry around in their cars certain 'props' to insert into pictures. A well-known ploy used to be to have a child's shoe, or teddy bear available, so that photographers covering disasters like train or air crashes, could set this prop among the wreckage for a 'poignant' picture. Such pictures have now become a cliche. Besides, there was always the danger that the passenger list, when finally issued, would reveal that there were no children aboard. Deliberate fakes, or at least the detected ones, are very rare. Perhaps the most famous recent example was Janet Cooke's Pulitzer-winning story in the Washington Post. It was called 'Jimmy's World' and told the story of an eight-year-old heroin addict. Jimmy, however, did not exist.

The story was an invention from beginning to end. When the fiction was revealed the Post saw that, with hindsight, there were many warning signs. Some staff, for instance, had harboured doubts about the story at the time, but had either thought it best to keep quiet, or thought the story 'too good to check'. This journalistically-lethal attitude was encouraged by Cooke's warnings that her (and Jimmy's) life would be endangered if checks were made. Nor did anyone think to check Cooke's own credentials. She said she was a graduate of Vassar, had a master's degree from Toledo, studied at the Sorbonne, was an accomplished pianist and spoke four languages. No editor thought this a tall order for someone aged just 25. Among these executives, ironically, was Watergate hero Bob Woodward.

Using information you have acquired in order to make a commercial gain before the story is published is a temptation most likely to be faced by business reporters. A few years ago a reporter for the Wall Street journal called R. Foster Whinans co-wrote a column based on information from sources that traded stocks. He decided to sell information to a stock-broker friend. He was paid $31,000 to leak the contents of the column to several stock-brokers, enabling them to buy and sell shares in companies before this information became public and thus would affect the price of the stock. The brokers made about $690,000 from the leaked information. Whinans and the brokers were eventually caught and found guilty in court of violations of the Securities Exchange Act by misappropriating confidential information. Whinans was sentenced to 18 months in prison, five years' probation, 400 hours of community service and a $ 500 fine. Many Western papers now make their financial staff declare their investments and financial dealings.

Important Issues

The above issues are clear-cut. But a lot of issues in reporting are more complicated. Hard and fast rules are difficult to design and apply. Take phoney by-lines, for example. Plainly wrong if used routinely to give the impression a paper's staff is several times what it is, the practice is a good deal less harmful when sports editors use it to disguise the identity of, say, staff reporters from a daily moonlighting to cover events for a Sunday. Since the story purports to be written by someone who does not in fact exist, I would still contend phoney by-lines are a deceit. It is particularly unsafe where the story may be challenged, or even end in a law suit. Who do you produce in court', An actor taking the name of the fictitious reporter?

There have been many attempts to be dogmatic about privacy, but none can be sustained beyond the most simplistic instances. We all agree that if a President fools around with a junior employee in his office, there is a legitimate story. If someone is asking for our votes (and our taxes to pay their wages), we have a right to know about them, their lives and how they impact on their duties. On the other hand, few would suggest writing a story about a second junior employee fooling around, in their own time, with a third. The sex lives of private citizens, however fascinating, are not regarded as a legitimate target for a story, unless the law is broken. But between these two extremes, in all the less clear-cut cases, is the gaping space where we argue about privacy.

The conventional, and largely sensible, guideline is that the person should be a public figure and the invasion of their privacy must have a legitimate justification based on the public interest, not merely tickling the public's curiosity. If a man standing for public office makes a great deal of public fuss about morality and the virtues of family life, but you can prove he has a string of mistresses, then it is right to publish a story. His double standards are clearly relevant to public life. There are two problems with this conventional wisdom. First, if a paper thinks the story is sufficiently entertaining or salacious, almost any 'public interest' pretext can be dredged up. Second, justifications tend to be applied in a partisan way: papers defend the privacy of those they admire and invade the privacy of those they seek to destroy.

Part of the answer lies in that traditionally most unjournalistic of qualities: sensitivity. Journalists must have very good reasons for invading someone's privacy and should also be aware of the consequences of such reporting. A few years ago in Britain a policeman began an affair. His wife learnt about it and persuaded him to give up his mistress. The jealous lover then told a national paper and her account was printed under the headline, 'The Love Life of a Detective'. As a result, the couple's child was teased at school, the husband had to give up his job and the family had to move. Some may think that a fitting punishment for his original sin. I do not think so, and neither would I like to justify that reporting.

An issue which comes up less frequently is where journalists get involved in wrong-doing in order to investigate it. This is not a good idea. Breaking the law in pursuit of a story is both wrong and unsafe. It removes whatever moral legitimacy their reporting may otherwise have had. Sometimes reporters investigating drug-dealing, crime or prostitution learn information that should be passed straight to the police. I think you should do that. Otherwise you are compromising your legitimacy, and may also be putting the lives of innocent citizens at risk. Only the police—not you—can judge that. (This condition about the safety of citizens also applies to the situation where journalists are accused of merely ehpectating in disaster or war situations and not doing anything to help those who are in danger. Our rule should be that if you can have any influence on the outcome of a situation you should follow your normal instincts and act to help.) : Never accept a free ticket from a theatre manager, a free ride from the chamber of commerce, or a favour from a politician.

Establishing Again

Regretfully, All India Radio (AIR) performance in informing, educating and entertaining its listeners has not been impressive and it has failed to come up to its promise as an instrument of mass communication. Its failure has been twofold: it has failed to provide a broadcasting service satisfactory to the community and it has failed to fulfil the purpose of the state to inform and educate the masses, to enthuse them with plans of social and economic progress and to enlist their cooperation in fulfilling them. This failure is attributable to many factors; basically they arise from organisational deficiencies and inadequate financial resources.

According to the Indian Telegraphs Act of 1885, as amended, the Government of India has the exclusive privilege of establishing, maintaining and working a broadcasting service. The Act provides that a licence may be granted to others also. This permissive provision was used when in 1926 the Indian Broadcasting Company Ltd., was granted a licence for the two stations at Calcutta and Bombay. Since 1930, when the broadcasting service was taken over by government as 'The Indian State Broadcasting Service' no licences have been issued except for small agricultural stations at Allahabad and Dehra Dun, both since defunct, and to the Madras Corporation for a restricted city service until the Madras station came on the air in 1938. AIR thus enjoys a monopoly in the field.

Various Faculties

Since its inception AIR has been a department of the government. At present, its status is that of an attached office of the Ministry of Information and Broadcasting. The minister is responsible to the Cabinet and accountable to Parliament for all broadcasting activity. Except for short spells during the period 1947-65, the minister has not been a member of the Cabinet. Since January 1966, the ministry once again is put under a minister of state. It is unfortunate that it has been so. Effective mass communication in a developing country is essential for its economic and social regeneration. The minister at the helm should have suitable authority and status for the purpose. It is equally unfortunate that the Cabinet Committee on Information and Broadcasting has been recently discontinued. This again makes-the link between the minister and the Cabinet tenuous.

The Director General is responsible to the ministry for the working of AIR as its executive head. He is appointed by the government in consultation with the Union Public Service Commission. It is usual to appoint an officer of the programme cadre of AIR to be the Director General, though the post is not specifically reserved for the cadre. There have been occasions when officers of the Indian Civil Service were drafted to be Director General.

Though the pay of the Director General is the same as that allowed to a Joint Secretary, he has not been equated in status to a Joint Secretary nor does he exercise any powers of government. The heads of two other similar organisations, namely, the Director General, Posts and Telegraphs, and the Director General Tourism, both have ex-officio Secretariat status and the former is remunerated by a higher salary.

The Director General is supported by a Chief Engineer ranking next only to him and three Deputy Directors General, one each for Programmes, Inspection and Administration.

The Deputy Director General (Programmes) is in charge of the preparation of programme schedules and recruitment and utilisation of staff artists, their emoluments etc. He is assisted by eight Directors, in the rank of Station Directors, nine Chief Producers, two Deputy Chief Producers and other staff.

The Station Directors of AIR administer the various stations on behalf of the Director General. Similarly, there are Directors in charge of Units such as the Staff Training School, the TV Service, the Transcription and Programme Exchange Service, the External Services, and the News Services. They are assisted by Station Engineers/Assistant Station Engineers, Assistant Station Directors and Producers or Assistant Producers.

Like all other departments of government, the entire expenditure of AIR is met by appropriations made by Parliament. In theory, the licence fee on receivers is levied to sustain the broadcasting service. But in practice, revenue derived from licence fees, after deducting collection charges, is credited to the Consolidated Fund and both the capital and revenue budgets of

AIR are debated and voted upon annually by Parliament. There is thus no direct link between licence fees collected and amounts appropriated. In many countries the entire collection of fees reduced by the cost of collection is placed at the disposal of the broadcasting organisation either directly or through a vote of Parliament without a detailed control over its activities.

The Process

We should now consider whether organised as it is today as an attached office of a ministry with concomitant financing arrangements, AIR can develop as a national organisation and provide a countrywide service of quality and excellence.

In the first place, a theme of centralisation runs through the fabric of India's administration. It is more marked in the field of financial administration. This by itself is a deterrent to the growth of departmental initiative and expeditious transaction of business. Even the ministries of government do not enjoy full financial powers over the appropriations made to them for purposes embodied in the estimates as approved by Parliament. They derive financial authority by delegations made from time to time by the Finance Ministry. The principle that all executive levels should have administrative authority and financial power commensurate with their responsibilities and functions has yet to find acceptance. There is also a general disinclination to part with power and the Director General in his turn has been chary in delegating powers to the Station Directors.

A government department is subject to the discipline of rules and regulations both in regard to its employment policy and utilisation of resources allocated. These rules and regulations framed for administrative purposes are not wholly suitable for the commercial activities of government or for a creative medium like AIR. It is on this consideration that industrial and commercial activities of government have been entrusted to statutory corporations on companies. In the case of AIR no such dispensation has yet been made. The purpose of adopting the corporate form was to free the commercial activities of the state from inappropriate rules and regulations and to place them on a comparable footing with private enterprise.

We do not wish to overload this report with details but would refer to a few major limitations which impinge on the efficiency of AIR's administration. In the administrative field the Director General's powers for creation of posts only extend to minor posts of clerks and peons.

Similarly, he can order transfers of only junior officials, not of Directors and not even of Assistant Station Directors if they hold independent charge of a station. His disciplinary powers are also extremely limited and hemmed in by archaic regulations. In this situation, it is difficult for him to administer the department efficiently nor can he command the respect of his subordinates.

His financial powers are even more limited. He cannot send out any officer on tour for more than ten days at a time and he cannot authorise air journeys where necessary. Even his powers in regard to programme planning do not allow him to make worthwhile adjustments. One might well say that he has responsibility without the authority necessary to fulfil it.

We now consider whether basic requirements of AIR would be met by enlarging the powers of the Director General.

First, he has to work within the limits of funds appropriated by Parliament In the framing of estimates AIR's proposals are first scrutinised and usually pruned down by the Ministry and the process is repeated in the Finance Ministry. Thus, it is seldom that the reductions are made in a constructive way keeping in view the main purpose for which funds were demanded. Secondly, the Director General cannot spend the amounts voted according to his requirements without adhering to detailed allocations to different activities. He has hardly any powers of reappropriation.

Thirdly, the capital grant is determined by the Planning Commission's decision regarding the rate of development and the priorities in this development. As we have mentioned earlier, broadcasting does not figure in the list of priorities drawn up by the Planning Commission. We were informed that AIR's plan has just undergone a fifth revision to accord with the Commission's proposed total allocation of resources in the Fourth Plan. This has at one stroke nullified AIR's earlier intention to provide a medium-wave network to serve 95 per cent of the people by the end of the Fourth Plan.

Fourthly, the Director General is not competent to engage the type of people he needs and offer them salaries they are worth, as all recruitment has to be made through prescribed government channels and remunerations paid according to scales laid down by government. There is thus little flexibility in the selection of staff and in determining the terms and conditions of service'. And the Director General has no authority to dispense with the services of unsuitable staff.

We say all this to pinpoint the present disabilities of AIR, but we do not for a moment suggest that the Director General should be allowed to function without control and guidance or that he should be given all the resources he demands. He should, however, be brought into closer collaboration in the shaping of policy and programmes and given greater flexibility in their fulfilment.

Before we discuss what would be the most suitable organisation for AIR, we should make one point of substance and that is that the stations and other units of AIR must be given greater autonomy than they enjoy at present. It is the stations which are actually concerned with broadcasts and the test of a broadcasting organisation is the quality of its programmes. The need for speedy decisions and initiative at the stations is indisputable but cannot be met if their Directors have to obtain the Director General's approval for every little thing that they need or propose to do. Their status in the organisation has been progressively whittled down over the years.

For reasons we have developed earlier, it is not possible in the Indian context for a creative medium like broadcasting to flourish under a regiment of departmental rules and regulations. It is only by an *institutional chance* that AIR can be liberated from the present rigid financial and administrative procedures of government.

We first explored the possibility of adopting the form of one or other governmental agency which has greater freedom in movement than departments of government. The Railway Board, the Atomic Energy Commission, the Council of Scientific and Industrial Research, were suggested by some as a possible model for AIR. Anxious as we were to limit structural changes to the minimum, we studied these organisations but came to the conclusion that none of the patterns would meet the needs of AIR. The reasons for our conclusions are as follows: There is a clear division of functions in Railway operations and it is not so in broadcasting. Secondly, the Railway Board is not engaged in creative activity. And thirdly, as a ministry of government, the Board has to work within the limitation of rules and regulations framed for recruitment, promotion, etc. On all these counts, the Railway Board pattern would not meet the needs of AIR.

Similarly, both the Atomic Energy Commission and the Council of Scientific and Industrial Research are engaged in specialised activities which do not make it necessary for them to be in constant touch with political, cultural and social developments with which Radio is intimately involved. We, therefore, proceed to consider whether it would not be best to give AIR the corporate form which has been successfully adopted by broadcasting organisations in countries with a democratic constitution. In this consideration it would be relevant to examine the policy resolution which led to the acceptance of the corporate form for state industrial enterprises.

It was acknowledged that subject to the observance of certain general principles, the organisation of management suitable for each undertaking must necessarily be determined with reference to its particular requirements. The method of recruitment, the regulation of scales of pay, conditions of service and discipline of employees, the procedure for financial control, the system of accounting applicable to the normal activities of government could not obviously be adopted for the efficient administration of industrial enterprises. We feel that the same considerations apply with equal force in the case of AIR.

Experience has shown that the corporate form by itself has not brought about a psychological transformation nor given flexibility in operation because the Boards as constituted do not ensure independence implicit in the form. It is necessary to safeguard this position by making AIR a *national authority* in which major national interests would be represented to give it balance, quality, poise and purpose. Secondly, even with such a constitution the autonomy of the corporation would not be real unless it is financially independent and viable. We have carefully studied in detail the major types of broadcasting organisations in different parts of the world. Major broadcasting systems are either in private hands largely exploited for profit, or they are owned by the state but entrusted to autonomous corporations subject to specified control over policies and programmes.

It is necessary at the outset to make the point that all radio and television organisations are subject to control and regulations by the state. First there is the international obligation in the use of wave lengths and frequencies. This requires the issue of a licence to operate as prescribed by the International Telecommunication Union. The grant of licence is subject to certain legal formalities and regulations framed by each government. Apart from legal requirements, no state can allow unrestricted authority to a broadcasting organisation to embark on programmes which offend against social and moral values.

These media have a tremendous potential in moulding public opinion; they can equally enslave or liberate the human mind. The state has to safeguard the public interest through its regulatory power. It is largely on this consideration that the Supreme Court of the United States of America had declared: 'Unlike other modes of expression, radio inherently is not available to all. That is its unique characteristic. That is why unlike other modes of expression it is subject to government regulations.'

The outstanding example of private ownership and management is provided by the United States of America where licences to operate Radio and Television Stations are issued by the Federal Communication Commission subject to certain laws and regulations. This system also operates in many other countries, notably, Japan, Canada and Australia. All the three countries have each a public corporation owned wholly by the state, but they have also licensed private stations which operate in competition.

There is a variation of this form which provides for joint state and private collaboration. The best examples of blending of public and private ownership are provided by the Italian and Swedish organisation. RAI, the Italian organisation, is a private limited company which has been granted a monopoly of Radio and Television and wire distribution. The majority of its shares are held by the Institute of Industrial Reconstruction which is a government agency. Although RAI enjoys a considerable measure of independence, it is subject to obligations and inspections by the state. The Board of Management and the Board of Auditors have government members.

In Sweden, programming rights are vested since 1925 solely in a company known as Sveriges Radio. The state owns the transmitting network and is responsible for its maintenance and operation. The programme company is privately owned; the state has no financial interest in it. Two-fifths of the shares are held by the Press, another two-fifths by large national organisations and popular movements and one-fifth by business and industrial interests. The government, however, reserves the right to appoint the Chairman and one half of the members of the Board of Governors; the other half being elected by the shareholders.

In the other category are public corporations constituted by Royal Charter of Statute. They are run independently by a body specifically set up for the purpose and are largely independent of government financially. All governments, however, retain overriding control by prescribing regulations under which the corporations must operate and also have discretion to alter the regulations from time to time. Theoretically the supervisory powers vested in the governments are extensive but in practice they are invoked only if the corporations tend to behave in an irresponsible manner or offend against the public interest.

Unlike privately owned corporations, they are not actuated by the profit motive. They are under an obligation to utilise their income to promote denned objectives. The best known examples of this type of broadcasting organisation are the corporations and commissions in the United Kingdom, Canada, Japan, Australia, France and West Germany.

We reproduce below an extract from the Beveridge Report on Broadcasting in the United Kingdom as an example to show how autonomy has been reconciled with control:

> The formal power of the government over the British Broadcasting Corporation is absolute. The Governors who constitute the Corporation can be removed at any time by order in Council and can be replaced by others. The licence can be revoked by the Postmaster General, if at any time the Corporation in his opinion is failing in its duties. The Postmaster General can veto any proposed broadcast or class of broadcast, and in doing so can require the Corporation to refrain from announcing that a veto has been imposed. Any government department can require the Corporation to broadcast any announcement or other matter desired by it.

In practice it has become the agreed policy of successive governments, accepted by Parliament, that the Corporation should be independent of the government in the day-to-day conduct of its business, including both the making of programmes for broadcasting and general administration.

We now discuss the suitability or otherwise of the two forms we have outlined. On many consideration we are not attracted to the idea of entrusting radio and television to commercial interests. First, there is the consideration that no commercial interest would be able to undertake the enormous capital outlay involved in setting up a radio and television organisation, unless it were given unfettered discretion to earn revenue from advertisements. They might not also provide requisite time and resources for programmes of educative value, and indulge in sensationalism, sacrificing objectivity and integrity in presenting news. We must, therefore, turn our face against this form of organisation.

The most important consideration on which we have rejected this form, however, is that radio and television have a purposeful role to fulfil in our developing economy. They have to mobilise public opinion to support the plans of development, they have to educate and inform the people and strive to better their social and economic life. That should be the major role and purpose of radio and television in India.

Several witnesses including some Union and state ministers and officials were in favour of allowing private stations to operate side by side with the national network. They felt that the national network should be supplemented by private endeavour to meet the requirements of the local communities. They also felt that independent private stations would be able to provide programmes which would give greater satisfaction to the listening public. This in our view is a danger. It may lead to a lowering of standards. We, therefore, are unable to subscribe to this view and would retain for the national network a monopoly in the field of broadcasting.

We are also averse to the system in which these two media are used primarily for purposes of propagating a particular ideology and regimentation of its citizens. We are thus left with the only alternative of entrusting the broadcasting services to an autonomous corporation set up by statute which would clearly define the authority and control which government would exercise over its activities. We found overwhelming support for this idea from the officials of AIR, distinguished witnesses whose advice we sought and from others who either sent in written memoranda or gave evidence in addition. The Press also largely supported the transformation of AIR into a Corporation.

There are other valid considerations which influence us in making this recommendation. AIR must not be considered by the people as an instrument of the government of the day as it is widely regarded today. If its organisation were to be made autonomous and its programmes based on the concept of social responsibility, its value and effectiveness would be considerably enhanced. It would create public confidence and lead to the acceptance of its programmes as objective and unbiased and consequently their impact would be far greater.

Polity at Work

There is also a political consideration which cannot be lightly dismissed, more so in a federal state. If some of the states come to be controlled by parties other than the one in power at the Centre, AIR would be exposed to stresses and strains which are best avoided.

We now turn to the nature of the Corporation we recommend. The Corporation should be set up by an Act of Parliament in which its objectives should also be clearly defined and be free of ambiguity. The right to require the Corporation to broadcast certain programmes as also the right to veto broadcasts in certain subjects may be reserved to government. It must be understood that such powers must be sparingly used and only when the national interest so demands. These reservations would automatically define the accountability of the minister to Parliament.

We also consider that the Act itself should lay down the authority and powers of the Governors to prevent possible encroachment.

The constitution and composition of the governing body are all-important. The Chairman of the Corporation should be a *public figure* with a national reputation for his integrity, ability and independence. The members, the number of whom we consider should not exceed seven, should similarly be drawn from diverse fields of national life, each enjoying a reputation in his particular field. One of the complaints in the functioning of autonomous corporations, here as elsewhere, had been that the ministers are able to influence their policies without issuing directives, thus escaping parliamentary accountability. This position can be safeguarded only when the composition of the Board is such that it will not be amenable to undue and unreasonable pressure.

The people who constitute the Board must understand fully the purposes of broadcasting and see that they are fulfilled. They must also take note of public opinion and ensure that the programmes respond to it.

Various suggestions for ensuring independence have been made. One is that appointments should be made by the President, the other that they should be made by him on the recommendation of the Chief Justice, a third is that public organisations and associations with related activities should each submit a panel and selections should be confined to the names included.

We do not favour any of these suggestions. A responsible government is expected to function in a responsible way and we would much rather leave selections to government indicating only the broad principles to be observed. Secondly, experience has shown that once selected to such autonomous bodies people act independently and do not sacrifice the interest of the organisation to outside pressure.

It now remains to consider whether members of Parliament and service personnel should be categories specifically excluded as suggested by some. We are against such a blanket ban and would not demur if, by reason of eminence and specialisation, one or two were drawn from these sources.

The term of office of the Chairman and Governors should, we feel, be six years and it should be provided mat for the sake of continuity two members should retire every other year in rotation.

The Director-General: The selection of the Director General requires equally careful consideration. As Chief Executive, on him will devolve the responsibility for maintaining objectivity, ensuring efficiency and economy and building up an attractive image of the organisation. He has undoubtedly to be a person with a dynamic personality endowed with drive, imagination and initiative, capable of creating a well knit team of devoted workers and giving it resolute leadership. It is difficult anywhere to find one with all these attributes.

It will be more so in India, particularly if according to present practice the selection is confined to government servants. The net will have to be cast much wider. It may even become necessary to persuade an outstanding personality in the fields of journalism, advertising, the film industry and the academic world to accept this assignment in a spirit of dedication and service. If a civil servant is selected by the Board of Governors, there should be a stipulation, as in the case of the Reserve Bank, that he should resign from service.

The question of the status of the Director General was also mooted by some, it being suggested that in a protocol-ridden society it is important that the Director General should be accorded a high rank commensurate with his responsibilities. We, however, do not attach importance to his suggestion. The status of the Board and its Chief Executive would automatically come to be determined by the place the organisation comes to occupy in our national life and the public esteem it is able to command by its independence, integrity and excellence.

Though the details of the organisation and the rules or business should be drawn up by the Board, we should suggest certain broad principles so mat in inheriting the organisation it does not inherit the deficiencies.

Even at the risk of being repetitive, we should stress once again the need for decentralisation of authority and functions. This is necessary in the interests of efficiency in any organisation, it is more so in a broadcasting organisation. For example, in a country so vast as ours with a multiplicity of languages and cultural patterns and with, regions in different stages of development, central control of programme planning and the imposition of uniformity in their contents and presentation would not only be inappropriate but would defeat the basic purposes of the broadcasting system. We would, therefore, give the Station Directors complete freedom in the matter and subject them only to policy directions as to the types of broadcasts which should be discouraged.

We do not suggest that this decentralisation should be absolute. It should be obligatory to relay the national news bulletins and other national programmes of interest. It is necessary though that determination of themes of broadcasts as national should be made with circumspection and discretion. Another way to achieve decentralisation is to have several channels of broadcasting, one of which would provide the national programme, the other regional programmes and the third a local service on local transmitters which we have recommended earlier. The only practical way as we have stressed, is through such local stations.

The establishment of competitive channel of broadcasting was advocated by several witnesses. They argued that a monopolist enterprise tends to become complacent, stale and ineffective. It needs the stimulus of competition to make its staff more alert and enterprising and the programmes more lively. It was said that the establishment of the Independent Television Authority in Britain had a tonic effect on the BBC's TV Services.

We have considered this question carefully. We have come

to the conclusion that having regard to the availability of resources both in manpower and in funds, and the role we envisage for broadcasting, we should not at this stage bring in considerations which might well come in the way of the development of radio.

We should, however, encourage universities to instal closed circuit radio and television services, or the state governments and major municipal corporations to set up local transmitters for agricultural, social and educational purposes to meet the needs of local communities which cannot be effectively served by the national network.

It is necessary to consider how the Corporation we have proposed should be financed. The question falls into two parts: capital expenditure to add to the network by installing additional transmitters, studios and other equipment; revenue expenditure for sustaining and improving the service.

We now turn to the question how future capital expenditure should be financed and how best the revenue of AIR should be augmented. In the case of state enterprises, government have provided both equity capital and loans to maintain a proper ratio between the two. While interest is chargeable on the loan (there has been a period of moratorium in many cases), the return on equity investment depends on the profits, if any earned. This is the policy adopted in the case of commercial activities. Similarly, government meet the capital expenditure on welfare measures, on education, health and activities necessary to increase agricultural production.

Broadcasting is not a commercial activity, though a monopoly, it cannot, unlike other monopolies, adjust prices, rates and fees to meet interest liability on capital expended. On all considerations and having regard to its primary role as a medium of education and information, we consider that capital expenditure is a legitimate charge on public revenues.

We propose, therefore, that the assets of AIR should be

transferred to the Corporation without any interest or any other financial liability. Similarly, the allocation in the Fourth Plan should be made available to the Corporation free of charge. We consider that thereafter the proposals we make on revenue account, would make the Corporation fully viable, able to expand with its own resources taking resource to borrowing, if necessary, on its own financial standing.

We have one important observation to make in regard to capital expenditure. We find that organisationally AIR is geared to an expenditure of about Rs 2 crores a year. To enlarge its spending capacity efficiently, it would be necessary to bring about a reorganisation and the sooner it is undertaken the better it would be. The allocation in the Fourth Plan is bound to be larger and we have recommended certain priorities for providing local transmitters and the reorientation of the external services.

To fulfil this plan, AIR needs organisation and effort which should be pre-planned.

There has been a suggestion that licence fees should be discontinued. We do not accept this suggestion. It would be unfair to burden the community at large to support a service when the beneficiaries are small in number. The fee should continue to be recovered from users of the service. (Licence fee has since been abolished).

We consider that considerable improvement in the recovery of licence fees is possible. It is common knowledge that a number of sets in the country are unlicensed; some suggest that it is as high as sixty per cent.

The steps we have recommended would give elbow room to AIR but would not make it fully viable nor enable it to finance.

By far the most fruitful source of additional revenue would be the acceptance of advertisement in programmes. In dealing with Television we have marshalled the arguments in favour of its acceptance with certain safeguards and restrictions. We do not feel that there are any special considerations which would justify making a distinction on this question between television and sound broadcasting. Consistent with our thinking on this subject, we would limit advertisements to the Vividh Bharati channel alone. By timing the spot advertisements suitably there need be no interference with a programme or its continuity. Vividh Bharati is a light programme predominantly of film music and the inclusion of advertisements is not likely to infringe on its quality or appeal.

Television is a comparatively new medium far more sophisticated than radio. There are basic differences between radio and television in important matters of technique and financing of operators and planning and execution of programmes. Television also presents other problems infinitely more complicated.

Even so, many countries with well-established broadcasting systems found it convenient to entrust the development of television to their existing organisations. This arrangement soon proved to be little more than a marriage of convenience. The rapid growth of television, the remarkable advances in its technology and programme planning, and its versatility in use, brought new responsibilities which could be hardly fulfilled within the resources of existing organisations. This difficulty has been sought to be met by investing the television wing with virtual autonomy. In the United Kingdom, the Union of Soviet Socialist Republics and in Italy, the television centre has now become a distinct, separate and powerful entity with tenuous links with the parent organisation.

In the light of these developments, it has to be considered whether it will be possible or wise to place television under the aegis of AIR. This possibility has to be ruled out as AIR is not organisationally and financially equipped to shoulder this responsibility. It would also be unfair to tag on television to AIR and expose it at its birth to prejudices which exist against AIR. On all these considerations, we would strongly advise against the development and management of this new medium, requiring a dynamic and imaginative approach and ample resources, being linked as an ancillary to an organisation which itself needs a major overhaul and refurbishing.

The question still remains whether the new organisation should follow the pattern of AIR and become an attached office of a ministry or whether it should be made an autonomous corporation, created by a special statute of Parliament. Having carefully considered the question in all its aspects, we have come to the conclusion that to develop on correct lines television must not be hampered by the limitations of a department; it should have a broader outlook, greater flexibility and freedom of action which the corporate form alone can give.

While discussing the future organisation of AIR we have already stated in detail the reasons for our recommendation that an autonomous statutory corporation would be the best form of organisation for providing a broadcasting service. These consideration apply with equal, if not greater force, in case of television.

We consider that to give shape to our recommendations immediate steps should be taken to invite a competent agency to prepare the project report. An officer of the status of a Chief Engineer, should be associated with their team in its preparatory work, who could later be selected to head the technical wing.

To ensure that the two processes of project study and operation planning go hand in hand, it would be necessary to form the Television Corporation with the nucleus of staff necessary to access the ultimate requirements of staff, organise training, draw up the programme policy and prepare an estimate of the finances required. It should also initiate negotiations with potential collaborators but keep government closely informed of developments. The agreements reached should naturally be subject to government approval.

We have already given our views on the staffing of AIR and suggested reorganisation. The staffing pattern and employment policy of the Television Corporation we propose will have to be differently conceived and designed.

As mentioned earlier, television is basically a different medium from radio and cannot be given the same treatment. Being, however, a part of AIR, the Delhi Television Centre has unfortunately the same organisation as a radio unit and has developed unsuitable trends and nuances. For one thing, it has tended to become a top-heavy organisation in which the more expensive technical staff was until recently being incorrectly employed; for another, its programmes being produced on the basis of radio techniques and experience, are indifferent and even colourless. It is essential that the two activities should be separated at the large scale inception of television, to give it a fair wind.

We are in agreement with our Consultant mat 'television needs a lively, decisive, imaginative, adventurous yet responsible staff. This implies that its control and operations should be in the hands of those who have these attributes. Taking a look at the Delhi Centre, the first point that struck us was the strength of the staff deployed for its limited output. It appeared that there had not been a proper assessment of the staff required in different categories and that as problems arose they were sought to be met by hurriedly transferring whoever was conveniently available in the radio wing. As a consequence of this haphazard and irrational staffing, the sanctioned strength has been raised to 271 to allow for the recent extension of the service.

The Centre provides a one-hour evening programme of news and entertainment of which only about a third is produced at the Centre itself, the rest being films or recorded material obtained locally or from abroad. It also provides three twenty-minute school lessons a day for six days a week for each of the two shifts in the schools, giving a total broadcast time of about 120 minutes a day. But of these lessons one or two a week are repetitions of old lessons already recorded and telecast, thus reducing the output of the studio to about eight hours a week.

In the opinion of our Consultant, the Centre is grossly overstaffed. Our Sub-Committee concurs in this assessment on the basis of its study abroad. 'Telescuola' in Italy, running school and adult literacy programmes, is on the air for 41½ hours a week but it employs a total of 128 people only including 27 technicians and 16 teachers, e.g. Admittedly, its telecasts do not require certain categories of staff which an inclusive service of information, education and entertainment would need, but even so the contrast is striking.

Our Consultant also informed us that a firm International Television Consultants had recommended a total staff of approximately 50 for certain African countries embarking on television with a daily programme output of four hours. Similarly, a UNESCO Mission, which advised Israel on the introduction of television, recommended a total staff of 226 distributed between the three organisations of the Central Administration (the equivalent of the directorate general of AIR), the Jerusalem and the Tel Aviv Studio Centres. This requirement was based on a suggested output of 23 hours of programmes a week of which over 12 hours were to originate in the two Studio Centres.

The second point that struck us was that at its inception the Television Centre was manned largely if not entirely by people drawn from sound broadcasting without a mature consideration whether this arrangement was suitable either for the installation or the development of this medium.

Training is essential for the success of all human endeavour. The more difficult the objective, the greater is the need for training for its attainment. Yet the necessity of advance training of the required number of people in the difficult and varied techniques of television had been ignored before the Delhi pilot project was launched in 1959.

It was only after six years, in 1965, that a producer was obtained on loan from the BBC to give a course of training to a small number of selected production staff. We consider that this is totally inadequate even to sustain the extended programmes of the Centre and to improve their quality, leave alone to handle the expansion we recommend.

We have earlier mentioned that the installation of a television network needs massive financial outlay, a large part of it in foreign exchange. On both these counts, some acceptable form of foreign collaboration will have to be considered. Financing of the television service is another matter; it needs a different treatment.

Because of the low priority given to broadcasting, the allocation of Plan resources has so far been minuscule. We have already adduced many considerations why television should receive equal priority with industrial and agricultural schemes of development. Even so, the competing demands of other nation-building activities might make it difficult to allocate to television all the money it needs for developing a countrywide network by the end of the Fifth Plan. We have perforce to consider alternatives which would ensure adequate financial support.

We have made as detailed a study as is possible, in the absence of complete documentation, of developments elsewhere and the manner in which countries similarly situated have set about to bring the benefits of television to their people.

Foreign collaboration in two different forms has been adopted to cover fully the foreign exchange component of the project for the supply of capital goods such as transmitters, studio equipment, installation of links and other ancillary facilities. It has either taken the shape of participation in the equity issue of the corporation or it has been a straight loan with a period of moratorium before repayment commences.

Some countries have adopted the former method in which a consortium of industrialists has a minority financial interest, the controlling interest being retained by government. Some others have preferred the latter method but have not encountered any lack of response because of this choice. We also consider that we must not have any foreign equity participation in the proposed Television Corporation. It is needles to add that the provision of a loan must not give any voice to the donors in deciding the policy of the Corporation.

In addition, it has been arranged either separately or as a part of the same scheme that the foreign exchange requirements of manufacturing television sets and the essential equipment would be provided by the foreign associates, the inducement being that they would themselves supply the television sets until, manufacture has been established but without an appreciable outflow of foreign exchange.

It is found impractical for a single county to provide the required financial support, the formation of a consortium might become necessary. The idea of forming a consortium has caught on even in the matter of international aid to developing countries. It should not, therefore, be difficult to bring about the formation of a consortium to assist our project should this become necessary. We contemplate a package deal in which the collaborator would also accept responsibility for the manufacture of television sets and other equipment. It may be necessary to set up a separate manufacturing unit.

The willingness to collaborate with technical assistance and a loan will naturally depend on the viability of the project and its ability to generate enough resources to be able to repay the loan in agreed instalments. Under the plan we later discuss, we have no doubts that the revenues of the Corporation will be ample to meet all its commitments. We are confident that foreign collaborator would feel equally reassured.

The question will still remain how the rupee finance of the project can best be found. The allocation of a high priority for television together with the realisation that the acceptance of the plan we later unfold would make television a viable and even a productive venture should make it possible for the Planning

Commission to release necessary resources. The expectation that television would become self-financing within a short time, if not at its inception, and that it would not, therefore, make annual demands for its running expenses should be a weighty consideration in the allocation of resources. It would imply that the initial investment needed would be little more than a capitalisation of a few years recurring expenses, provision for which would have to be made otherwise, being inherent in the acceptance of a television scheme, however, unambitious it may be.

There is another aspect developed earlier, that is the extensive use of television for educational, agriculture, health and other socioeconomic purposes. On a long term view, it may be found more economical, yet more effective to invest in television than, for example, to build schools for which teacher cannot be found, or equipment provided, or build health centres which can only be manned by indifferent and unimaginative people. Similarly, recurring expenditure on publicity to give an impetus to programmes for self-sufficiency in the production of foodgrains and other expenditure now incurred for popularising the introduction of improved strains of seeds, the use of fertilisers and pesticides, the rotation of crops, etc., could be considerably minimised by visual presentation which television alone can provide.

These savings would be a recurring annual feature and should give welcome relief to the budgets of these departments. Once his important aspect of television is realised, there should be no difficulty in either increasing the allocation for television by corresponding reduction in the capital budgets of the ministries concerned; alternatively, they should invest a part, albeit a small part, of their capital grants in building up a countrywide television network. A small advisory body of the participants in programme planning should ensure the allocation of adequate time to each.

The cost of operating the network depends on its output, the standard of the producers and artists it employs, the level of remuneration it pays, and the type and quality of programmes it provides. It must obviously be the aim to give the optimum output within the capability of the network and to plan and produce programmes of the highest quality employing first class artists. This implies that there must be resources available for establishing and sustaining a high professional standard comparable to other television services.

The method evolved by the British Broadcasting Corporation, and followed by some other broadcasting systems, is to levy a licence fee from the owners of receiving sets and to allocate the proceeds, after deducting the cost of collection, to broadcasting. The yield is thus directly related to the number of receiving sets held and licensed. The limitation of this arrangement is that the rate of levy cannot be easily adjusted to accord with the needs of the service. There are many factors including public resistance which have to be taken into account in a revision of the fee.

When the British Broadcasting Corporation entered the field of television, a separate and higher scale of levy was designed to finance its programmes and other operating costs. This levy has been adjusted upwards from time to time to sustain an expansion of programmes, to improve their quality and to neutralise rising costs. The public had gone along with these increases. More recently an Independent Television Authority was created by statute and was given freedom to run its services with advertising revenues without sharing with the British Broadcasting Corroboration the licence fees collected. This brought a new concept of financing television in tradition-bound and conventional Britain.

The programmes controlled by the Independent Television Authority not only proved attractive but were made available without any payment by the viewing audiences. We shall refer to the ITA later in the narration but mention it at this stage because of its indirect impact on the recent demand of the British Broadcasting Corporation for a substantial increase in licence fees both for existing services and for opening up a fourth channel which has become available. Government considered the increase demanded unreasonable and also unfair to licence-holders and conceded a smaller increase. This has left the British Broadcasting Corporation in a quandary.

It has to be appreciated that in a country like India the licence fees have to be kept reasonably low to accord with the people's capacity to pay. On the one hand, the number of sets in private hands in the initial stages will be small and the yield of licence fees negligible, on the other, there will be the need for a wide network to bring the social programmes within the reach of the community which needs them most. It will thus become necessary to accept commercial advertisements to supplement the revenue derived from licence fees.

We are aware of the opinion which still persists against the acceptance of commercial broadcasts. There is the apprehension that were commercial advertisements to be accepted television would become largely dependent on revenues derived from commercial interests and this might well lead to the political, economic and social policies of the organisation being influenced and even indirectly controlled by these interests. There is also the apprehension that the advertisements to have a popular appeal, might tend to become somewhat vulgar and demoralising.

Experience elsewhere has shown that the acceptance of advertisements to accord with the programme policy of a television organisation does not bring it even remotely under the control of commercial interests nor does it lead to the presentation of material which is in questionable taste.

It is necessary to review in a brief compass, the policy adopted by different organisations, discussing later their merits and demerits. In the United States of America and Latin American countries as also in Iran, Lebanon, Thailand and the Philippines, television is in the hands of private interests who finance their operations, including the setting up and expansion of their existing networks, from revenues derived entirely from the sale of time to advertisers.

In the United States of America and most of these countries, the advertisers not only buy time but also provide programmes of their choice which go with the advertisements.

In Australia, Japan and Canada this system has been adopted by a number of comparatively small television stations which operate in competition with the national organisations which are maintained out of licence revenues. The acceptance of commercial programmes, known as 'sponsored programme' has resulted in the largest and most prosperous television network in the world being built up in the United States of America and it has also given impetus to the growth of television in the countries mentioned and in Latin America and some countries of Asia. The major undesirable feature of this system is that the television organisation has very little control over the programmes put on the air with the result that they are often in questionable taste and have a demoralising effect on impressionable and immature minds. It has been suggested that the increase in the rate of child delinquency in the United States of America is attributable to these programmes.

Benefiting by the experience of the United States of America, countries which entered the television field later, more particularly the European countries, evolved a new system. While accepting commercial advertisements as inescapable for supporting the growth of a sound television system and also the U.S. practice of selling time, they safeguarded the quality and standard to the programmes by refusing to allow the advertisers to produce them or even to have a say in the programmes which would include their advertisement material. By this method commonly known as 'spot advertising' or 'spot announcements', the organisations retained full control over their programme policy. An additional safeguard was also introduced, by stature where necessary, but mainly by a code of conduct voluntarily agreed upon by the organisations and the advertisers, to control the make-up of the advertisements. Italy went a step further and set up a corporation to handle and produce all advertisement shots.

Television stations in West Germany, Ireland, Italy, Spain, the United Arab Republic, Iraq, Pakistan, to mention a few countries, have adopted this system of spot advertising to raise resources to supplement revenues from licence fees. Some countries such as Italy and West Germany have introduced the practice of presenting in a single special programme all advertisements within an allocated period of time, usually 20 to 30 minutes, at an excellent viewing hour, between eight and nine o'clock in the evening. Other countries intersperse the spots, not exceeding five or six minutes in an hour, in their daily programmes.

It is necessary to discuss the two practices, their merits and demerits and their revenue potential. The practice of concentrating all advertisements in one programme has two attractive features: First, it enables the viewers who are not interested in commercials to switch off at the hour when they are on the air; secondly, by not breaking into a programme, it preserves the continuity and entertainment value of the programme and also the atmosphere it creates. The advertisers, however, do not consider this method as attractive as spots in regular programmes. They also consider that a spot should be repeated in a number of programmes in any one day to have worthwhile advertisement value.

The latter practice has undoubtedly greater advertisement value, as it provides a captive audience and a repeated presentation of the same spots in different programmes at different viewing hours. The irritation caused by the spots breaking into a programme has been sought to be removed by putting the advertisements at the beginning, the intermission and the end of the programmes. This is an improvement from the viewers point and meets the advertisers' demands to a certain extent. The revenue potential of this practice is undoubtedly greater.

We have very carefully considered which of the two systems, the U.S. one of sponsored programmes or the European one of spot advertisement to recommend, or whether a combination of the two would be more suitable. We do not feel that one need be squeamish about sponsored programmes as such so long as they have an educative and cultural value and do not include any advertisement material except to mention at their commencement or conclusion that they were presented by the courtesy of so and so (naming the sponsors).

Such programmes do not have the connotation or implications of sponsored programmes in the United States of America and should even be welcome as being useful and valuable additions to the repertoire of the television organisation. Such programmes are not uncommon elsewhere and have been viewed and appreciated by some of us abroad. These 'prestige' programmes are presented by sponsors who are inspired to contribute to the growth of the television system and incidentally bring their names and contributions to the notice of the viewing public. However, the revenues from this type of sponsored programmes will not be substantial but that should be no reason for excluding them.

The acceptance of advertisements should be considered only if it brings significant financial support to the growth of television. There is nothing non-ethical in accepting advertisements prepared in good taste provided that they do not affect the quality of the telecasts or make excessive demands.

If the educational, social and children's programmes do not carry spots and they are confined to the entertainment programmes, there should not be any objection in adopting a practice which has now become more or less universal.

A 12-Member Working Group headed by B.G. Verghese was set up on August 17, 1977, to go into the working of AIR and Doordarshan and suggest changes. The following were the other members of his Group: V.G. Rajadhyaksha, Dr. Malcolm S. Adiseshiah, Chanchal Sarkar, P.L. Deshpande, Umashankar Joshi, A.G. Noorani, G.R. Subramanian, Mrs. Nayantara Sehgal and Dr. Ishwar Das (Member Secretary).

The group made wide-ranging recommendations to transform

All-India Radio and Television into a more responsive organisation from a mere government department. The two-volume report running into 405 pages was presented to Parliament on March 9, 1978. In its unanimous report, the working group suggested that the national broadcasting services should be vested exclusively in an independent impartial and autonomous organization established by law to act as a trustee for the national interest.

The legal framework of the autonomous national trust, as envisaged by the working group, was that the establishment of the corporation should not await a constitutional amendment. The law establishing the corporation could be enacted and the organisation brought into being to be followed subsequently by an amendment of the Constitution.

The autonomy of the corporation and its independence from government control should be entrenched in the Constitution itself and the idea of a trust woven into it.

In making recommendations, the working group was guided by a factor that mass media, radio and television must fit into a wider perspective of national communication policy or philosophy.

It rejected a proposal to create two separate corporations for All-India Radio and Television. However, it conceded the need to recognize the distinctive identity of radio and television within the ambit of a new integrated structure.

The group also did not favour the creation of autonomous regional corporations or even a federation of State Government corporations. While rejecting the proposal to create two separate corporations or set up autonomous regional corporations, the working group argued that there would be a large measure of power delegated to the regional and local level.

This was kept to the fore so that the organisation enjoyed the advantages of quick decision making, sensitivity to local problems and tasks, and close linkages with various governments and institutions.

In recommending the new set-up, the working group did not apparently follow any model operating in any other country.

At the apex of NBT, the working group suggested a board of trustees consisting of 12 persons, and not exceeding 21 persons. The trustees would be guardians of the charter given to the NBT by statute.

The Controller-General of Broadcasting (CGB), heading the central executive board, was conceived by the working group as a link between the trustees and the entire broadcasting organisation. He would be ex-officio secretary to the board of trustees so as to provide an organic link between these two tiers.

Apart from the Chairman, the board of trustees would have three other full-time members to devote themselves to the fields of current affairs, extension and culture. They will operate through the CGB.

In addition to the Chairman and the three full-time trustees, the board would have two part-time trustees—one highly experienced in the field of finance and management and the other an eminent scientist or engineer familiar with the technology of broadcasting.

For the first time in the history of over half-a-century of broadcasting in India, there would be a complaints board comprising persons selected by the Chief Justice of India.

The recommendation of the working group for constituting a complaint board assumed significance in the light of the experience gained during the Emergency when the broadcasting system was blatantly used by the previous regime to further partisan ends.

According to the report, the board of trustees would be responsible to Parliament through its budget and an annual report. Together with accounts and auditor's comments, reports of the complaints board, among other things, would also figure in the annual report.

The complaints board would deal with complaints from the public relating to charges of unjust or unfair treatment including unwarranted invasion of privacy and misrepresentation, provided the right of resources to court was waived. The findings should be published by NBT in the programme 'Journal' and broadcast in special programmes.

In order to ensure the independence of the proposed NBT, the report recommended that the trustees, with six-year terms of office, would be appointed by the President on the recommendation of the Prime Minister from a list of names forwarded to him by a nominating panel.

The nominating panel for trustees would consist of the Chief Justice of India, the Lokpal and the Chairman of the UPSC. It would be a healthy convention if the Prime Minister consulted the leader of the Opposition before submitting the list of names to the President.

The trustees would enjoy the status of Supreme Court judges.

In regard to financial autonomy, the report recommended several measures. Initially, the government should make up the revenue deficit for a period of five years, after transferring the existing assets of All-India Radio and TV.

Later, NBT should be expected to stand on its own feet or raise additional resources by charging for broadcast time, made available by it to various users, including the Central and state governments.

It also felt that the Trust should undertake a comprehensive review of commercial broadcasting rates and procedures. The group also recommended an increase in broadcast receiver licences for certain categories of radio and TV sets.

The report comprehensively surveyed the entire scene of broadcasting and television network since the Chanda Committee submitted its report on radio more than 12 years ago. The Chanda

Committee had also recommended an autonomous set-up for AIR.

According to the report, there were now some 20 million radio receivers and 600,000 TV sets. 'With population rising to say, 950 million by 2000 A.D. and 'an end to destitution' and fuller employment, at least 80 to 90 per cent of all households should possess radios,' the report added.

In a perspective study for 2000 A.D. there would be 160 to 180 million radio sets and between 12 to 15 million TV sets by the turn of the century.

In the opinion of the working group, AIR and TV combined in themselves the characteristics of the marketplace, newspaper, university, national extension agency and cultural academy. As such a unique institution must enjoy a unique autonomy.

The report called upon the National Broadcast Trust to bridge the urban-rural divide and combine modernity with relevant tradition.

It recommended the establishment of a strong audience research division. It noted that the audience research unit had a very limited staff and budget. It was, therefore, impossible to conduct any regular audience surveys or to operate on more than very small samples.

The audience research reports should be made available simultaneously and directly to the board of trustees, since these reports would constitute one of the most important antenna of the broadcasting organisation.

Prasar Bharati Bill : The Prasar Bharati Bill was introduced in the Lok Sabha on December 30, 1989, by the National Front Government led by V.P. Singh. The purpose of this Bill was to grant autonomy to the electronic media, that is AIR and Doordarshan.

The Lok Sabha passed the Bill on August 30, 1990 and the

Rajya Sabha approved it on September 6, 1990. The President accorded assent to the Bill soon after.

The changes in the original Bill ran as follows :

> The autonomous Prasar Bharati or Broadcasting Corporation of India will be directly answerable to three authorities—a Parliamentary Committee, the Central Government and the proposed Broadcasting Council.
>
> The original draft of the Prasar Bharati Bill introduced in the Lok Sabha did not contain any provision for the Parliamentary Committee. The government inserted this provision on August 29,1990, as one of the 65 amendments proposed by an all-party consensus. Members of the committee will be elected by proportional representation and will ensure that the Corporation functions in the manner set out in the Bill.

There was no opposition in Parliament to this particular provision as it was only intended to make the autonomous body accountable. Besides being answerable to the Committee, the corporation has to submit annual reports of its activities to Parliament.

The powers envisaged for the Central government, however, have given rise to immense misgivings. The initial draft said the Central government could give directions to make or not to make a certain broadcast only when 'the security of the state or preservation of public order' was at stake. But the August 29 changes widened the ambit by saying that the Central government can also issue directions 'in the interest of sovereignty, unity and integrity of India'. These concepts are very subjective and have been left undefined, tremendously increasing the scope for abuse of power.

Further, the Central government has been empowered to

demand any information from the corporation. This means, for instance, that it can order Doordarshan to divulge the source of a news report. If the corporation 'persistently' refuses to comply with any direction, the Central government has been empowered to recommend to Parliament any action, including supersession of the Prasar Bharati Board. The government's recommendation has been given such weight that a ratification by a simple majority will be enough to supersede the board.

The only constraint is that the President, before issuing the notification of supersession, will have to give 'a reasonable opportunity to the board to show cause as to why it should not be superseded'. The maximum permissible period of supersession is six months. The powers and functions of the board during that period will be discharged by 'such person or persons as the President may direct.'

The third authority which will be vested with some power over the corporation is the Broadcasting Council, which corresponds to the Press Council. The original draft of the Bill, envisaged as a watchdog to protect the interests of the citizens, empowered the Broadcasting Council to decide complaints against the corporation and recommend appropriate remedial action to it. What happens when the corporation rejects the Broadcasting Council's recommendation? An amendment provides for such a contingency:

The Broadcasting Council will have the authority to force the corporation to broadcast the recommendation. This, in fact, is the only form of vindication the Bill offers to a citizen aggrieved by the corporation.

If Doordarshan or Akashvani, after they are unfettered, broadcast a programme or news report defamatory to somebody, he cannot sue or initiate criminal proceedings against the corporation or anybody in it. This is due to a clause granting immunity against all legal action to the corporation and its employees.

Thus, on the one hand, the proposed corporation is sought to be given the freedom enjoyed by newspapers, on the other, the producers and reporters in the broadcasting field will not be liable for their mistakes as their counterparts in the print media.

The relevant section (24) in the initial draft grants the legal immunity 'for anything which is in good faith done or intended to be done in pursuance of this act or of any rules or regulations made thereunder.' The language is general enough to enable anybody in the corporation to take refuge under this clause for any error committed by him. Yet this section has surprisingly managed to survive the radical amendments made in the Lok Sabha to the original draft.

The Prasar Bharati Board which forms the core of the legislation has also undergone many changes. In the first place, its name was 'Board of Governors'. But the high sounding 'governor' has been replaced by the simple 'member'. The strength of the board has been increased by the inclusion of two ex-officio members—the Director-General of Akashvani and Doordarshan and two elected members from among the employees of the Corporation. The whole-time chairman has been made a part-time one.

All the whole-time members of the board have been made employees of the Corporation.

Among other amendments are: the inclusion of four MPs (two from each House) in the Broadcasting Council, the stipulation on the Broadcasting Council present an annual report to Parliament, deletion of the power to dismiss an employee without being given an opportunity to defend himself and the bar on the Corporation from ceiling its assets.

The Verghese Committee which also advocated autonomy to the electronic media wanted the Ministry of Information and Broadcasting to shed its control over Broadcasting. But the Prasar Bharati Bill puts a representative of the Ministry on the Board of the Corporation.

The most controversial clause as stated earlier is Parliament's power to supersede the Prasar Bharati Board.

In the original version of the bill, this power was sought to be vested in the government.

The present dispensation is an improvement but the effect is the same to ensure that the Prasar Bharati behaves. BJP leader, L.K. Advani sought to soften the blow by suggesting during the discussion of the Bill, an amendment that would have required any resolution on supersession to be passed by two-thirds majority instead of a simple majority. But surprisingly except for one member, nobody supported his suggestion. Strangely, the CPI(M) appeared particularly averse to Mr. Advani's plea.

Voting in Parliament is on strictly party lines and it is unimaginable that if an official resolution is moved for supersession of board of governors, the ruling party members would vote against the resolution.

The official justification for such sweeping Parliamentary control is that if the Prasar Bharati were to be left completely to its devices there was a danger of its being taken over by big business. According to P. Upendra, all autonomous corporations are accountable to Parliament and their functioning is supervised by the Committee on Public Undertakings.

This according to him, has not led to interference in their day-to-day affairs, so why should there be fears about such interference in the case of Prasar Bharati.

The fact is that no political party, especially the Left and the Congress wanted an absolutely free Prasar Bharati. They wanted to avoid a situation when the corporation could go 'amuck' in the name of autonomy.

The Congress party also opposed the decision to transfer the assets of AIR and Doordarshan to Prasar Bharati. It is on the insistence of the Congress party that the Bill was amended to say that the new corporation would use the assets in accordance with the terms and conditions prescribed by the government.

Commenting on the question of how autonomous would be the electronic media under the new set up, B.G. Verghese said that the concept is to de-governmentalise broadcasting, both radio as well as television, by placing it under an autonomous corporation—as against where it is now as a subordinate department of the government. Its autonomy would be safeguarded by two or three things.

One is that, according to the Bill, the corporation's accountability is not to the Information & Broadcasting Ministry, but to Parliament. Secondly, the appointment of its top board will be done by a selection committee consisting of the Chairman of Rajya Sabha, the Chairman of the Press Council and a third member to be selected by the President and their decision will be final. This prevents the body from being packed by government favourites.

The third safeguard is that if these people are to be removed it will have to be by a special procedure which is applicable to the members and chairman of the UPSC. They cannot be sacked. And now, they have also added the clause that if the board collectively misbehaves by persistently defying the government directives, then the ministry can make a report to Parliament in which it could recommend supersession, and following a decision of Parliament, supersession can take place. According to Mr. Verghese, Parliamentary control is unnecessary and he feels that the contingencies in which these powers would be used are extreme. They are theoretically possible but in practical terms, they are unlikely to be used.

According to Mr. Khushwant Singh, the well-known journalist, freeing the electronic media from government control deserves to be applauded as the National Front government's biggest achievement of its nine-month rule. All our past Prime

Ministers and Ministers of Information and Broadcasting paid lip-services to the principle of freedom of expression for Press, Radio and Television, but everyone of them meddled with their free functioning when they found themselves at the receiving end of criticism.

Jawaharlal Nehru was no exception. He was riled by what Durga Das (father of Inderjit, Member of the Lok Sabha) wrote about him and did his best to damage his career. His Minister of Information and Broadcasting, Keskar, had Nirad Chaudhuri dismissed from AIR and then blacklisted for eulogising the British in the dedication of his autobiography of an unknown Indian. Keskar had not bothered to read the book.

Mrs. Gandhi had scant respect for Press freedom and blatantly misused Radio and Television to propagate herself and denigrate rivals like Jayaprakash Narayan. She pressurised proprietors of newspapers to remove editors she did not like. Her sycophantic ministers like N.K.P. Salve and H.K.L. Bhagat (Vasant Sathe was one exception) went a step ahead to cancel programmes like 'The World of Nature' which had nothing whatsoever to do with politics for the sole reason that it was written by someone who Mrs. Gandhi regarded as her critic.

It was the same during the short regimes of Morarji Desai and Charan Singh: editors were fired, broadcasters, they did not approve, removed. Blacklists continued to be maintained by AIR and Doordarshan throughout Rajiv Gandhi's tenure as Prime Minister. Who is the Congress (I) to talk about freedom of speech and expression? For Messrs Salve, Bhagat and their likes to extol them is like harlots extolling the virtues of chastity.

It is still not clear how free from political meddling will be the board that will control Radio and Doordarshan. However, a very bold and significant step has been taken. Full credit for this must go to P. Upendra and V.P. Singh.

This is what Mr. Nikhil Chakarvarty, a columnist, said about the electronic media's autonomy. He said there was little consultation even with the media circles before the Bill was drafted, but the criticism was more than negated by two things. First, the speech made by Information and Broadcasting Minister, P. Upendra, while introducing the Bill had a ring of sincerity that reassured many that the present government was earnest about autonomy for the government owned media.

Second, the Minister, on his own, announced that there would be free and wide-ranging national debate on the proposed legislation and the criticisms, suggestions and comments to be made in such discussions would be taken into consideration in amending the bill before it was taken up by Parliament. Not only that, his ministry promoted such discussions all over the country. But after the much publicised computerisation of proposals and suggestions, the amendments which the government announced came as a big shock. These were largely retrogressive.

Meanwhile, the government has been remiss on another count. Upendra had promised that there would be a non-official committee to oversee the functioning of the Akashvani and Doordarshan in the interim period until the proposed Prasar Bharati Corporation took over. It was stated that within a couple of weeks this interim set-up would start functioning. Nothing of this kind happened.

Looking at the amendments so far tabled in the Lok Sabha, I for one cannot be optimistic about our setting up a genuinely autonomous corporation. For instance, there is an amendment seeking to establish a Parliamentary Committee to control the set-up. This sounds very impressive as evidence of democratic control but in practice it would have meant not the autonomy of the media but its domination by the party bosses in Parliament.

Vasant Sathe, one of the more competent among the long line of Information Ministers, has been harping on behalf of the Congress, on the need for functional autonomy instead of a new autonomous set-up as envisaged in the Bill. Functional autonomy would mean that the functionaries of the Radio and Television set-up would be ensured autonomy irrespective of ownership—government or a corporation. In fact, such functional autonomy would be needed even if and when the Prasar Bharati is set up.

The Prasar Bharati Bill was supported by the Congress under Rajiv Gandhi and received the President's assent on September 12, 1990. The election manifesto of the Congress party issued in April, 1991, contained a pledge to implement the Act. But the Congress government has now developed cold feet towards its implementation.

In March 1992, the Information and Broadcasting Ministry, in a note to Prime Minister P.V. Narasimha Rao, observed that the 'circumstances have changed' since the time when the idea of autonomy to the electronic media was mooted.

The note cites some of the fruits of the government's recent liberalisation policy on media, including the advent of satellite broadcasting, video news cassettes and cable TV networks as evidence of the fact that the government no longer holds a monopoly over the electronic media.

The ministry wanted the Prime Minister to consider whether the notification on Prasar Bharati should be deferred.

The note also sought the Prime Minister's opinion on whether second Doordarshan channels in the four metropolitan cities should be simultaneously leased out to one or more entities who may share time among themselves.

With regard to cable television, the I&B Ministry note solicited the Prime Minister's opinion on whether permission should be given for the cables to operate with or without dish antennae. It has asked whether such permission, if given, should be through a system of licensing, or a mere registration with a local authority would suffice.

The government constituted an interdepartmental committee

on September 3, 1991, under the Chairmanship of K.A. Varadan, Additional Secretary, Ministry of Information and Broadcasting, to suggest options available for implementation of the scheme for offering broadcasting rights to public corporations. The committee submitted its report in October 1991.

A major recommendation of the Varadan Committee relates to leasing out the second channel of Doordarshan in the four metropolitan cities to suitable licencees. At the same time, additional radio channels including FM stations wherever available, could also be leased out. The government proposed to set up a Broadcasting Council of India. The Council could, among other things, serve as the agency for redressal of complaints emanating from individuals or institutions in regard to any programme broadcast by a new channel. The Varadan Committee's Report on leasing out broadcasting rights of Doordarshan and Radio channels has offered a way out to the Congress government dilemma of liberalising the media without upsetting the existing power structure or losing its propaganda advantage.

It has achieved this by watering down and moderating many of the radical reforms that the government had earlier proposed.

The government has refused to give broadcasting rights to individuals and private firms. Instead, it has recommended that the government would lease out parts of Doordarshan's second channel and extra channel of AIR to potential licences.

In addition, the Varadan panel has recommended that the so-called 'public limited companies' to which such broadcasting rights are to be granted are to be decided by a single statutory or autonomous body known as the Broadcasting Council of India. By adopting a more cautious approach towards privatisation, the Committee has done well to ensure that the autonomy does not mean replacement of state control with market ownership.

In a developing society like India, privatisation would only succeed in promoting elitism and consumerism which could be socially disastrous. It would help prevent perpetuation of monopoly by industrial houses running the newspapers.

Unfortunately, the Varadan Committee does not effectively tackle the two most important questions before it—the threat of foreign TV networks' invasion and the related issue of improving Doordarshans' fallen credibility. While cognisant of and cautioning against the evil design of media Multinational Corporations (MNCs) which subject newly freed countries to cultural imperialism, the Committee pleads that nothing can be done to stop these transmissions or ban their receptions. The government must establish some kind of regulatory mechanism to monitor the programmes being beamed into the country from outside.,

At the same time the government must implement the Prasar Bharati Act at the earliest. It is only by injecting professionalism and credibility into Doordarshan that the government can hope to wean away Indian audiences who are getting hooked to alien broadcasting networks.

8

Team Work

Chief Reporter

The chief reporter has a team of reporters working with him. He holds discussions with the news editor regarding the coverage of news. He plans the special coverage of the expected news. On the basis of his planning he allocates duties to the reporters. Many of the reporters are specialists of different fields like politics, sports, business, crime etc. It is the duty of the chief reporter to see that all the activities are covered properly and nothing important is missed by the reporters.

The chief reporter decides regarding the relative importance of the happenings in the city which should be covered and reported. He receives many invitations for press conferences, public meetings, demonstrations, agitations, strikes etc. He deputes his reporters to cover these events after assessing their relative importance. Many social and voluntary organisations also invite him to cover their annual functions and other activities.

The chief reporter also receives a lot of Government handouts, press releases and other publicity material for publication. He selects the important items for printing after assessing their newsworthiness. Sometimes, he also goes out to cover some very important news or function especially when there is a heavy rush of work. Sometimes he also looks after the administration side of the reporter's holidays and other routine matters.

He has also to keep contacts with the various sources of news. He tries to cultivate new contacts of likely information. He keeps in touch with all the important happenings. He tries to be fully aware of the activities of the rival newspapers. He also plans new investigative and interpretative reports by deputing his men.

Press Representatives

There are different kinds of correspondents who work for a newspaper. Some of these are discussed below:

The Liner : The liner is not a full time journalist. He may be living in a small town. From time to time he may send news stories to the newspaper. He is paid on the basis of the lines of the news stories published in the newspaper. He is only a part time journalist whereas he regularly pursues some other profession.

The Stringer : The stringer is also not a full time journalist. His whole time profession is quite different which he is doing in addition to writing for some papers. But he is in a little better position than the liner. Because he is attached to a newspaper through a string on payment of a small amount to cover his expenses. He is generally paid some fixed amount to retain him for the newspaper.

The Correspondent : There are various categories of correspondents. The most important of them are special correspondents. They generally cover some specified fields in the capital of a country. Some of these attend the Parliament sessions. They keep in touch with the government agencies and other news sources. Sometimes, they are also assigned to cover

> other special areas. Then there are the foreign correspondents. Some people consider the foreign assignment as the most glamorous part of the job. They are stationed in the capitals of important countries of the world.

A newspaper may also have its correspondents at important district headquarters. Generally, they are full-fledged journalists. The correspondents of a newspaper at the stale capitals are called 'staffers'. They do full time reporting work and are the regular employees of a newspaper or an agency. The correspondents in the different state capitals are in direct contact with the newspaper office. Generally, messages and reports from them are received on the teleprinter. Similarly, instructions are also sent to them on the teleprinter.

Agencies for News

Sometimes, important national newspapers also have their own special news service. This news service is run by a chief of news service in consultation with the editor. The chief of the news service keeps in touch which its correspondents stationed in the country and in other parts of the world. These correspondents, spread all over the world, send their reports to the chief and the sub-editors working under him to shape them into news stories. Sometimes they also revise or even rewrite them. These sub-editors are experts in rewriting the reports sent by the correspondents. The chief of the news service keeps himself in touch with all the important happenings in the world through his correspondents. As a head of his department he also looks after the administration side of the staff under his control.

People Working for Press

The staff of a big newspaper consists of many persons, those who work on the front desks, like the employees in the advertising and circulation departments, and those who work behind the scenes, like the editor, leader writer, sub-editor, manager etc. But the most interesting and the most familiar person for the public is the reporter. For the public the reporter is the press itself. At all important meetings, demonstrations, national or international gatherings, and trouble spots the presence of the reporter represents the mysterious and invisible power of the press.

There is no doubt that no other single member of the staff has a greater influence upon the life of the newspaper than the reporter. The reporter is in touch with life every day under all sorts of conditions. It is his duty to go out to see, find, hear, and know about the latest events and happenings and then write about the same in his newspaper. The newspaper today is a reflex of the day to day life and this reflex is made possible through the stories of the reporter.

Prime Duty : It should be the duty of every reporter to make his copy pulsate with life and full of interest for the readers. His stories should be bright and sparkling, something that should make people think and talk and look forward to the next issue. To do this a reporter has to put his heart and soul into his work. Of course, the reporter of today has to work at a greater speed and under more stressful conditions than his predecessors in the past. But he also gets more remuneration today as compared with the past. It goes without saying that a reporter has also to sacrifice many of the pleasures of home life to answer the call of duty, at all odd hours.

A reporter must appreciate the importance of having a good reputation for absolute reliability. For this purpose he must be systematic in his habits and punctual in keeping his appointments. He should be quite careful while making inquiries to know the facts and should be fair in his comments. The most important thing is that he should be efficient and prompt in turning out his copies. By observing these principles, every reporter can make his path smooth and trouble free.

A reporter should have the ability to write good English or the language of his paper. He should possess the quality to write in a condensed manner according to the availability of space. This goes without saying that whenever a reporter writes his copy in his own hand, it must be readable. In fact, he should write his reports in such a way which obviates any possible chance of mistake and subsequent query regarding spellings of words and meanings.

The reporter should type or write his reports clearly only on one side of the paper in double space so as to allow enough space for sub-editorial corrections. Every good reporter should develop the habit of turning out a neat and clean copy. Sometimes a reporter may give headlines to the report, but generally the headlines are given by the sub-editor. Now-a-days the reporters usually type out their stories but whenever a hand written copy is to be filed, it must be written in ink.

Unique Position : The reporter of a local newspaper occupies a unique position and he becomes quite popular with the people of his town. He reports the local events, functions, fairs, socials etc. and comes closer to the social life of the town. A reporter should follow some professional ethics in his work. Sometimes, while engaged in his profession, he may come closer to some persons and develop confidential relations with them.

Some persons may also tell him their personal, private and business affairs. But a reporter should never betray their confidence under any circumstances by divulging their secrets which they have told him in good faith. This quality of trustworthiness increases the popularity of the reporter and he is welcomed wherever he goes. This will also enhance his reputation in all sections of the society.

Sometimes, a reporter may be asked to write short length paragraphs regarding the local intelligence or about the city news. For this he should keep his eyes and ears open and develop a nose for local news. He should develop a system to ensure that none of the interesting news is missed by him. He should try to know the secretaries of social, religious, political, musical, dramatic, legal, official and other organisations and should call upon them regularly to get some interesting stories. He should make inquiries from the police regarding news of accidents and crime. He should also contact the fire station for the particulars of local fires.

Similarly, he can contact hospitals for collecting information regarding accidents and deaths. In the same fashion, he can get a lot of good news from the sports clubs and other organizations.

Systemised Working : Every reporter should keep an engagement diary. In this way he can systematise his working and attend to all his appointments properly and punctually. By keeping an engagement diary he can know about the important engagements and other events in the future and cover them without fail. Now-a-days, it is very necessary for a reporter to possess a good knowledge of shorthand and typing. This helps a reporter greatly in writing down verbatim reports of political meetings and speeches made at some political functions.

Generally, the reporter types the copy in the office or telephones it to a copy taker. Whenever the reporter types the copy in his office, he should prepare it in such a way that it should not need much sub-editing. It should be so neat and clean that it could be photographed and put in the paper as it is.

The reporter should not forget to give a catch-line to this copy. Every copy which goes to the printer to be set is given a catch-line. The catch-line is a key-word, because during the production it identifies all the sheets of the copy. The catch-line is given on each sheet so that the printer can collate the whole story. The catch-line should be chosen very carefully. It is better to choose an uncommon word, which may not resemble with another catch-line.

If you choose a very common word as a catch-line like 'accident', it might be confused because there may have been half a dozen accident stories in that edition of the paper. The word chosen as a catch-line may not have a very close identification with the story. But there should be some mental link with it. You should put the catch-line and the page number at the top.

Before starting the story you should leave half page of the first sheet. At least two inches margin should be left on the left side of every page. The space which you have left at the top of the first sheet can be used by the sub-editor for writing the headlines or any other instructions for the printer. On the left side margin, the editor might write corrections if any. As already mentioned you should always type the copy in double space to leave some space in between the lines for corrections which might be made by the sub-editor.

Good Rules : It is a good rule to end the page at the end of a paragraph. Similarly, you should not continue a sentence on to the next page. At the end of each sheet you should type the word 'more', or the letters 'm.f.' or "more follows". Whenever you finish your story you should write at the end of the last page the word 'end'

All these things are very necessary, otherwise, sometimes a page or a paragraph of your copy might be lost on the printer's desk. You should also try to follow the house style adopted by your newspaper thoroughly. Every newspaper has its own style, which must be adhered to.

Besides the above a reporter should also remember the following points :

(i) As already discussed above, a reporter should never repeat a story which has been told to him confidentially or in good faith, unless he takes the prior permission of the person concerned to make it public.

(ii) While collecting the local news, a reporter should keep in mind the great value of giving the names of persons in his stories. However, the names should be spelled correctly.

(iii) Every reporter should try to develop the qualities of a descriptive writer.

(iv) A reporter must remember that practice makes a man perfect. Therefore, he should always try to improve his method of reporting and his style.

(v) Every reporter should use plain English. He should avoid difficult words. He should enable his reader to visualise the scene described by him as clearly as if he had seen it with his own eyes.

(vi) A good reporter should avoid the use of stereotyped phraseology.

(vii) A reporter should try to be accurate in his reporting. Whenever his accuracy is called in question, he should be able to produce his original note-book.

(viii) One main cause of the complaint against misrepresentation in newspapers is that certain persons in the heat of excitement say things, which they do not mean. And when reported accurately in the press, they deny having said such things.

(ix) Whenever a reporter has to report on the court proceedings, he should be very careful in his report. For example, use of a wrong name or adverse comment might land him into legal problems.

(x) While reporting ordinary public meetings, a reporter has to produce only a summary, which he should try to write up as the meeting progresses.

(xi) The reporter must master the art of condensing while reporting the speeches made in the public meetings. This will greatly help him in writing his summaries.

(xii) A reporter must know what is news-worthy and what is not. Recognition of news values implies the need of "news nose". Without it a reporter cannot hope to achieve success in his career.

Experienced Reporters

There was a time when Indian newspapers had two kinds of correspondents at New Delhi: the Special Representative and the Special Correspondent. The former species seems, for a variety of reasons, to be dying. But the Special Correspondent remains, the aristocrat of the profession, often better known to readers than the editor himself since it is the former's by-line that often features on the lead story on the front page.

Special Representatives : The Special Representative, however, ruled the roost for a long time, in fact from around the turn of the century when leading newspapers used to keep high-powered; influential special representatives at Simla whenever the government shifted its headquarters there from Calcutta (the then capital) during the summer.

The era of the Special Representative, then, may be said to have started in 1899 during the Vice regality of Lord Curzon. The reason for sending a special representative to Simla grew out of the fact that there was no powerful daily in the Delhi area at that time, the nearest one being the *Civil and Military Gazette* at Lahore. Leading newspapers wanted one of their men to be where power was, not only to get news, which an ordinary reporter may have obtained without great difficulty, but to negotiate favours and facilities with the high and the mighty.

Since those in power were Britishers, with their own sense of racial superiority, it was inevitable that those appointed to hobnob with them were also Britishers, naturally of some eminence, so that they could easily socialize with their fellow compatriots and wrangle favours from them. Such a one was Howard Hansman of the *Pioneer* of Allahabad who quickly earned the reputation for getting exclusive interviews. The *Pioneer*, it may be remembered, was very much a British-owned paper; so was *The Statesman* which had its own Special Representative in Everard Coates. *The Englishman*, another paper, had Sir Edward J. Buck and the *Indian Daily News* a man called Dallas. Viceroys, Governors,

Commanders-in-chief and their minions patronized these men, who wore the right sort of ties and came from the right sort of schools. It was the world of the whiteman into which the brown man had no entry. It was many years later that K.C. Roy and Ushanath Sen joined that strange band of lobbyists and preened themselves as a special breed of newspaperman, with more interest in newsprint than in news.

All Powerful : Today, however, it is the Special Correspondent who is accredited to New Delhi and his fare is special news. He is expected to rub shoulders as did his professional forebears again with the high and the mighty, and while 'it is no more necessary to know how to tie your knot or to wear formal dinner dress, it certainly helps to have the right kind of contacts in ministerial circles. Indian ministers these days have no use for formal dinner wear and at least one minister decided he could even dispense with a tie when he was appointed Minister-in-waiting to President Carter when the latter visited India in 1977.

Nevertheless the glitter is there. As Sir Philip Glbbs, no mean. Special Correspondent himself, once said: "The noblest and most amusing career in journalism is that of the special correspondent, because the special correspondent sees a great deal of life at other people's expense and it is very much worthwhile."

That is looking at it somewhat cynically and while it is true that a special correspondent enjoys a great number of privileges, dines and wines (when that is permitted) with the powerful in the land travels abroad at some one else's (usually his government's or newspaper's) expense and comes to see a great deal more than other ordinary mortals, it is not roses, roses all the way.

Often, it is necessary to remember, the special correspondent does not reach his eminence overnight. He has probably come up the hard way, via reporting the police courts and the municipal corporations of his home town, though it is not unusual for some leading newspapers to pick up a bright young man with a foreign degree to do the job, probably on the theory that if the young man had an opportunity to study abroad, he comes from a sufficiently high social stratum that ensures self-confidence in dealing with the world of officialdom.

For certainly the Special Correspondent has not only to meet the dhoti-clad minister who would probably be only too glad to talk to him, but he will also have to deal with the Chief Secretary to a Department and some of his minions who may think they are a cut above the elected representatives. In this, as in other spheres, self-confidence and the air of a man who knows he represents a major paper and can afford to swank about, helps. If word goes round that his salary, not to speak expense account, is measurably higher than that of his less fortunate brethren, he would find that he has entry into normally reticent circles.

In Delhi, a Special Correspondent, once he is accredited, gets certain facilities that go with the job: reserved seats at public functions, entry into the Secretariat, housing facilities and of course, the right to ask questions from the Prime Minister and other ministers and get answers. This puts him in the category of a man who has access to news at the highest level. If he is familiar with ministers he would call them at their homes or be invited as their guest. All too often, if he represents a national daily, he may find that instead of his calling up ministers, the ministers, or their men may be wanting his ear. If the Special Correspondent wants news, the minister, on occasions, may be only too willing to provide it. One feeds on the other.

This, of course, puts a terrific burden on the Special Correspondent. He has to be familiar to-and not necessarily with-the minister, but he must know how to keep aloof from his source as well. He has to be especially aware of the planted story, the deliberate leak intended to damage some one else's reputation or power base. News is not always what a minister tells the Special Correspondent. It is the latter's job to find why a minister is confiding him and what axe the latter has to grind. In the circumstances, a Special Correspondent is the sifter and the interpreter, the guide and the diplomat. James Gordon Bennett once described a Special Correspondent as "half diplomat and half detective" which is a pretty good description of the job.

It is his dexterity to interpret news, as much as to get it, that marks the Special Correspondent from the run-of-the-mill reporter. A good Special Correspondent will not only get news-that, after all, is his major responsibility-but will make it meaningful to his reader. Facts, admittedly, stand by themselves and are self-explanatory. But only partly. What do the facts mean in terms of a possibly emerging pattern? What does it mean to say that the rate of industrial growth was three per cent in a given year? Is it low or reasonably high against a background of economic stagnation? What was the rate of growth a year ago?

How does it compare with the rate of growth in the neighbouring countries? It is the Special Correspondent's special responsibility to inform the reader of the *meaning* of facts. This is where his talents are most called for. He has to express an opinion. But the opinion must be so interwoven with information that together they provide the reader with the full story. Facts without opinion are barren; opinion without facts is arrogance. What the Special Correspondent has always to beware of is the tendency to offer opinion without supporting data. It is difficult enough to give an opinion with available data; it is unjournalistic, if not unethical to spout opinion with no hard information to base it upon. A columnist may get away with it but a Special Correspondent cannot.

Sometimes what passes for special correspondence is a caricature of what it should be. A Special Correspondent may be called upon to provide an "intro" to long parliamentary proceedings or to. "open" stories such as are meat to the news agencies, but that is not really what a Special Correspondent is paid for. It is poor journalism to stay put in one's own office or home and then, when the evening is over, pore over the news agency reports and condescend to write an "intra." It will be more professional if the

Special Correspondent attends parliament and sits through the often tedious proceedings to make his own assessment at first hand. Then his effort at providing an "intra" becomes relevant and sound.

A good news editor will ask the Special Correspondent not only to provide an "intro" but to give a running story as well, telling the reader what the parliament was discussing, with adequate background as to the importance and significance of the debate. If the newspaper has plenty of space to allot to parliamentary proceedings, it may be left to the agencies to report who said what. In any event, that is the function of the agency. But it is the Special Correspondent's particular responsibility to place debates in their proper perspective. This calls for in depth study not just of past parliamentary proceedings, but of political science, history, economics and allied subjects. Special Correspondence does not come easy. It is earned by dint of hard work and home studies. To believe, as some do, that all that a Special Correspondent does is to attend cocktail parties and drop names, is not to appreciate his avocation.

Home study includes poring over voluminous government reports and publications of all sorts relevant to a Correspondent's job. One never can tell where one can get a good lead. The Correspondent may pick one in the day's newspaper by sheer chance because he notes that a report reveals a missing link that is worth chasing. Or he may get it in a report that is hard to read but should, perhaps for that very reason, be read with greater attention. Even usual government handouts under trained eyes could yield profitable leads to be developed by further research and interviews.

So a Special Correspondent will perforce have to do a large amount of reading, not only of reports and documents available in India, but similar ones from abroad. His reading has to be very catholic and embrace a wide range of interests such as foreign affairs, defence, agriculture, industry and commerce, trade, imports and exports, taxation policy. Well might he say with Terence: *Homo sum; humani nil a me alienum puto.* (I am a man, I count nothing human indifferent to me).

Friends and Foes : A high powered Special Correspondent attracts equally high powered friends and not a few enemies. He has to learn to live with them. Friends may-and often will provide him with valuable information. He should know how to use such information. Some of it may be spurious; it will have to be checked for accuracy. Some will be confidential and then the Special Correspondent will have to use his judgment. A confidence betrayed is a friend lost for ever. But sometimes an important source will deliberately provide information in the hope that it will be used, even though he may swear you to secrecy. To assess such situations requires experience and confidence. The best thing in such circumstances is to refuse to be party to confidential secrets and information dubbed "off the record." This calls for courage. It is some what flattering to be taken into confidence by ministers or high officials. But ministers may want to take you into confidence precisely because they do not want the Special Correspondent to delve deeper into certain kinds of news.

Besides, the Special Correspondent may be aware already of what the high official seems eager to tell on an "off the record" basis. Even if he is not, the chances are that he would soon learn of it from other, independent sources and so why tie oneself to observing secrecy? It is certainly not prudent for a Special Correspondent to receive conditional information when for all he knows, his rivals may be getting it from other sources unconditionally, thereby scoring a scoop. A Special Correspondent's loyalty is not to his ministerial or official friends but to his newspaper and to his readers.

A Special Correspondent cannot afford to live in an ivory tower, nor can he disdain social life. It is at putties that he makes important contacts under relaxed conditions. But it is a woeful mistake to believe that he can get information while swapping drinks.

Some notable Special Correspondents do not touch a drop of liquor. One does not have to be a drunk to get news. Senior officials-who, after all, are the real source of meaningful news-do not pass information to Special Correspondents over a gin-and-tonic.

And not even two Patiala pegs may loosen their tongues. If that happens they may find that they are transferred. A cocktail party is not a place to gather news; it is a place to make friends in congenial surroundings. It will not hurt to have a drink or two; but it will certainly be no handicap to be a teetotaller. Drinking does not make a journalist, though a journalist may drink. If that was all to journalism, pubs in every city would provide the best correspondents.

Writing in the mid-fifties, Krishnalal Shridharani, himself a distinguished journalist summed up the qualities that a Special Correspondent should possess. These are :

(1) Vast and varied contacts with official sources, with opposition sources, with embassy sources, with fellow reporters, with private secretaries and with one or two high and mighty.

(2) Ability to keep a confidence.

(3) Courage, occasionally to refuse confidences with strings attached. Ability to avoid hearing things that bind one to secrecy.

(4) A bent for research based upon previous training in social sciences and the humanities. A craving for facts.

(5) A bit of brass (especially in foreign countries and in a war zone), the knack of bluffing one's way through forbidden areas.

(6) The art of conversation which primarily consists of encouraging others to talk, without yourself being a wet blanket.

(7) The ability to get along with people and in difficult situations. A friendly smile. This will invoke "human interest" confidings.

(8) Physical stamina and moral courage. The ability to do with out sleep on occasions.

(9) Ability to be freshly impressed by action, colour, life.

(10) Imagination, and a simple, sparkling style.

Shridharani then went on to outline the pitfalls in the path of a Special Correspondent which he said are more numerous than in the case of the routine reporter. And what were the pitfalls?

They are deeper, too and their openings more obscure. He may begin to take himself too seriously because of the stir he creates and that is the beginning of the end. Then again, he might begin to accept the wishful thinkings of his 'important sources', and thus lose the power to judge and predict. And exclusively top-level contacts might make his stories hollow: they supply leads, but meat is to be found with men who work out the details. Exclusively top-level connections may turn him into a party-going butterfly, progressively more and more incapable or applying the seat of his pants to his working chair. Just when things become easy, he stands in the need of doing things the hard way.

Much of what is said about Special Correspondents holds good' for Foreign Correspondents as well. A Foreign Correspondent comes to his job with a good deal of experience behind him. He would probably have spent some years in New Delhi as a Special Correspondent, learning the nuances of being a diplomatic correspondent at home. That ought to stand him in good stead when he leaves for foreign capitals.

Indian correspondents abroad at one time were mostly concentrated in London which used to the most important capital for India in pre-independence days. After all there was a need to know the pulse of the British public and what Parliament did or said about India and its nationalist movement. Indian newspapers regularly sent correspondents to cover the Round Table Conferences come of them like Dr. Shelvankar stayed on. London increasingly became the home of Indian Foreign Correspondents.

But as the centre of political gravity shifted to the United States, so did to some extent the interest of Indian newspapers which first began to send correspondents to the United Nations and then, as the United Nations' glamour and relevance began to' fade, to Washington. Indian correspondents sent to Washington were simultaneously accredited to the United Nations as a matter of course.

Accreditation rules to Washington are simple enough. The news paper informs the State Department through a letter from the editor of its intention to appoint the correspondent-named, for guidance-to his post in the capital. The letter is processed and the correspondent thereafter is duly informed that his appointment is accepted. He is then given a press card that permits him to enter the State Department and to attend news briefings and other press conferences. He could then join the State Department Correspondents' Association which also issues him a card acknowledging his membership of the Association. He will meanwhile have to be processed by the security offices and be fingerprinted after which he will get a White House press card that will enable him to attend White House press briefings and also presidential press conferences. Armed with these he could apply for membership of the Senate and Congressional Press Association; membership would qualify him to observe Congressional sessions from the press gallery, and also to attend hearings. He will also be entitled to receive the *Congressional Record* gratis.

Foreign Correspondents : Time was when a Foreign Correspondent would have had to take his copy to the nearest telegraph office where he would have been asked-unless, by then, he was sufficiently well-known-for his press card, his telegraphic or cable authority and identity card. But time marches on and so does technology. These days it is easy to apply for and quickly get international telex machines that link one with one's own office and the world at large.

The correspondent therefore does not have to go to the cable office to hand over his copy. He can have a telex machine installed in his own office or home and send his message directly to his office and have the satisfaction of knowing that it has been received without any distortions.

The telex is a major boon to Foreign Correspondents. The author had the mortification to find out, while covering the non-aligned conference that met in Algiers that his copy did not land in Bombay for four days. By then naturally, the story was dead.

As long as the Foreign Correspondent remains in his chosen capital, his problems are easily handled. It is when he is sent to another capital or country that he has to be familiar with a number of items of professional interest, such as the place where the international conference is held, the facilities available for cabling, the availability of hotel accommodation, costs, distances to be covered in commuting from hotel to conference site or to cable, office, the nature and cost of transportation, the kind of medical and dental service available at short notice etc.

Sometimes the government of the host country will provide the information; at other times it will be necessary to call on the local residence of the Indian Ambassador or at the Chancery to register one's presence. Certainly it is a wise Foreign Correspondent who will stay in touch with the Embassy of India, not only as a source of information but for safety reasons also.

It is presumed, of course, that a Foreign Correspondent will know the language of the country to which he is assigned, Russian if he is in the Soviet Union, German if in Bonn, French in Paris and Spanish in many Latin American countries.

The Foreign Correspondent will be under pressure to say kind things about the host country. He should have the courage to resist such pressures. It is also unwise to run down the host country, no matter how much its society and administration differs from one's own. It is not the task of a Foreign Correspondent to sit in judgements on alien governments and institutions but rather to explain them in the context in which they chanced to be set up.

Different countries have different historical backgrounds and they are what they are because of their special and unique pasts. Wisdom lies in understanding the process of history and to interpret each nation in the context of its own history and immutable past. Wisdom also lies in knowing that several international conflicts and controversies have no simple, immediate solution, that the conflict generally is between right and right and not between right and wrong and that one's patriotic bias, although justified, is not always just. And that takes some time to learn; especially at the United Nations where the urge to take sides, to pontificate and to prejudge can be very pressing indeed.

The Foreign Correspondent, under all circumstances, will keep to the law of the host country and never break it wittingly or even unwittingly. The Foreign Correspondent is an Ambassador of the press of his own country and has to be on the best of his behaviour.

A Foreign Correspondent who cheats, who indulges in questionable practices where foreign exchange is concerned and who gets a notoriety for being unscrupulous not only brings disgrace on himself, which is his private business and should be of no concern to anyone but his own office, but will make it difficult for fellow correspondents from his country to follow him. Foreign Correspondents are usually under constant and quiet observation, a fact that they must be aware of, especially in communist or authoritarian countries. Getting into trouble of any kind just would not do.

In this regard the Foreign Correspondent cannot do better than take guidance from his Embassy which could give him some simple obvious do's and dont's. Embassies are generally helpful to correspondents if only because they themselves do not want adverse publicity. Also, they would like to be briefed on what the

Foreign Correspondents have learnt in the course of their work. In most instances, there is a fair exchange of information between Foreign Correspondents and their Embassies but the correspondent must remember and realize that he works for his newspaper and not his country's government and should, at all times, learn to keep his distance from officials, if for nothing else, to respect his professional ethics of independence.

Over dependence on Embassies will result in Foreign Correspondents relying on what for all practical purposes become government or embassy handouts. A Foreign Correspondent is sent abroad to give his personal assessment of the situation prevailing in the host country or countries, not to peddle Embassy views on the same. To retain one's independence in foreign lands is not always easy and embassies sometimes come under pressure from host governments to keep the writings of the correspondents in check, but this is part of the game and must be faced with courage, good humour and firmness.

Of all types of correspondents, the War Correspondent is in a very special class by himself. Think of the names: Winston Churchill, William Howard Russell, Edwin Lawrence Godkin, Richard Harding Davis, James Creelman, Luigi Barzini, Irvin S. Cobb, John Reed, Ernest Hemingway, Evelyn Waugh, Herbert Matthews, Wilfred Burchett, David Halberstam.

There are very few Indian war correspondents and such wars as India was compelled, after independence, to participate in have happily been of short duration. Frank Moraes, D.R. Mankekar and D.F. Karaka, among others covered the second world war. But they are in a different class form Ernie Pyle or Edward R. Murrow.

Actually, the war correspondent is comparatively new to history. In years gone by Generals preferred to report their own victories and resented a civilian snooping around the battlefield as William

Howard Russell of *The Times* of London quickly discovered in the Crimea. During 1914-1918 the war correspondent was very much part of the military machine and kept quiet about the extent of the slaughter till the war was over. Not until Vietnam did the war correspondent begin to emerge as a partisan for truth and compassion. The British press failed miserably during the Russian Revolution. Looking back on its own coverage of the Revolution 35 years later, *The Times* in fact, admitted its shortcomings:

> "The idea of a *campaign ad maiorem proletariatis gloriam* was so foreign to Wilton (the correspondent) that he never understood it. More unfortunately still, the idea was equally foreign to Steed (the Foreign Editor), Dawson (the Editor), Northcliffe (the proprietor), to Lloyd George (Prime Minister) and to Milner (soon to be Minister of War). No one had heard of the forces of the Left except in terms that indicated them to be madmen.

Not all War Correspondents were so dumb, though some were more Jingoistic than stupid. James Creelman, along with J.A Mac Gahan' and the Italian Luigi Barzini, was one of the few correspondents to protest the conduct of war and write with truth and-compassion. His report of the Japanese massacre at Port Arthur in 1894 caused the Japanese to offer him a bribe to tone down his report, but he refused. American opinion was changed overnight. Barzini was a misfit among war correspondents of his time for he saw no glory or heroics but only senseless slaughter in war. Yet news-dealers had only to shout "Article by Barzini" for his paper, *Corriere della Sera* to sell out. American journalist and poet John Reed, author of *Ten Days' That Shook the World* and correspondent for the radical publication *The Masses* achieved journalistic greatness with his unparalleled description of the November 1917 events in Petrograd. Ernest Hemingway, reporting from Spain for the North American Newspaper Alliance (NANA) became the most influential figurehead in the fight against fascism.

The Spanish Civil War remains a watershed in the annals of journalism. No other war has left such a profound and lasting impression on those who reported it. "Today wherever in this world I meet a man or woman who fought for Spanish liberty, I meet a kindred soul" wrote Herbert Mathews.' "In those years we lived our best and what has come after and what there is to come can never carry us to their heights again."

The second World War had its crop of outstanding war correspondents like Ernie Pyle, Drew Middleton and Edward R. Murrow. It must have taken Murrow some courage to depart from the propaganda line that the fall of Dunkirk was Britain's "finest hour" and to assert, if somewhat, mildly, that "there will be disagreement an that point" Ernie Pyle won renown by speaking up far the infantry soldier. "I have the infantry because they are the underdags. They are the mud-rain-frost-and-wind,bays. They have no comforts and they even learn to live without the necessities. And in the end they are the guys that wars can't be won washout" was his credo.

The wars since 1914-18 have made many war correspondents heroes in their awn right. Same have 'been killed. This is the price that wars exert even an journalists. A revolution, Mao Tse-tung once said, is not a tea party. Nor is war. Those who have reported one do not glamourize it, Vietnam was probably the most dangerous affairs-far correspondents. Forty five of them have been killed there and eighteen listed as missing.

Fortunately wars are not as regular as international conferences; true, they provide all the drama far a correspondent to work an. "If you have not seen a battle" Herbert Matthews once wrote, "your education has been same what neglected-far after all, war has never been one of the primary functions of mankind, and unless you see men fight you miss something fundamental" Other journalists may fervently pray they may be spared such fundamental education but the fact remains, as another War Correspondent, Charles Mohr said, wars, "in an add way provide good stories." The hell they do.

The trouble is that many correspondents fight shy of telling the truth about war far a variety of reasons: ignorance of what really is going an, a false sense of patriotism, fear of being sent back far reporting reality. In his fascinating book *The First Casualty,* Phillip Knightley, himself a special correspondent, recalls instance after instance of War Correspondents failing to tell it all, of Ernest Hemingway suppressing the unpalatable facts about Republican Spain, Evelyn Waugh making a mess of covering the Abyssinian-War but gathering material far his navel *Scoop* and the Russians crushing Quentin Reynolds because they believed that Western correspondents were spies. Perhaps they were. War is a distressing affair in many ways and the first casualty turns aut to be truth.

The Vietnam war was better reported than any other war since the Crimean was a casualty to truth. As journalist Murray Kemptan has remarked, with a million-dollar corps of correspondents in Vietnam, the war in Cambodia was kept hidden for a year.

That takes something. The best comment on war coverage is perhaps given by Gavin Young, a British newspaperman who covered Vietnam. "Correspondents" he wrote, "are bound to be haunted by the feeling that there is probably only one way to work the various elusive aspects of the war into one wholly satisfactory picture.

Apart from the aid programmes, the military operations, the political ups and downs, how can one depict the human facets of such a complete tragedy? What of the thoughts and feeling of the Vietnamese? How has the war affected their lives and art, their outlook on foreigners, and different cultures? How if at all, have the Americans been changed by contact with the Vietnamese?.. The Vietnamese war awaits its novelist."

Knightley asserted that on the whole, writers-be did *not* call them War Correspondents-for non-daily publications like *Tom* Buckley in the *New York Times Magazine,* Jonathan Schell of *The New Yorker* and Sol Sanders of *U. S. News & World Report* came out better than most of their news colleagues because, he said, they were "free from the tyranny of pressing deadlines" and could look at the war in greater depth.

Are regular war correspondents, then, a useless tribe? One suspects that even at the risk of not being able to tell the whole story every day, the War Correspondent will be necessary though wars may not. Only, the War Correspondent must know his limitations and be honest enough to admit to them' It is the most important service he could do to his reader who otherwise depends upon him to tell the truth as he sees it.

The Benefit

Every capital has its own rules of accreditation. Given below are rules for accreditation of news media representatives to New Delhi.

(1) These rules apply to the accreditation at the headquarters of the Government of India of news media representatives.

(2) An application on the prescribed form should be submitted by the editor in the news media organization concerned to the Principal Information Officer, Government of India, New Delhi. Full details about the professional experience of the representative seeking accreditation should be furnished with the application. The Principal Information Officer will refer the application to the Central Press Accreditation Committee for their advice and approval.

(3) The applicant should fulfil the following condititions for accreditation:

  (a) His residence should be the headquarters of the Government of India during the period of accreditation.

  (b) He should be working journalist as defined by the Working Journalists (Conditions of Service and Miscellaneous Provisions) Act, 1955 and should be whole time engaged as a correspondent or cameraman or correspondent-cameraman or a cartoonist.

(c) At the time of application he should have spent five years in the profession of journalism.

(4) The professional norms applicable to Indian newsmen will also govern the grant of accreditation to applicants on behalf of foreign media.

(5) Editors of news media may in exceptional case be granted accreditation if CPAC is satisfied that the applicant is genuinely engaged in covering current affairs and needs accreditation for this purpose. Such applications will only be considered by the CPAC. No temporary accreditation will be granted by the PIO in such cases.

(6) The Central Press Accreditation Committee may grant accreditation, as an exceptional measure, to journalists of long and distinguished service of at least 25 years who may be contributing special articles to a number of newspaper regularly but not attached to any newspaper which qualifies for accreditation.

(7) Accreditation will be granted only on behalf of a news media-organization having a minimum circulation or coverage as prescribed by the Central Press Accreditation Commitee. The Central Press Accreditation Committee will lay down, from time to time, the number of accreditations for various classes of news media organizations, taking into account the coverage required by the organizations and the service limitations of the Press Information Bureau.

(8) In the case of news, features, photo and TV news and feature agencies, following factors will be taken into consideration for determining the entitlement for and the number of accreditations:

(a) The news, features, photo or TV news and features should be based on the news emanating from the capital.

(b) The agency should provide regular service to media network on commercial basis. For the purpose of classification of the agency, only the revenue, as certified by a Chartered Accountant by way of subscriptions from news media for supply of news material will be taken into consideration.

(c) An agency whose service operations extend to at least half of the State of the Indian Union or to electronic media network shall be deemed to be an all-India agency.

(d) In case of agencies of all classes and types, accreditation will be given to the whole-time employees only.

(9) In case of daily newspapers and weeklies, the following factors will be taken into consideration for determining the entitlement for and the number of accreditations.

(a) The paper concerned should be published regularly.

(b) Its circulation should not be less then 5,000 copies as certified by the RNI.

(c) The contents of the concerned weekly should be mainly related to current affairs.

(d) For newspapers and weeklies with circulation above 50,000 copies, only full-time employees of such organization will be granted accreditions.

(e) In the case of smaller newspapers combined circulation may be taken into consideration if they ask for accreditation for a common representative or a journalist himself seeks accreditation jointly on their behalf.

(10) Periodicals of longer than a week's periodicity will not be granted accreditation. However, fortnightlies and monthlies published abroad for the benefit of Indian communities or for dissemination of Indian news would be granted accreditation on the merits of each case.

(11) A press card will be issued to each accredited representative. Admission to special functions including press conferences however, will be governed by invitation.

(12) Accreditation is personal and not transferable.

(13) Accreditation does not confer any official or special status on the news media representative. It merely recognizes and identifies him as a representative of the media organization which employ him. It must be used only for journalistic purposes. The words "Accredited to the Government of India" should not be used on visiting cards, letter-heads or any other literature.

(14) When the representative ceases to represent the media organization for which he is accredited, the fact should be brought to the notice of the principal Information Officer in writing within 15 days by both the representative and his editor. Failure to comply with this may result in withdrawal of facilities.

(15) The list of accredited news media representatives will be subject to review every year by the Principal Information Officer in consultation with the Central Press Accreditation Committee.

For the purpose of review, the PIO may call for : (a) information about the revenue of the Indian agencies (b) dipping of published dispatches or photographs of dope sheets from the concerned news media organization or representative. To ensure that only genuine news media representatives remain accredited on behalf of foreign media organizations, the PIO may, from time to time, go through their published dispatches or enquire through the Indian missions abroad about the representative's work.

(16) The Principal Information Officer may:

(a) accord accreditation by issuing a temporary card in case both the applicant representative and the media organization qualify

(b) accept substitution of an accredited representative for a temporary period

(c) grant temporary accreditation to visiting pressmen

(17) A representative will be liable to dis-accreditation if:

(a) He engaged himself in work other than journalistic, such as soliciting business or advertisement.

(b) He uses for non-journalistic purposes information and facilities provided to him as an accredited representative.

(c) He publishes official secret the inviolability of which is accepted by general understanding and the Central Press Accreditation Committee concurs with this view after giving opportunity of a personal hearing to the concerned representative.

(d) In the course of his duties, he behaves in an undignified or unprofessional manner.

(e) He ignores or violates the conditions on which information and facilities are provided by government.

(f) News media organizations will also be liable to dis-accreditation if they are responsible for wilful publication of mala fide reports or abuse confidence.

(18) In all cases relating to dis-accreditation, the Principal Information Officer will take action warranted by the circumstances in each case in consultation with a locally-based sub-committee of the Central Press Accreditation Committee. All such cases will be referred to the Central Press Accreditation Committee within a period of not more than three months.

(19) These rules come into effect from 17 February 1978 and supersede the earlier rules.

9

Art of Expression

Shakespeare knew the value of a name. In *Othello* he had Iago say, "But he that filches from me my good name/Robs me of that which not enriches him/And makes me poor indeed." A name misspelled in a person mis-identified. Of all the errors a newspaper is capable of making, one of the most serious is a misspelled or a misused name. In radio and television it is the mispronounced name.

Important Jobs

One of the important functions of the copy-editor is to make sure that all names in the copy are double-checked. The proper form is the form the person uses. He may be Alex rather than Alexander, Jim rather than James, Will rather than William. He may or may not have a middle initial, with or without a period (Harry S. Truman). No one has yet explained why today's newspapers are so insistent on using middle names or initials of well-known men.

After seeing Richard Nixon's name in the news hundreds of times, most readers didn't have to be reminded that the story concerned President Richard M. Nixon instead of plain Richard Nixon. Men's first names are seldom used alone, except in sports copy. The same should be true for first names of women.

Anyone resents an attempt at cleverness where his name is concerned. Such "cuteness" should be felled on sight :

> Orange County will have a lemon as district attorney. Jack Lemon was elected to the job yesterday.
>
> Of the five patrolmen on the staff, two are crock.
>
> The last name was Crook.

A title generally precedes a name unless it is a long title. It is Harley F. Taylor, principal of Philip C. Showell School, rather than Philip C. Showell School Principal Harley F. Taylor.

Nor should the story make the reader guess at the identification. Here is an example.

Albert A. Ballew took issue with Mayor Locher today for announcing in advance that the post of administrative assistant in the Safety Department will be filled by a black. The president of the Collinwood Improvement Council commended the mayor for creating the post, but added... Now then, who is the president of the Collinwood Improvement Council? Will readers assume it is Ballew? The solution is so simpler "Ballew, president of the Collinwood Improvement Council, commended the mayor. ..."

The first reference to any person is by full name and professional, scholastic or religious title, if appropriate. Titles may be used on second reference to aid the reader.

Newspapers traditionally have used Mrs. on first reference only with the husband's given name: *Mrs. John Smith* and *Mr. Smith* thereafter; or, if it is her preference, *Gladys Smith* and *Mr. Smith thereafter.*

Women on second reference are identified by Miss, Mrs. or Ms., according to the women's preference. It is the responsibility of the reporter to determine which the woman prefers.

Editors may determine which women are sufficiently well-known in their professions to be referred to on second reference by last name only. Billie Jean King and Joan Sutherland, for example, could be identified as King and Sutherland, but the mother of a high school swimmer or the lead in a civic theater production probably could not be, unless that was their stated preference.

It may be Mrs. Richard Harris Jr., but not Mrs. Dorothy Harris Jr. Her husband may be Jr., but she is not.

Newspaper style may dictate that certain positions be neuterized (chairperson for chairman) but even this rule could lead to the absurd *(person kind for mankind).*

Editor's can be fair to both sexed by eliminating purely sexist adjectives before women of accomplishment and by using plural forms when possible and substituting the relative pronouns *they* or *them* instead of *he* or *him.*

All males on second reference are identified by surname only although some newspapers use Mr. on second reference in obituaries of prominent persons.

Newspapers have no firm rule about when to identify a person as a girl or a woman, or as a boy, youth or man. Generally, a girl becomes a woman at 18; a male is a boy until he is 13, a youth from 13 to 18 and a man from 18 on. Appropriateness should determine whether males and females 18 and older or even those under 18 should be referred to by the familiar given name.

A surname alone is used in half-column cutlines except when two or more half-column photographs of persons with the same last name are used with an article. In that case, first names or initials are needed.

Pupil describes a person attending grade school; *student* applies to those attending junior high school, high school, college or university.

A maiden name can cause trouble: "He married the former Constance Coleman in 1931." This is incorrect; Constance Coleman was Constance Coleman when he married her. He married Constance Coleman. His wife is the former Constance Coleman.

Woman is used as a general descriptive possessive—woman's rights. *Women's* is used as a specific—women's club (but Woman's Christian Temperance Union). It is women fliers. Young Women's Christian Association, women workers, but woman suffrage. It is never the Smith woman.

Foreign names are tricky. In Spanish-speaking countries, individuals usually have two last names, the father's and the mother's—Adolfo Lopez Mateos. On second reference, Lopez Mateos should be used. In headlines, Lopez Mateos is preferred, but Lopezs will do.

A Chinese family name is usually given first, and the second part of the hyphenated name is given in lower case—Chiang Kai-shek, Lee Su-kun. On second reference, use Chiang, not Kai-shek.

In Arab names, *al* generally is hyphen, Al-Azhar. Some Arabs drop the article—Mamoun Kuzbari, not al-Kuzbari. Compound names should be left intact—Abdullah, Abdel, Abdur Pasha and Bey titles have been abolished. Royal titles are used with first names—Emir Faisel, Sheik Abdullah. *Haj* is used with the first name in both first and subsequent references—Haji Amin-al-Hussain, Haji Amin.

The U in Burmese names means uncle, our equivalent of *Mr. Thakin* means master. *Daw* means Mrs. or Miss. Many Burmese have only one name—U Thant. If a Burmese has two names, both should be used—U tin Maung, Tin Maung.

Some Koreans put the family name first—Park Chung Hee. The second reference should be Park, not Chung Hee, the given name.

Many Indonesians have only one name—Sukarno, not Ahmed Sukarno.

Swedish surnames usually end in *son,* and Danish names usually end in *sen.*

Art of Headline

Few editors have escaped letters that begin something like this: "Dear Sir: the attached clipping from your paper of July 14th contains a mention of our product and we very much appreciate this unsolicited publicity. However, the name of our product was used with a lower case 'c' As you know. . . ."

Makers of trade-name products want to protect their rights under the Lanham Trademark Act of 1947 and insist that in any reference to the product name the manufacturer's spelling and capitalization be used. This is to protect the trade name from becoming generic, as happened to aspirin, cellophane, escalator, milk of magnesia, zipper, linoleum and shredded wheat.

Much of the confusion and protest can be eliminated simply by using a generic term rather than the specific trade name—petroleum jelly for Vaseline, freezer for Deepfreeze, fiber glass for Fiberglass, tranquillizer for Miltown. Where the product is trade-named and there is no substitute, the trade name should be used, especially if it is pertinent to the story. The withholding of such information on the ground of free publicity is niggardly.

Institutions should be labelled correctly—Bell Telephone System, not Bell Telephone Company; Lloyd's, not Lloyd's of London; D'Oyly Carte: J. C. Penney Co. (Penneys in ads. Penney's in other usages); American Geographical Society; National Geographic Society.

It is the Tomb of the unknowns, not the Tomb of the Unknown Soldier.

Jewish congregations should be identified in news stories as Orthodox, Conservative or Reform, and the terminology of the congregation concerned should be followed in naming the place of worship as a temple or a synagog. When grouping, the generic term is "Jewish houses of worship."

To help readers, the copy-editor should insert "Branch of Judaism" or whatever other phrase might be necessary to convey the proper meaning.

Most Orthodox congregations use *synagogue*. Reform groups use *temple* and Conservative congregations use one word or the other, but *synagogue* is preferred. It is never *Church,* which applied to Christian bodies.

Sect has a derogatory connotation. Generally it means a church group espousing Christianity without the traditional liturgical forms. *Religion* is an all-inclusive word for Judaism, Moslemism, Christianity and so on. *Faith* generally is associated with Protestants. *Denomination* should be used only when referring to the church bodies within the Protestant community.

Religious labels can be misleading. *Jews* and *Judaism* are general terms. *Israelis* refer to nationals of the state of Israel and *Jews* to those who profess Judaism. The state of Israel is not the centre of or the spokesman for Judaism. Some Jews are Zionists; some are not.

Not all denominations use *Church* in the organization's title. It is the First Baptist Church but the American Baptist Convention. It is the Church of Jesus Christ of Latter-day Saints (not Mormon Church); its units are Missions, Stakes and Wards. It is the Episcopal Church, not the Episcopalian Church. Its members are Episcopalians, but the adjective is *Episcopal* : Episcopal clergymen.

Mass may be *offered or celebrated.* High mass is *any;* low mass is said. The rosary is *recited* or *said.* If mass is sung, the "high" should be omitted. The copy-editor can avoid confusion by letting the statement read something like this: "The mass (or rosary) will be at 7 p.m." An official presides at solemn high mass. Requiem mass is not necessarily high, but it usually is. It is *offered,* never "celebrated" or "sung". The Benediction of the

Blessed Sacrament is neither "held" nor "given", services close with it.

The order of the commandments varies depending on the version of the Bible used. Confusion can be spared if the commandment number is omitted. Also to be deleted are references to the burning of a church mortgage unless there actually is a burning ceremony. It is an elegant but ridiculous way of saying the mortgage has been paid off.

The usual style in identifying ministers is the *Rev.,* followed by his full name on first reference and *the Rev. Mr.* on second reference. If he holds a doctorate, the style is *the Rev. Dr.,* or simply *Dr.* on subsequent references. *Reverend* should not be used standing alone, nor should plural forms be used, such as the Revs. John Jones and Richard Smith. Churches of Christ do not use the term *reverend* in reference to ministers. They are called *brothers.*

Rabbis take *Rabbi* throughout. Catholic priests who are members of orders take the initials of their order after their surnames: S.J., S.S., etc. Priests who are rectors, heads of religious houses or presidents of institutions and provinces of religious orders take *Very Rev.* and are addressed as *Father.* Priests who have doctorates in divinity or philosophy are identified as *the Rev., Dr.* and are addressed either as "Dr." or "Father."

The Church of Christ is not the same as the United Church of Christ. It is Seventh day Adventist, but Seventh Day Baptists. When used as an objective, Bahai is spelled *Ba-hai.*

The words *Catholic* and *parochial* are not synonymous. There are parochial schools other than Catholic schools. The writer should not assume that a person is a Roman Catholic simply because he is a priest or a bishop. Other religions also have priests and bishops.

Not all old churches merit the designation of *shrine.* Some are just old churches. *Shrine* denotes some special distinction, historic or ecclesiastical. Usually, shrines are structures or places that have religious connections or that are hallowed by their associations with events or persons of historic significance, such as Mt. Vernon.

Use *nun* when appropriate for women in religious orders. The word sister is confusing except with the person's name (Sister Mary Edward).

Set-up for Working

Persons die of heart *illness,* not "failure"; after a *long* illness, not an "extended" illness; *unexpectedly,* not "suddenly"; *outright,* not "instantly"; *following* or after an operation, not "as a result of" an operation; *apparently of a heart attack,* not of an "apparent heart attack." A person dies of a disease, not *from* a disease!

The age of the person who died is important to the reader. The copy-editor should check the age given; with the year of birth. Generally, the person's profession or occupation, the extent of the illness and the cause of the death are recorded, but without details. The length of the story is dictated by the fame of the person. Winston Churchill's obit ran eighteen pages in the *New York Times.*

A person *leaves* an estate; he is *survived* by his family. Usage: varies as to whether he is survived by his wife or his widow. He is survived by his children if they are children and by sons and daughters if they are adults.

If the family requests that the story include the statement that donations may be made to such-and-such organization, the statement should be used. Whether such a statement should contain the phrase "in lieu of flowers" is a matter of policy. Some papers, in deference to flourists, do not carry, the phrase.

A straightforward account of a death is better than one told euphemistically. The plain terms are *died,* not "passed away" or "sticcumbed"; *body,* not "remains" or "corpse"; coffin, not "casket"; *funeral* or *services,* not "obsequies" "interment," unless interred in a tomb above the ground. Flowery expressions such as "two of whom reside in St. Louis" and "became associated' with the blank company shortly after college" show no more' respect for the dead than do the plain expressions "live in St. Louis" or went to work for the blank company."

Few stories in a newspaper are more addicted to formula writing than the obituary. Here is a lead from an Associated Press story: *New York—If you area movie fan, you will remember Mary Roland as the fluttery matron, the foolishly fond mother, the ladylike scatterbrain. The character actress who died yesterday at the age of 80 was none of these in real life.*

The Copy-editor should be on guard for the correct spelling of all names used in the death story and for slips such as "cemetery" for cemetery and "cremation" for cremation. Errors are inexcusable.

A postmortem failed to disclose the cause of death because the girls body was too badly decomposed.

Thousands followed the cortege. The thousands must have been *in,* not "following," the cortege (the funeral procession). Even after death, a medal won by serviceman is awarded to him. It may be presented to his widow, but it is not awarded to his widow.

If the service is at a funeral establishment, the name of the funeral establishment should be included for the convenience of mourners. It is not a "funeral home" A funeral service is *at* a place, not *from* it. A mass is *offered;* a funeral service is *held.* Even so, "held" usually is redundant, "The service will be at 2 p.m. Thursday..."

The passage should leave on doubt for whom the service was held. This one did leave doubt: "Services for 7-year old Michael L......., son of a Genoa Intermediate School District official who was struck and killed by a car Monday in Bay City, will be held..."

People are *people*, not "assaults" or "traffic deaths" or "fatals" or "dead on arrival":

A youth stabbed at a downtown intersection and a woman pedestrian run down by a car were among assaults on six persons reported to police during the night.

Hugo Woman/among nine/traffic deaths

Dead on arrival at Hurley after the crash was Oscar W-who was decapitated.

The events in a person's life that should be included in his obituary pose a problem for the desk. One story recited the death of a former school administrator who died at the age of 87. It said he had been the first principal of blank high school and had served in that capacity for seventeen years. Then the story recalled that he resigned two months before he was found guilty of taking $ 150 from the school yearbook fund and was fined $500. Should an account of a minor crime committed a quarter of a century ago be included in the obituary? To those who knew the former principal intimately the old theft was not news. Those who didn't know him so intimately could hardly care about the single flaw in a otherwise distinguished career.

The following death story illustrates several errors overlooked by the copy-editor : Two Jefferson children were killed when the automobile in which they were riding was struck by another auto Saturday night at the intersection of Eastern Boulevard and Brooks Avenue in Clarksville.

They were killed instantly due to skull fractures sustained in the accident, "according to Clark County Coroner Edwin M." Coots. Their father George M. Gilbert Sr., Morris Ave., was driving the car in which the children were riding.

"Three other Gilbert children were hospitalized. Lori and Brian are in satisfactory condition and Karen is in intensive care at Clark County Memorial Hospital.

Michael was an eighth grade student at Parkview Junior High School and Christine attended Eastlawn Elementary School.

In addition to their father, survivors include their mother, Mrs. George M. Gilbert Sr.,a brother George M. Gilbert Jr. : and grandparents. Mrs. Emma Cannon, and Mr. and Mrs. Gobel Gilbert, all of Jeffersonville. The funeral for Michael and Christine" will be at 2 p.m. tomorrow at Coots Funeral Home here, with burial in Walnut Ridge Cemetery.

Major Factors

Reporters and copy-editors have no business playing doctor, If a child is injured in an accident, the seriousness of the injury should be determined by medical authorities. To say that a person who was not even admitted to the hospital was "Seriously injured" is editorializing.

Hospitals may report that a patient is in a "guarded condition," but the term has no meaning for the reader and should be spiked. The same goes for "he is resting comfortably."

No one can sustain a "fractured leg." He may suffer a *fracture of the leg* or a *leg fracture* or *better still,* simply a *broken leg. Injuries are suffered, not received.*

A story described a murder suspect as "a diabetic of the worst type who must have 15 units of insulin daily." The quotes were attributed to the FBI. An editor commented, "In my book, that is a mild diabetic, unless the story means that the suspect is a diabetic who requires 15 units of regular insulin before each meal. A wire service should not rely on the FBI for diagnosis of diabetes and the severity of the case."

The name of the doctor can be used in a medical news story under these circumstances :

1. If he is the attending physician to a prominent person, such as a governor.

2. If he is the officially designated spokesman for his medical society.
3. If his medical society has furnished his name as one from whom authoritative information may be obtained in his speciality and he has consented to the use of his name.
4. If he is an official, such as a state epidemiologist, the doctor is treated the same as any other individual in the news.

Doctor and Scientist are vague words to many readers. *Doctor* may be a medical doctor, a dentist, a veterinarian, an osteopath, a minister or a professor. The story would be clearer if it named the doctor's specialty or the scientist's specific activity, whether biology, physics, electronics or astronautics.

Medical doctors diagnose the illness, not the patient. The proper term to use in determining the remedy or in forecasting the probable course and termination of a disease is *prognosis.*

Mothers *delivery;* babies are born.

Everyone has a heart condition. It is news only if someone's heart is in bad condition.

"The wife of the governor underwent major surgery and physicians reported she apparently had been cured of a malignant tumor." It is unlikely that any doctor said she was *cured* of a malignant tumor. They avoid that word with malignant growths.

"A team of five surgeons performed a hysterectomy, appendectomy and complete abdominal exploration." Why the unnecessary details? It would have been enough to say, "Five surgeons performed the abdominal operation."

Unless they are essential to the story, trade names of narcotics or poisons should be avoided. If a person dies of an overdose of sleeping pills, the story should not specify the number of pills

Also, *use Caesarean section or Caesarean operation.*

Usually, no sane person has his leg broken or his pockets picked. Use the passive tense: "His leg was broken;" "His pockets were picked."

Use the expression *physicians and dentists,* not *doctors and dentists.* The second suggests that dentist are not doctors.

A doctor who specializes in anaesthesia is an anaesthesiologist, not an anaeshthetist.

A person may wear a sling on his right arm. He doesn't wear his right arm in a sling.

"He suffered a severed tendon in his right Achilles' heel last winter". It was the Achilles' tendon in his right heel or his right Achilles' tendon.

"A jaundice epidemic also was spreading in Gaya, Indian health officials said. The second disease claimed 30 lives." Jaundice is not a disease but a sign of the existence of one or another of a great many diseases.

Technical Terms Should be Translated

Term	***Translation***	***Term***	***Translation***
Abrasions	Scrapes	Suturing	Sewing
Contusions	Bruises	Hemorrhaging	Bleeding
Lacerations	Cuts	Obese	Fat
Fracture	Break	Respire	Breathe

An editor said, "Ever since the National Weather Service started naming hurricanes alter females, reporters can't resist the temptation to be cute." He then cited the lead, "Hilda—never a lady and now no longer a hurricane—spent the weekend in Louisiana, leaving behind death, destruction and misery."

Thai, the editor said, is giddy treatment for a disaster causing thirty-five deaths and millions in property damage.

Another editor noted that a story referred to "the turbulent eye of giant storm." He remonstrated that the eye of the hurricane is the dead-calm centre. A story predicted that a hurricane was headed for Farmington and was expected to cause millions of dollars in damages. So the Farmington merchants boarded their windows, the tourists cancelled their reservations—and the hurricane went around Farmington. This is the trouble when an editor lets a reporter expand a prediction into a warning.

The headline *Freeze tonight expected/ to make driving hazardous* was based on this lead: "Freezing temperatures forecast for tonight may lead to a continuation of hazardous driving conditions as a result of last night's snow and freezing rain." The story made no mention of anyone's saying there would still be dampness on the ground when freezing temperatures arrived. There wasn't and driving was unimpeded.

A lead said, "One word, 'miserable,' was the U.S. weatherman's description today of the first day of spring." The head was *Snow predicted/It's spring, miserable.* It was the weatherman's prediction, not his description. The sun stayed out all day, the clouds stayed away, and readers of the paper must have wondered where this U.S. weatherman was located.

Temperatures can become higher or lower, not "cooler" or "warmer."

On flood stories, the copy should tell where the flood water came from and where it will run off. The expression *flash flood* is either a special term for a rush of water let down a weir to permit passage of a boat or a sudden destructive rush of water down a narrow gully or over a sloping in surface in desert regions, caused by heavy rains in the mountains or foothills. It is often used loosely for any sudden gush of water.

Weather stories, more than most other, have an affinity for the cliche, the fuzzy image, overwriting, mixed metaphors, contrived similes and sundry other absurdities.

"A Houdini snow did some tricks yesterday that left most of the state shivering from a spine-tingling storm." Houdini gained fame as an escape artist, not as an ordinary magician. Did the snow escape, or was it just a tricky snow? After the lead, the twenty-two- inch story never mentioned the angle again, Spine-tingling means full suspense or uncertainty or even terror. Sports writers are fond of using it to describe a close game, called a heart stopper by more ecstatic writers, often in conjunction with a gusty performance. If a cliche must-be used, a very cold' storm is spine-chilling; not "spine-tingling."

"Old Man Winter yesterday stretched his icy fingers and dumped a blanket of snow on the state." How would reporters ever write about the weather without Old Man Winter, Jack Frost, Ice Fingers and Old Sol? Why do rain and show never fall? They are always "dumped."

"Atleast two persons were killed in yesterday's snowstorm, marked at times by blizzard-like gales of wind." By Weather Service standards, this is an exaggeration and a contradiction. By any standard, it is a redundancy. A blizzard is one thing. Gales are something else. Gales of wind? What else, unless may be it was gales of laughter from discerning readers.

An editor's moral: Good colourful writing is to be encouraged. But a simply written story with no gimmicks is better than circus writing that goes awry. To quote a champion image-maker, Shakespeare, in *Sonnet 94,* "Lilies that fester smell far worse than weeds." The writer who plants the festering lilies is only a little more guilty than the copy-editor who lets' them grow. They have a way of reproducing.

Blizzard are hard to define because wind and temperatures may vary. The safe way is to avoid calling a snowstorm a *blizzard* unless the Weather Service describes it as sudi Generally, a blizzard occurs when there are winds of 35 m.p.h. or more that whip falling snow or snow already on the ground and when the temperatures are 20 degrees above zero Fahrenheit, or lower.

A severe blizzard has winds than: are 45 m.p.h. or more, temperatures 10 degrees above zero or lower,, and great density of snow either falling or whipped from the ground.

The Weather Service insists that ice storms are not sleet. Sleet is frozen raindrops. The service uses the terms ire *storm, freezing, rain and freezing drizzle* to warm the public when a coating of ice is expected on the ground. A cyclone is a storm with heavy rain and winds rotating about a moving centre of low atmospheric pressure.

A hurricane has winds above 75 m.p.h.

A typhoon is a violent cyclonic storm or a hurricane occurring in the China Seas and adjacent regions, chiefly from July to October. The word *Chinook* should not be used unless so designated by the Weather Service.

Temperatures are measured by various scales. Zero degree centigrade is freezing, and 100 degree centigrade is boiling. On the Fahrenheit scale, 32 degrees is freezing, and 212 degrees (at sea level) is boiling. On the Kelvin scale, 273 degrees is freezing, and 373 degrees is boiling. To convert degrees centigrade to Fahrenheit, multiply the centigrade measurement by nine-fifths and add 32. To convert degrees Fahrenheit to centigrade, subtract 32 from the Fahrenheit measurement and multiply by five-ninths. Thus, 10 degrees centigrade is 50 degrees Fahrenheit. To convert degrees Kelvin to centigrade degrees, subtract 273 from the Kelvin reading.

Weather Cliches

Fog rolled (crept or crawled) in

Jupiter Pluvius

Fog-shrouded city

Winds aloft

Biting (bitter) cold

Hail-splattered

Mercury dropped (dipped, zoomed, plummeted)

Rain failed to dampen

Hurricane howled

Storm tossed

Conjecturing about possible damage to settlements from forest fires is as needless as conjectures on weather damage. The story should concentrate on the definite loss. Stories of forest fires should give the specific area burned, the area threatened and the type of timber.

Most stories of earthquake attempts to describe the magnitude of the tremor. One measurement is the Richter scale, which show relative magnitude. It starts with magnitude 1 and progresses in units with each unit ten times stronger than the previous-unit. Thus, magnitude 3 is ten times stronger than magnitude 2, which, in turn, is ten times stronger than magnitude 1. On this scale the strongest earthquakes recorded were the South American earthquake of 1906 and the Japanese earthquake of 1933, both at a magnitude of 8.9. Intensity generally refers to the duration or to the damage caused by the shock.

In train and plane Crashes the story should include train or flight number, the place of departure, the destination and times of departure and expected arrival, "Passenger train" is adequate, "Crack passenger train" is a cliche. Airplanes may collide on the ground or in the air (not "midair"). Let investigators *search* the wreckage not "comb" or "sift" it.

In fire stories, the sad truth is that in nine of ten cases when somebody is "led to safety," they're not. Except for an occasional small child, they simply have the common sense to beat it without waiting for a fireman to "lead them to safety."

In both fire and flood stories the residents of the area are rarely taken from their homes or asked to leave. Instead, they're always told to "evacuate" or they're "evacuated." What's wrong with *vacate?*

Eliminate terms such as *three-alarmfire* and *second-degree burns.* "An estimated $ 40,000 worth of damage was done Jan. 29... Damage isn't worth anything. Quite the contrary."

"The full tragedy of Hurricane Betsy unfolded today as the

death toll rose past 50 and damages soared into many millions." *Damage* was the correct word here. You collect *damages* in court.

Disaster Cliches

Rampaging Rivers	Tinder-dry forest
Weary firefighters	Raging brush fire
Fiery holocaust	Traffic fatals or triple fatals
Flames licked (leaped, swept)	(police station jargon)
Searing heat	

Labour Disputes : Stories of labour controversies should give the reasons for the dispute, how long the strike has been in progress and the claims by both the union and the company.

Copy-editors should be on guard against wrong or loaded terms. Examples: In a closed shop the employer may hire only men already members of the union. In a union shop, the employer may select his employees but the workers are required to join the union within a specified time after starting work. A conciliator or mediator in a labour dispute merely recommends terms of a settlement. The decision of an arbitrator is binding. There is a tendency in labour stories to refer to management proposals as "offers " and to labour proposals as "demands." The correct word should be used for the correct connotation.

Strikebreaker and *scab* have no place in the report if used to describe men or women who act as individuals in accepting positions vacated by strikers. The expression "honoured the picket line" frequently appears in the report even though a more accurate expression is "refused (or declined) to cross a picket line."

Union leader is usually preferred to *labour leader.* A longshore man is a waterfront leader. A stevedore usually is considered an employee.

On estimates of wages or production lost, the story should have authoritative sources, not street-corner guesses. An individual, however voluble, does not speak for the majority unless he has been authorized to do so. Statements by workers or by minor officials should be played down until they are documented.

If a workers gets a 10-cent an hour increase effective immediately, an additional 10 cents a year hence and another 10 cents the third year, he does not receive a 30-cent-an-hour increase. His increase at the time of settlement is still 10 cents an hour. "The company has been on strike for the last 25 days." No. The employees are on strike. The company has been struck.

Criminal court terms should not be applied to labour findings unless the dispute has been taken to a criminal court. The National Labour Relations Board is not a court, and its findings or recommendations should not be expressed in criminal court terminology. In most settlements, neither side is "found guilty" or "fined." A finding or a determination may be made or a penalty may be assessed.

Financial News : A news release from a bank included the following: "The book value of each share outstanding will approximate $ 21.87 on Dec. 31, and if the current yield of 4.27 per cent continues to bear the same relationship to the market price it should rise to $ 32 or $ 33, according to ..." The copy-editor changed the ambiguous *it to the book value.* Actually, the release intended *it* to refer to the market price, which shows what can happen when copy-editors change copy without knowing what they are doing.

Another story quoted an oil company official as saying that "the refinery would mean $ 7,000,000 in additional real estate taxes." It should have been obvious that this was a wholly unrealistic figure, but for good measure there was an ad in the same paper that placed the total tax figure at around $ 200,000 and said "The initial installation will add about $ 7,000,000 a year to the economy of the state, not including taxes."

A story and headline said the interest on the state debt accounted for 21 per cent of the state government's spending. An accompanying graph showed, however, that the figure was for debt service, which includes both interest and amortization.

All who edit copy for financial pages should have atleast some elementary knowledge of business terms. If they can't distinguish between a balance sheet and a profit and loss statement, between earnings and gross operating income, and between' a net profit and net cash income, they have some homework to do.

This was brought home by a syndicated financial columnist who cautioned business news desks against using misleading headlines such as *Stocks plummet—Dow Jones average off 12 points.* It may be a loss, the columnist noted, but hardly a calamity. Dow Jones may indicate that the market is up, whereas it is actually sinking. Freak gains by a few of the thirty stocks in the Dow may have pushed up that particular indicator. Nor does a slight market drop call for a headline such as a *Inventors loss millions in market value of stocks.* They lost nothing of the sort. On that day, countless investors the nation over had substantial paper profits on their stocks. If they sold, they were gainers on the buying price in real terms; if they held, they had neither gains nor losses.

The Dow Jones Industrial Average is one of several indexes used to gauge the stock market. Each uses its own statistical technique to show market changes. The Dow Jones bases its index on thirty stock. It is an index number change, not a percentage change.

Reports of dividends should use the designation given by the firm (regular, special, extra, increases, interim) and show what was paid previously if there is no specified designation such as regular or quarterly. The story should say if there is a special, or extra, dividend paid with the regular dividend and include the amount of previous added payments. When the usual dividend is passed, or reduced, some firms issue an explanatory statement, the gist of which should be included in the story.

Newswire stylebooks recommend that news of corporate activities and business and financial news should be stripped of technical terms. There should be some explanation of the firm's business (plastics, rubber, electronics) if there is no indication of the nature of the business in the firms's name. The location of the firm should be carried.

Savings and loan firms object to being called banks. Some commercial banks likewise object when savings and loan firms are called banks. There need be no confusion if thc institution is identified by its proper name. In subsequent references the words *firm or institution* are used.

Some newspapers permit *S & L Firm* in tight headlines. Actually a *firm* is a partnership or unincorporated group. It should not be used for an incorporated company. *Concern* is a better word for the latter.

Jargon has no place in the business story, "Near-term question marks in the national economy—either of which could put a damper on the business expansion—are residential housing and foreign bade, the Northern Trust company said in its December issue of *Business Comments.*" Are near-term question marks economy question marks? If so, can they put a damper on anything? Isn't all housing residential?

Major producers scrambled today to adjust steel prices to newly emerging industry-wide patterns...' .The welter of price changes was in marked contrast with the old time industry practice of posting across-the-board hikes.

This approach apparently breathed its last in April, 1962 when it ran into a Kennedy administration buzzsaw, and a general price boost initiated then by United States Steel Corporation, the industry giant collapsed under White House Fire.

Readers of financial pages read for information. False colour is not needed to retain these readers. The following story should have freely butchered on die desk:

Stock of the Communications Satellite Corporation went into : an assigned orbit yesterday on three major stock exchanges, rocketing to an apogee of $ 46 a share and a perigee of $ 42 and closing at $ 42.37, unchanged.

It was the first day of listed trading on the exchanges. The stock previously was traded over the counter.

The countdown on the first transaction on the New York stock exchange was delayed 12 minutes by an initial jam of buy and sell orders.

Percentages : Two types of errors appear frequently in stories dealing with percentages. One is the failure to distinguish between percentage ., and percentage points; the other lies in comparing the change with the new figure rather than the original one. For example, when a : tax rate is increased from $5 per $ 100 assessed valuation to $ 5.50, the increase is 10 per cent, New figure less old figure, divided by

$$\$5.50—\$5; = \frac{50}{\$5} = 10 \text{ or } 10 \text{ per cent.}$$

"Jones pointed out that the retail markup for most other brands is approximately 33 per cent, whereas the markup on Brand] is 50 per cent, or 17 per cent higher/' No. It is 17 percentage points higher but 51.5 per cent higher,. Divide 17 by 33.

"Dover's metropolitan population jumped from 16,000 ten years ago to more than 23,000 last year, an increase of better than 70 per cent." Wrong again. It's a little less than 44 per cent.

Is the figure misleading or inaccurate? The story said, "A total of $6,274 was raised at each of the four downtown stations." This adds up to $ 25,096. What was meant was that "A total of $ 6,274 was raised at four stations." A not-so-sharp copy-editor let this one get by: "Almost 500,000 slaves were shipped in this interstate trade. When one considers the average price of $800, the trade accounted for almost $20 million."

Are terms representing figures vague? In inheritance stories, it is better to name the amount and let the reader decide whether the amount is a "fortune." One of the wire service editors noted, "Fifteen thousand might be a fortune to a bootblack, but $200,000 would not be a fortune to a Rockefeller."

For some reason, many stories contain gambling odds, chances and probabilities. When a princess gave birth to a son, reporters quickly snatched on to the odds on his name. Anthony was 1:2, George was even money and Albert was 3:1. One headline played up the third in the betting. The name chosen was David, an 18:1 shot. All of this shows the foolishness of newsmen who play into the hands of gamblers. If odds must be included in the story, they should be accurate. The story said that because weather records showed that in the last eighty-six years it had rained only nineteen times on May 27, the odds were 8:1 against rain for the big relay event. The odds mean nothing to readers except to those who like to point out that in the story just mentioned the odds actually were

"Dr. Frank Rubovits said the children came from a single egg He said the chance of this occurring 'probably is about 3 million to 1," He meant the odds against this occurring. The chance of this occurring is 1 in 3 million.

"The Tarapur plant will be the world's second largest atomic generator of electricity. The largest will be the 500-ton mega watt plant at Hinkley Point in Britain." A 500-ton megawatt plant makes no sense. What the writer meant was a 500-mega watt plant.

Some readers may rely on the idiom and insist that "five times as much as" means the same as "five times higher than" or "five times more than." If so, five times as much as $50 is $ 250 and five times higher than $50 is still $250. Others contend that the second should be $300. If earnings this year are 3½ times as large as last year's, they are actually *2½* times larger than last year's.

Insist on this style: 40,000 to 50,000 miles, not 40 to 50,000 miles; $3 million to $5 million, not $3 to $5 million.

"The committee recommended that a bid of $ 26,386.60 be accepted. After recommending the higher bid, the committee also had to recommended that an additional $326.60 be appropriated for the fire truck, since only $26,000 was included in the budget." The sum is still $60 short of a bid.

Equivalents should be included in stories that contain large sums. Most readers cannot visualize $20 billion, but they can understand it if there is an indication as to how much the amount would mean to each individual.

Here is an editor's advice to the staff:

We can do a service for those important people out there if we use terms they are most acquainted with. For example, to most of our readers a ton of come is more easily visualized if ; it is reported as bushels, about 36 in this case. We normally report yields and prices in bushels and that is the measurement most readers know. The same goes for petroleum; barrels is probably more recognizable than tons. When the opportunity presents itself, translate the figures into the best-known measurement.

Nothing is duller or more unreadable than a numbers story. If figures are the important part of the story, they should be related to something—or atleast presented as comparisons.

Two of the most common mathematical errors in news copy are the use of millions for billions and vice-versa and a construction such as "Five were injured. . . " with only four persons listed.

Ships and Boats : Belay using nautical terms unless they're used properly, "Capt.

Alberts. Kolly, the 75-year-old pilot, who manned lite Delia (JueenX tiller yesterday. . . " What he manned was her *helm or her wheel.* Few vessels except sailboats are guided with a tiler.

A story referred to a 27-foot ship. Nothing as small as 27 feet is a *ship. Ship* refers to big seagoing vessels such as tankers, freighters and ocean liners. Sailors insist that if it can be hoisted onto another craft it is a boat and that if it is too large for that it is a ship. Specific terms such as *cabin cruiser, sloop, schooner, barge and dredge* are appropriate.

"A rescue fleet ranging from primitive by you pirogues to helicopters prowled through the night," That should send the copy editor to a dictionary so he can explain to readers that a pirogue is a canoe or a dugout.

"The youths got to the pier just before the gangplank was lowered." When a ship sails, the gangplan is *raised.*

Commercial ships are measured by volume, the measurement of all inclosed space on the ship being expressed in units of 100 cubic feet to the ton. Fuller description gives passenger capacity, length, age, and so on. Naval vessels are expressed in tonnage, the weight in long tons of a ship and all its contents (called displacement). A long ton is 2,240 pounds. All this is "Greek" to many readers. Copy-editors should translate into terms recognized by readers, who can visualize length, age and firing power more readily than tonnage: "The 615-foot Bradley, longer than two football fields, ..."

A knot is a measure of speed, not distance (nautical miles an hour). A nautical mile is about 1— land miles. "Knots per hour" is redundant.

Some readers may understand when the story says, "The limestone carrier was enroute home in ballast," All will understand if the story says simply that the ship was enroute home empty.

Some of the best writings in American newspapers appears in the sports pages. So does some of the worst.

Many of the weaknesses could be minimized if sports copy were submitted to a universal desk for editing or if the sports copydesk were permitted to edit for all readers—the women, the teenagers and those with only a lukewarm interest in sports, as well as the sports experts. Too often, the sports copydesk permits the abuses of sports copy and magnifies the excesses.

Sports pages should be, and are, the liveliest in the paper. They have action photos, a melange of spectator and participant sports and an array of personalities. Sports writers have more latitude than do other reporters. The good ones are among the best in the business; the undisciplined ones are among the worst.

Attractive pages and free expression meant little if the sports section is unintelligible to half the paper's readers. Too often, the editing reflects the attitude that if readers don't understand the lingo they should seek elsewhere in the paper for information and entertainment.

The potential for readers of the sports section is greater than ever because of the growing number of participants in golf, bowling, fishing, boating and tennis. The spectator sports, especially automobile racing, football, golf, basketball, baseball and hockey, attract great audiences, thanks to the vast number of television viewers. Thus the sports pages, if edited intelligently, can become the most appealing section in the paper; But first, writers and copy-editors must improve their manners.

A report of a contest or struggle should appeal to readers if, it is composed in straightforward, clear, honest English. The style can be vigorous without being forced, honest without being awesome. Sports fans do not need the fillips to keep their awesome. Sports fans do not need the fillips to keep their interest whetted. Those who are only mildly interested won't become sports page regulars if the stories are not understandable.

Know the Game : One of the elementary rules in sports writing is to tell the reader the name of the game. Yet many stories talk about the Cubs and Pirates but never say specifically that the contest is a baseball game. Some writers assume that if the story refers to the contest a "dribble derby " all sports page readers must understand that the story concerns a basketball game.

The story may contain references to parts of the game yet never mention the specific game.

Here is an example.

Three teams tied for low at 59 in the sweepstakes division as the 11 to annual Sliceroo got under way Thursday at Lakewood County Club

Deadlocked at 59 were the team of. . .

In the driving contest, it was. . .

In the putting and chipping contest. . .

A best ball is set for Friday and a low net for Saturday, final

day of the Sliceroo. A $5,000 hole-in-one competition on the 124-yard 11th hole is set for both final days.

Golfers will understand this story. But non-golfers, even many who enjoy watching golf matches on television, should be told outright that the story concerns a golf tournament. The added information would not offend the golfers. It might encourage a non-golfer to read on.

Some stories fail to state categorically who played whom. Again, the writer assumes that if he names the opponents managers, all hard-core sports readers will recognize the contestants. Perhaps so, but the general reader might like to know too. The legend under a two-column cut read, "They cant' believe their eyes. Coach Andy S—, left, and Manager May S—, right, showed disbelief and disgruntlement as the Braves belt Pitcher Don C— for five runs in the eighth inning of their exhibition baseball game. Wednesday at Clearwater, Fla. The Braves won, 10-2." Now, whom did the Braves play?

Not all readers understand the technical terms used to describe a sports contest. It might be necessary to explain that a seeded team gets a favoured placement in the first round, and that if Smith beats Jones 2-1 in match play it means that golfer Smith is two holes ahead of golfer Jones with only one hole left to play and is, therefore, the winner. The name of the sport should be used in reference to the various cups. The Davis Cup is an international trophy for men tennis players. The Heisman Trophy is an award presented annually to the most outstanding college football player in the nation.

America's Cup refers to yachting, and Americas Cup to golfing. Technically, it is *All America,* not "All-American."

Unanswered Questions : Answering more questions is one way to win more readers for the sports department. The key questions frequently overlooked are how and why. Why did the coach decide to punt on fourth down instead of trying to make one foot for a first down? How does a tournament get the funds to award $200,000 in prizes?

"The shadow of tragedy drew a black edge around a golden day at Sportsman's park yesterday, bringing home the danger of horse racing with an impact that cut through the $68,950 Illinois Derby like a spotlight in darkness," So, what happened?

The best training for copy-editors or the sports desk is a stint on the news copydesk. But before they go on the sports desk they should become familiar with the intricacies of all sports so they can catch the technical errors in sports copy. Here are examples:

"Centre fielder Tony Cafar, whose fine relay after chasing the ball 'a country mile', held Ripley to a triple." Unless Tony also made a throw of "a country mile," another player, the shortstop, or second baseman, made the relay throw after taking a good throw from Tony.

When a writer covering a basketball game refers to a "foul shot," his reference should be nailed on the sports desk rim. The fouled player gets a free throw from the free-throw line, not the foul line or the charity lane.

The copy-editors also has to be alert for some of the wild flights' of imagination used by sports, writers. "The Tar Heels hurdled their last major obstacle on the way to an unbeaten season but still had a long row to hoe." Is this a track meet or a country fair?

The following passage is a sure way to discourage sports page reader :

> Kanicki's troubles in yesterday's 27-c factory over the Dallas Cowboys before 72,062, largest crowd ever to see the Texans, was the reason. Gain was in the trenches to receive a shattering kick with 6:24 left in the game.,

This example suggests another tendency in sports copy—turning the story into a numbers game. Box scores, league standings and records have a place in the sports story, but generally they should have a subordinate rather' than a dominant role. It is questionable whether gambling odds or the role of gambles should be used in either the story or the headline. Such intrusion often comes in races with their extra special payoffs.

Abbreviated Sports : The addiction for abbreviation is strong in both sports copy and headlines. *Broncos get first AFL win over NFL* announces a headline. It means that Denver's professional football team scored the first victory of an American Football League team over a National Football League team.

The seventh paragraph of a story referred to NPSA. The reader, if he was interested, had to reread the lead to know that the initials stand for National Professional Soccer League. An editor told his colleagues, "There is nothing more exciting than a good contest. There is nothing duller than reading about it the next day." Yet many spectators who watch a Saturday contest can't wait to read about it the next morning. What were the coach's and player's reaction to the game? What was the turning point? How long was the pass that won the game? What's the reporter's comment on the crowd's behaviour?

This should argue that if there is an audience for the report of a contest, the story needs no special flourishes. Loaded terms such as "wily mentor," genial bossman, "vaunted running game," "dazzling run" and "astute field general" add little or nothing to the report. Adjectives lend false colour. The Associated Press reported a "vise-tight race," "the red-hot Cardinals" and the "torrid 13-4 pace" as if these modifies were needed to lure readers.

If all copy-editors were permitted to aim their pencils at copy submitted by the prima dogmas of the sports world, there would be no sentence structures like the following ones: "Benny (Kid) Paret showed 'very slight improvement' in his battle for life today while his embittered manager branded the New York State Athletic Commission's report absolving Referee Ruby Goldstein of blame for the boxer's condition as a whitewash." "Maris, who has been bothered by a sore rib this spring, played eight innings yesterday, collected two singles and drove in a run." He didn't collect them; he hit them.

"Oritiz threw his first bomb in the second round when he nailed Laguna with a left and right to the jaw." How can you nail something with a bomb? "Left-hander Norman, who started on the mound for Chicago, recovered from a shaky start and pitched six-hit ball for eight innings before a walk and a botched-up double play caused Manager Bob Kennedy to protect a 4 to 1 lead, as a result of a three-run homer by Ernie Banks in the seventh." The sentence is hard to understand because it is overstuffed and because the facts are not told in chronological order. Revised: "Left-hander Norman started on the mound for Chicago. He recovered from shaky start and pitched six-hit ball for eight innings. Then a walk and a missed double play caused Manager Bob Kennedy to bring in a new pitcher. Chicago was leading, 4 to 1 as a result of a three-run homer by Ernie Banks in the seventh."

Here is how to tell a story upside down: "Waldrop's 17 yard explosions for high eighth touchdown of the season punctuated a 65 yard march from Army's reception of the kickoff by a courageous Falcon team which had gone ahead for the second time in the game, 10 to 7, in the ninth minute of final period."

An overstuffed sentence of any sort will be just as damaging and harder to repair, than compound sentence leads. Note this one: 'The heaviest betting non-holiday Monday crowd in the Balmoral Jockey club's eight years at Washington Park poured $ 1,066,919 into the machines yesterday on a nine-race programme headed by the $ 7,500 Harvey purse, a six-furlong dash which drew six starters and was won by Mighty Fenriec, piloted by Bill Hartack" Revised: "Horse-race fans put $1,066,919 into the Washington Park machines yesterday on arrhae-race programme.

It was the heaviest betting non-holiday Monday crowd in the Balmoral Jockey club's eight years at the park. The $7,500 Harvey purse for the six-furlong race drew six starters. It was won by Mighty Fennec, ridden by Bill Hartack.""Statistics don't tell the story," he explained, "looking many straight in the eye." If he looked more than one person straight in the eyes while he said that, he must have been a long time between words.

It takes some editing to convert sports writers into Homers and Hemingways. At least, though, copy-editors can try to help writers improve their way of telling a story. Copy-editors can excise cliches such as "pay dirt," "turned the tables," "hammered (or slammed) a homerun," "Big Eight hardwoods," "circuit clout," "gridder," "hoopster," "thin dads," "tanksters," "sweet revenge," "rocky road," "free loads" (foul shots), "droughts" (losing streaks), "standing-room-only crowds," "put a cap on the basket," "as the seconds ticked off the clock," "unblemished records," "paced the team," "outclassed but game," "roared from behind," "sea of mud," "vaunted defense," "coveted trophy" and "last-ditch effort."

They can insist on the correct word. Boxers may have *altercations* (oral) with their managers. They have *fights* with other boxers.

They can tone down exaggerated expressions like "mighty atom of the ring," "destiny's distance man" or "North-western comes off tremendous effort Monday" (North-western tried hard).

They can cut out redundancy in phrases like "with 30,000 spectators looking on."

They can resist the temptation to use synonyms for the verbs *win, beats and defeats:* annihilates, atomizes, bayyers, belts, bests, blanks, blasts, boots home, clips, clobbers, cops, crushes, downs, drops, dumps, edges, ekes out, gallops over, gangs up on gouges, gets past, H-bombs, halts, humiliates, impales, laces, lashes, lassoes, licks, murders, outslugs, outscraps, orbits, over comes, paces, pastes, pins, racks up, rallies, rolls over, ramps over, routs, scores, sets back, shades, shaves, sinks, slows, snares, spanks, squeaks by, squeezes by, stampedes, stomps, stops, subdues, surges, sweeps, tops, topples, triggers, trips, trounces, troubles, turns back, vanquishes, wallops, whips, whomps and wrecks.

They will let the ball be *hit,* not always banged, bashed, belted, blooped, bombed, boomed, bumped, chopped, clunked, clouted, conked, cracked, dribbled, drilled, dropped, driven, hacked, knifed lashed, lined, plastered, plunked, poked, pooped, pumped, punched, pummeled, pushed, rapped, ripped, rocked, slapped, sliced, slugged, smashed, spilled, spanked, stubbed, swatted, tagged, tapped, tipped, topped, trickled, whipped, whistled, whomped and whooped.

They will let a bill be *thrown* and only occasionally tossed, twirled, fired and hurled.

They will let a ball be *kicked,* occasionally punted and never toed or booted.

They will resist the shopworn puns; Birds (Eagles, Orioles, Cardinals) soar or claw; Lions (Tigers, Bears, Cubs) roar, claw or lick: Braves (Tribesmen, Indians) scalp or tomhawk; Mustangs (Colts, Broncos) buck, gallop, throw or kick.

They will insist on neutrality in all sports copy, avoiding "home policy" slanting.

They will not make verbs out of nouns:" AP—Chicago manager

Eddie Stanky non-chalanted the White Sox strike-breaker, saying, 'My food's going to taste the same...'".

They will not string modifiers endlessly: "UPI—The Pistons won 29 and lost 40 under the guidance of the then only 24 years old Dubusschere."

Society : One of the brighter changes in newspapers has been the transformation of the society pages, with their emphasis on club and cupid items, to the Women's section or the family section with a broader-based appeal. The philosophy of the new approach has-been well expressed by two editors:

Pages of the Women's Section are edited not for the ladies who write the stories, not for the ladies who are the source of the stories and not for gruff voice of the advertising department. They're edited for the people who buy the paper. Women's pages were formerly edited for the few. Now the pages appeal to the woman as mother and working girl and as an intelligent human being involved in the total society. Such sections still carry engagement announcement and wedding stories, but their added fare is foods, fashions, finance, health, education, books and other cultural affairs.

They are edited for active women in all ranks, not solely for those in the top rank of society. They also are edited for the increasing number of men readers. The better editors regard readers of the women's section as alert individuals who are concerned with problems such as prostitution, racism, civil disorders, women's prisons, alcoholism among housewives and educational reforms. Such editors strive to make their pages informative as well as entertaining.

Improvements are likely to continue. Some executives argue that newspapers should not segregate women, that material of special interests to the family should be scattered throughout the paper. Some maintain the club and social news should be held to a minimum because of low reader appeal. Others argue that the preoccupation with foods, fashions and furnishings squeezes out important items of women's activity. A quarter of a page devoted to a picture of a cherry pie might be trimmed a bit to accommodate a good story.

Some papers now handle engagements, weddings and births as court of record items. And a few charge for engagements and wedding stories and pictures unless the event is obviously news, such as the wedding of the President's daughter.

To add some spice to its pages devoted to wedding accounts, the Gannett Rochester Newspapers started a "Wedding Scrap-book" page to its Saturday section, "Brides Book for Greater Rochester." Included are features on how the couple met, amusing incidents of the participants on the way to the ceremony, pictures of the couple in faraway places.

In many daily newspapers, especially the medium-sized and smaller ones, reports of engagement and wedding will perish slowly, if they will die at all. Still, some conventions may change—such as giving the bridegroom a break for a change. The point was delightfully argued by Paul Brookshire in his column in the South Dade (Homestead, Fla.) *New Leader,* and reprinted in *The Quill* (October, 1967). Here are some excerpts:

In these days when the world is quaking in its boots and news of great significance is daily swept into newspaper trash cans for lack of space, it is sickening to read paragraph after paragraph about some little girl changing HER name to HIS. The groom? He apparently wasn't dressed at all. . .if he was even there . But Mother and Mother-in-law? Yes. They were fashion plates in beige ensembles and matching accessories or something. I ask you. Is it a wedding or a fashion show? If it is a fashion show, why isn't it held in a hotel ballroom and why isn't the groom given a tiny bit of credit for the showing up with his clothes on?

The blackout of the bridegroom in wedding accounts is an unpardonable sin. If the groom is mentioned at all he is afforded as much space as an atheist gets on the church page. And pictures. Did you ever see a photograph of a bridegroom? May be in the Post Office but not in the newspaper.

I'm going on record right now in favour of wedding announcements being run as legal notices—payable in advance by the father of the bride. Better still, if the bride insists on giving a minute, detailed description of every inch of clothing she happens to have on her person, I suggest she take out a paid display advertisement. In this manner, trade names may be used and shops that sold the girl all her glorious gear could get equal space on the same page.

Newspapers would reap untold profits from this arrangement and readers might be able to get some world news for a change instead of bouffant skirts highlighted with tiers of lace and aqua frocks with aqua tipped orchids and maize silk linen ; ensembles with... whatever you wear with maize silk linen ensembles.

Even though many newspapers have refined the society section, some retain a static style, especially on engagement and wedding stories. Wedding story leads usually read like these: First Methodist Church in Littleton was the setting for the double-ring wedding rites of blank and blank.

Miss Blank has become the bride of Blank, it was announced by her parents, etc. After a wedding trip to Las Vegas) Nevada, Mr. and Mrs. Blank will live in. . .

All Saints Roman Catholic Church was the setting for the single-ring rites. Newspapers continue to use the following: Stock words and phrases—holy matrimony, high noon, Benedict's, exchanged nuptial vows. Descriptive adjectives—attractive, pretty, beautiful, charming, lovely. Non sequiturs—"Given in marriage by her parents, the bride wore a white silk organza gown with a sabrina neckline and short sleeves." "Wearing a gown of white lace cotton over taffeta with empire waistline, square neckline and short sleeves, the bride was given in marriage by her father."

Confusing collectives—"The couple is on a trip to Northwestern and will live at blank Fairmount Ave., Whitefish Bay, when they return." Generally a collective noun takes a singular verb when the noun indicates a group acting as a unit and a plural verb when it means individuals performing individual actions: "The Board of Park Commissioners gave its blessings. . ." "The platoon fought its way up the hill" "Their headquarter is in the Bennett building..." "The crew have returned to their homes." Therefore, make it couple *are,* not is.

Details—gown and flower descriptions and social affiliations that reflect status.

Euphemistic headlines—*Betrothal told, Holy voivs exchanged, Wedding ceremonies solemnized.*

Excerpts from an error-tilled account of a wedding (2½ pages of copy) reveal the unbelievable triteness of such stories:

A petite white United Methodist Church nestled below the towering Rocky Mountains in Lyons. Colorado was the setting for the marriage of Shirley Ann M—and Wesley William B—on August 4. A happy sun brought windows at precisely 3 p.m. when Gloria L. ... played The Wedding March, and guests stood from hand carved oak seats, curved into an intimate half-circle to witness the double-ring ceremony.

The Rev D.L.N.—officiated at the afternoon ceremony amid arrangements of mint-green carnations, white gladiolas, and white daisies with giant white satin bows which adorned the alter. Pews were delightfully enhanced with waterfall baskets of fresh greenery and wild mountain flowers plucked early that morning from beside that St. Vrain River and tied with lime and powder blue satin ribbons.

The Bride tossed her bouquet from the stairway and "went away" all dressed in white and yellow.

Copy-editors who handle news and features for the women's section will not allow writers to single out women's achievements by sex, such as housewife and woman doctor. They will delete phrases like "is affiliated with," "refreshments will be served,"' "featured speaker," "special guests," "noon luncheon," "dinner meeting." They will refuse to let a person "host (or hostess) a party," "gravel a meeting" or "chair a committee."

They will not let reporters go out of their way to use *female, feminine* and *ladies* in all manner of sentences where the word *women* would be proper and more appropriate.

They will catch slips such as "Mrs. Richard Roe, nee Jane Doe," *Nee* means "born" and people are born only with their surnames. The first (not Christian) name is given later.

They will remain on guard for awkward sentences:

Do you keep track of your weight and lose the first five or ten pounds too much?

Seniors realize the importance of proper dress more than younger students, but after a while they catch on.

All copy for this section, as well as for the other sections of the paper, should be edited for its news value. This should apply to the syndicated features as well as to the locally produced copy.

The copy-editors should not allow any story aimed at younger readers to contain anything that patronizes these readers. Even terms like *teen, teenager* and *Youth* can be avoided, or at least can be held to a minimum. Copy-editors should make sure that both copy and headline talk up, not down to these readers.

10

News Sources

The Debate

Speeches are a major source of news and every day many news items that appear in the newspapers can be traced back to some speech or the other. Sometimes several speeches from part of one report. This happens in reports of seminars, symposia and legislatures. In such situations the most important speech, normally from the most important speaker, gets prominence.

While covering political party conferences and international conferences on various subjects, one has to deal with several speeches in a row. Depending on the content and the speaker a reporter has to decide who should come first. Effort should also be made to generalise observations if possible and then mention who said what. In such cases the most important things said by different speakers should be mentioned and there should be no repetition of ideas.

If there are contrary opinions expressed by different speakers they should be mentioned and then supporters of different schools of thoughts should be quoted. Here again repetition of ideas should be avoided.

The importance of speeches and speakers varies from occasion to occasion and relative importance of other speakers. A reporter must evaluate various factors and use judgement while writing the story. For example, if many ministers speak in a party their speeches are important and what they say will be important according to the content of the speech. But if the prime minister speaks and he touches upon points which have been covered by other ministers already and adds something to it, he will get the maximum space and the rest of the ministers will be mentioned in the story with very little of what they said.

If in a special debate in a house of parliament the speech of a minister of state gets prominence in case the cabinet minister of the same department does not speak. If the cabinet minister of the same department does not speak. If the cabinet minister also speaks then the state minister is normally pushed out of intro. If the prime minister intervenes during the debate and says something on the subject even the cabinet minister is pushed below in the body of the story. So while reporting multiple speeches the reporter must evaluate all these factors.

There are occasions when copies of a speech may be supplied in advance. Sometimes the story is prepared based on the advance copy and a reporter goes to the site when the speech is made-just to check whether the speech was made and if so whether it followed the advance copy. The advance story is subject to an embargo which is released automatically at the time up to which it is embargoed (should not be used before/ should be used on or after...).

A reporter or sub-editor who writes the story from such a speech has enough time to his disposal and should 'read the speech carefully and write the story on the top of which 'not to be used before ... on...' as mentioned in the embargo should be typed. Normally, this embargo time is the time of the event where the speech is to be made. News agencies sometimes creed the embargoed story in advance. It should be used only after the embargo is lifted.

Where advance copy is not made available the reporter must reach the place where speech is to be delivered and check from the organisers if they are supplying a copy of the speech. If the copy is supplied before the speech then the reporter should start working on it immediately. He should go through it carefully and mark what he considers as important points.

He should also mark the order of their importance so that he loses no time when he has to type or dictate his story. He should carefully check the copy when the speech is made and see if there are any major deviations from the text supplied. Sometimes what is said by the speaker outside the supplied text is more newsworthy than all what is given in the text. Such departures from the prepared text should find place in the intro or body depending on their news value.

Many a time a speaker does not read the prepared speech and says that the speech be taken as read while what he says is in addition to that in that case the reporter is supposed to listen to the speaker carefully and read the text also before writing the story.

If the organisers promise that the copy of the speech will be supplied but it is not distributed when the speech begins, the reporter should start taking notes from the beginning of the speech imagining that the copy is not available. Many such promises of the organisers prove false and if the reporter does not take notes or record the speech when it is delivered, he will be in difficulty. Moreover he will miss any departures from the text.

A reporter should make use of the copy if he gets it within a few minutes after the event, otherwise he should rely on his notes and do the story. The copy can be used for quotations from the speech.

But there are occasions when the copy of the speech is not supplied. This happens in seminars and almost all the public meetings of political parties. A reporter can record them on a tape recorder. He must taken care to take down important points in his notebook. In this way he can do the story quickly, for he will not have enough time to replay the full speech and then write. A tape recorder is useful for it helps the reporter in reproducing exactly what the speaker might have said on a controversial or important issue.

A speech can sometimes yield more than one story. In certain circumstances a reporter can add colour to the story by describing the atmosphere or some sidelights. Such opportunities should not be missed.

It is interesting to see how the same speech is covered by different newspapers. Following is the address by the President of India to Parliament (February 20, 1986):

Honourable members :

1. It gives me great pleasure to welcome you to this first session of Parliament in 1986. I felicitate the new members.
2. The year has seen Parliament transact its business in a purposeful manner and in an atmosphere of cooperation. I extend to you all my best wishes for the successful completion of the budgetary and legislative business that lies ahead.
3. In July, 1985, the Government took a major initiative to resolve the complex and difficult problems in Punjab. Our prime concern was to strengthen the forces of unity and integrity. Policy was governed by the perspective of serving the highest national interest. The democratic process triumphed over terrorism. The peaceful elections in Punjab testified to the desire of the overwhelming majority of the people for peace and normalcy in the State.
4. A great responsibility rest on those who have secured the mandate of the people. The supreme task is to isolate those who are resorting to violence to, disturb communal harmony and peace. In this task they will have the support

of all political forces committed to the unity and integrity of India. There cannot be and must not be, any compromise with the forces of disintegration. It is imperative that all secular and democratic forces join hands in a mass campaign to safeguard the values enshrined in our Constitution-nationalism, secularism, democracy and socialism-the bedrock of India's unity.

5. The Assam settlement was followed by elections to the Legislative Assembly and the Lok Sabha. A new Government has taken office.
6. Government are committed to the fullest implementation of the Punjab and Assam Accords.
7. Government express their deepest sympathy with the families of all those who lost their lives, or were injured, or suffered loss of property in violent incidents in different parts of the country. Violence in public life is the very antithesis of the ethos of our civilization. The frequent resort to violence to settle what are perceived as grievances of one group or another should deeply disturb those who uphold democratic values. While governments must firmly put down violence wherever it may occur, it is essential that political parties committed to democratic values should deal with the root causes of violence through purposive and sustained work among the people. The temptation to seek short-term advantages from communal and other types of violence must be eschewed.
8. Communalism continues to pose a serious threat to national unity, it is being reinforced by religious fundamentalism and fanaticism. These trends represent a reactionary social outlook, directed against the struggle of the poor and the underprivileged against the vested interest. The reconstituted National Integration Council will have to act decisively and systematically to strengthen secularism.
9. In my Address on January 17, 1985, I had outlined the

major policies and programmes of the Government. I recapitulate the main points:

(i) Commitment of a clean public life;

(ii) Administrative reforms;

(iii) Judicial reforms;

(iv) A new national education policy;

(v) A new national programme for women;

(vi) Participation of youth in programmes for promoting national integration and achieving excellence;

(vii) Establishment of a Wasteland Development Board;

(viii) Formation of a Central Ganga Authority;

(ix) A new textile policy; and

(x) Thorough examination of safety measures for industrial establishments.

10. My Government have fulfilled in substantial measure the tasks they had set for themselves for the past year.

11. The anti-defection Act is now on the statute book. Contributions to political parties by the companies have been permitted by law. Government have endeavoured to set a new tone in public life. This has strengthened national confidence. A strong sense of involvement in public affairs among all sections of the people and a buoyant spirit have characterised the year that has gone by. We have to build on these assets to raise the standards of public life.

12. Vigorous steps have been taken to combat corruption and to improve the performance of the public services. Strong emphasis has been laid on sound personnel management and training of personnel at all levels. Machinery for redressal of public grievances is in place. Its results are being continuously evaluated. A new Ministry has been set up to monitor the implementation of various programmes. All Departments of Government have been

directed to formulate detailed action plans for the coming financial year, against which their progress will be judged. Administrative reform is a continuous process. Detailed exercises are underway to reorient the system to speedier decision-making and better implementation.

13. Government are determined to eliminate delays in dispensation of justice. The experiment of Lok Adalats has proved that an innovative approach is required to cure this malady. The establishment of Administrative Tribunals will also lighten the burden of the courts, enabling them to devote more time to the liquidation of arrears. However, these are just the first steps in tackling the basic problem of making justice inexpensive and easily accessible to the poor. Drastic changes are needed. Government have entrusted to the Law Commission the task of recommending such changes.
14. Government published in August 1985, a status paper entitled "The Challenge of Education". This was intended to stimulate wide and intensive national debate on issues and alternatives. Government note with satisfaction that the debate has involved all sections of the people and many useful ideas and approaches have emerged. A draft of the new Education Policy will be presented shortly to Parliament.
15. Government have set up a new department to look after the development of women. A comprehensive national programme for women is being worked out. It will aim at enabling women to play their full part in developing a strong and modern nation.
16. Programmes for youth development have made considerable headway but much more has to be done in this area.
17. The Wasteland Development Board has been set up and has started work on an ambitious programme of

afforestation. In a recent meeting, all the State Governments endorsed an integrated approach to a National Land Use Policy as well as the strategies and policies for wasteland development.

18. The Central Ganga Authority has come into existence. With the cooperation of the concerned State Governments, work has started in full swing on stopping the population of the Ganga.

19. A new textile policy was announced in June 1985. It aims at production of cheaper cloth for the people. An equally important objective of the policy is to protect the interests of handloom weavers. It is envisaged that in the Seventh Plan the entire production of 700 million sq. metres of controlled and janta cloth will be transferred to be handloom sector. The Handlooms Act, 1985 has been passed to strengthen this vital sector which provides livelihood to millions. Steps are being taken to ensure full and efficient implementation of the policy.

20. Government have completed examination of issues relating to industrial safety and management of hazardous substances and legislation will be introduced in this session of Parliament.

21. Government will establish seven zonal cultural centres-three have already been set up-to promote a sense of cultural cohesion. These centers, cutting across territorial and linguistic boundaries, would project the rich diversity of regional cultural traditions and their underlying unity. They "Would take the best of our culture to the masses, harmonising it with their lives and struggles. Their essential thrust would be to break the artificial barriers created during the colonial era between the masses and the living tradition of India's age-old culture in all its forms. The centres will also aim at revitalising folk art which has enriched the country's culture life."

22. I would now refer to the major trends in our economy.

23. The seventh Five Year Plan was approved by the national Development Council. The basic strategy of the Plan is cast in a longer term perspective of eradication of poverty and building a strong, self-reliant and modern economy. The plan sharpens the focus on the anti-poverty programmes which will have an expanded coverage. It also envisages adequate investments in the core sectors to strengthen the growth potential of the national economy.

24. The fulfillment of the- Plan required total commitment and determination to mobilise adequate resources for investment. To translate the vision of a strong, prosperous, self-reliant India into reality requires unremitting to and capacity to sacrifice and to bear hardship. Adequate savings have to be mobilised to pursue a non-inflationary path of development. More importantly, these savings have to be used effectively. The challenge has to be met. There are no short cuts to development, no alternatives to hard work.

25. Vigorous implementations of anti-poverty programmes yielded significant results. The Sixth Five Year Plan aimed at assisting 15 million families under the integrated Rural Development Programme; 16.6 million families were actually covered, of which 6.4 million belonged to the Scheduled Castes and Scheduled Tribes. These programmes are being strengthened and surplus foodgrains stocks will be used in 1986-87 to expand the National Rural Employment Programme and the Rural Landless Employment Guarantee Programme to cover one million additional families. An amount of Rs. 100 crores has been provided annually during the Seventh Five Year Plan for the construction of housing for the Scheduled Castes/ Scheduled Tribes and freed bonded labour.

26. By the end of March, 1985, of a total of 2.31 lakh problem

villages lacking safe drinking water supply, 1.92 lakh villages had been provided with at least one source of water supply. During 1985-86 the programme was further accelerated.

27. In 1985-86 agriculture continued to make steady progress. In November 1985, foodgrains stocks with Government were higher by nearly 15% over 1984. This has enabled Government to launch a scheme for distributing wheat and rice at specially subsidised rates in tribal areas and to other vulnerable sections, especially the Scheduled Castes, expectant mothers, children, etc.-A comprehensive crop insurance scheme has been introduced in specified areas for the kharif crop. Government are considering further expansion of such schemes.

28. During the first seven months of 1985-86, industrial production grew at the rate of .3%. The policy initiatives of Government have created a buoyant investment climate. The infrastructural industries have performed well. Compared with the first nine months of the last year, power generation was up by 8.2%; saleable steel production by 12.9%; fertilizer production by more than 10%. Our ports handled 13.2% more cargo and the railways created an all time record in freight traffic movement.

29. In 1985-86 the Central Plan outlays were stepped up by 15% over 1984-85, especially on anti-poverty programmes human resource development and infrastructure. There was considerable increase in the outlays of State Plans. Government will have spent in 1985-86 Rs. 1,650 crores on food subsidy an and Rs. 2,050 crores on fertilizer subsidy. Public distribution system was strengthened and prudent management of supplies prevented shortages. It is gratifying that a significant increase in public investment was achieved.

30. Tax collections have been buoyant belying gloomy forebodings. The collection of direct taxes is up by about 23% compared to the corresponding period last year, indirect tax collection has increased by 22%. Total tax collections have increased by 22% which is the highest in the last decade. An effective drive was launched against tax evaders, smugglers and black marketeers. Action has also been taken against personnel found guilty of colliding with economic offenders. Government are determined to cleanse the economic life and to fight the evil of black money.

31. For the first time, a long-term fiscal policy coterminous with the Five Year Plan has been announced. A long-term direction to economic policy has been provided. Government are confident that the policy will ensure economic growth and speedier expansion of productive investment and employment opportunities.

32. It is necessary to focus attention on the structural problems of the economy to further our basic objective of growth with social justice. India's development depends upon steadily rising levels of public investment. How are these investments to be financed? Massive investments made in the previous Plans must yield adequate returns. Coasts of production on have to be reduced. Every pair of national savings has to be put to the most productive use. Otherwise it will be difficult to find real resources for the larger and larger investments required for maintaining the tempo of self-reliant growth, for enlarging our antipoverty programmes and for preserving our economic independence. Sooner or later, sooner rather than later, we have to face the realities of the situation. No one should be under the delusion that growth, social justice, price stability and self-reliance are achievable without efficiency, discipline and sharing of burdens. Contemporary history warns us of such pitfalls.

33. We must reduce the costs of our inputs and prices of final products and services. We cannot afford the luxury of pricing ourselves out of both the domestic and the export markets. A modern industrial society cannot rise on the basis of continuing low levels of productivity and high coasts of production. New jobs cannot be created if existing enterprises incur losses year after year. Operational inefficiency increases the cost of production and is inevitably reflected in increased prices which are a burden on the people. It raises costs all round, reducing real investment.

34. The future of the planning process depends on our capacity to face up to difficult questions and- to take hard decisions, decisions that may involve sacrifices but without which forward movement will not be possible. Growth is absolutely vital to raise the standards of living of the poor. Can we evade decisions that protect and strengthen this development process? Nations are built by generations that sacrifice for a better tomorrow.

35. The balance of payments position poses a similar challenge. Our exports have remained sluggish in 1985-86 but our imports have increased. The imports of petroleum products and edible oils are well above the limits the country can afford. The question basically is whether we want to stand on our own feet or not. If we do, there is no question that we have to curb the growth of consumption of petroleum products and we have to be self-sufficient in oilseeds. We also have to have a fresh look at our imports of capital goods. We do not want to shut out new technology because that will harm us, but we have to make sure that such technology meets the rigorous criteria of essentiality. External financial flows are needed but Government are determined that India is never at the mercy of foreign banks and institutions. Economic independence and self-reliance are central to our philosophy of development. We shall pay whatever price is required to maintain our economic independence.

36. The primary objectives of our foreign policy continue to be the promotion of non-alignment, advocacy of peace and nuclear disarmament, enlarging the area of friendship and cooperation and building of a just world order.

37. We welcome the resumption of high level dialogue between the Russian Federation and USA. It is imperative to take urgent steps to bring about a freeze in the nuclear arms race and a comprehensive nuclear weapon test ban treaty. The six-nation initiative has called for these measures. The Delhi Declaration of January, 1985 had a good impact on public opinion throughout the world. The leaders of the six countries are in touch with one another about further steps.

33. During the last one year the atmosphere in the subcontinent has distinctly improved. We have succeeded in making progress with our neighbours in many fields. But we remain concerned about the ethnic situation in Sri Lanka and Pakistan's continued pursuit of a nuclear weapon capability. We remain convinced that the situation in Sri Lanka can be settled only through political means; attempts to seek a military solution will fall and will only result in the loss of a large number of innocent lives.

39. The Government welcome the establishment of South Asian Association for Regional Cooperation launched in Dhaka in December, 1985. We expect that it will help strengthen forces of friendship and cooperation in our region.

40. The Government have made untiring efforts towards the resolution of the major areas of tension. At the Commonwealth Meeting in the Bahamas in October, in which the Prime Minister participated, our delegation played a leading role in the adoption of the Commonwealth Accord on South Africa. We continue to demand comprehensive mandatory sanctions against the racist

regime in South Africa. If the authorities there, and other Governments in a position to influence South Africa, do not act in time, violence on a large scale will become unavoidable.

41. The Prime Minister also attended the 40th anniversary of the United Nations. The Nassau Declaration on World Order adopted by Commonwealth leaders, contained a strong plea for adherence to international norms and principles and the strengthening of the United Nations. Support for the United Nations system is one of the corner-stones of our foreign policy. We are concerned at the growing threat to the multilateral institutions and the increasing tendency to resort to unilateral action. Government support international efforts to combat international terrorism, while recognising the rights to people under colonial occupation to use all means to attain their just objectives.

42. The Government deplore the fact that the Palestinian people continue to be denied their inalienable rights, including the right to an independent homeland of there own. Until this problem is tackled, West Asia will not see a basic lasting peace.

43. The Prime Minister paid official visits to the Russia, Egypt, France. Algeria, the USA, Bhutan, the UK, Cuba, the Netherlands, Vietnam, Japan, Oman and Maldives. Our traditionally close and friendly relations with the USSR have been further strengthened following the Prime Minister's discussions with Soviet leaders in Moscow. The visit to USA has significantly enlarged the content of our bilateral relations with the USA. The Prime Minister visited Dhaka to express our solidarity with the people of Bangladesh during the cyclone disaster and participated in the meeting of Heads of State and Government for launching the South Asian Association for Regional Cooperation. The Prime Minister addressed the UNESCO

during his visit to France. He addressed the annual conference of the I.L.O. in Geneva. We had the privilege to host visits by the Kings of Nepal and Bhutan, the Queen of the Netherlands, the Presidents of Mexico, Maldives, SWAPO, Sri Lanka, Tanzania, Indonesia and Pakistan, the Chairman of PLO, the Head of State of Ethiopia, and the Prime Ministers of Poland, Yugoslavia, Mauritius, Britain, New Zealand, People's Democratic Republic of Yemen and Trinidad and Tobago. The Crown Prince and Princess of Norway and the Pope also visited India.

44. Let me now outline some priority areas for 1986-87 and beyond.

45. The need of the hour is to enable the poor to better their lives. Science and technology have to support this fundamental objective. To this end, government are mounting technology missions in the following areas,

   (i) Drinking water for all villages;
   (ii) Eradication of illiteracy;
   (iii) Vaccination and immunisation of children;
   (iv) Production of oilseeds and manufacture of edible oils;
   (v) Improved communications.

46. In the course of the year more thrust areas will be identified with the object of using technology for improving productivity in industry and agriculture. In selected areas science and technology missions will endeavour to place India in the front rank of scientific activity.

47. A comprehensive agriculture policy will be formulated to promote an optimal cropping pattern, to improve water and soil management, to increase productivity of all crops to enhance the incomes of small and marginal farmers and to enlarge our hard-won self-sufficiency in foodgrains through production of oilseeds and pulses. A time-bound action plan will be drawn up to take the green revolution to the eastern region.

48. It is gratifying that a national consensus has emerged on treating water as a national resource. Government attach high priority to the evolution of a national water policy which would optimise the use of water for agricultural, industrial and other social needs.

49. Government have carried out an indepth analysis of our family planning programmes. Profiting from the experience of the past, an effective strategy for family planning is being worked out and will be announced shortly.

50. The focus on anti-poverty programmes will be sharpened. A new programme, which builds on the success achieved by the revised 20-Point Programme, is being formulated and will be announced soon. It will bring together all the elements, policies and programmes for a major national effort to tackle the problem of mass poverty in all its manifestations, specifically the problems of Scheduled Castes and Scheduled Tribes. Programme for the social economic educational and cultural development for the Scheduled castes, Scheduled Tribes and other weaker sections will be vigorously implemented. The implementation of the 15-Point Programme for thus development of minorities, with special emphasis on increasing economic opportunities will be closely monitored.

51. To rapidly increase employment to stimulate development in backward areas and to enhance the efficiency by Indian industry to serve the masses better, a more comprehensive framework of industrial policy is required. Many changes have already been made in our industrial policy which now reflects the new thrust for modernisaton, absorption of new technologies and promotion of indigenous technologies. High cost and inefficient industry hurts the poor, because it absorbs resources that are needed to create new jobs for them. A vast increase in the production

of goods and services for the masses in rural and urban areas is central to our strategy for he removal of poverty. This necessitates a fresh look at policies governing the scale of production, capacity utilisation, the role of indigenous technology, labour productivity, the detailed regulatory mechanism, thus future perspectives for small and medium industry and the existing administrative and management apparatus. Industry must serve the large masses.

52. To meet the challenge of maintaining a viable balance of payments position, a major thrust for promotion of exports and tourism is called for. Any slackening of progress on this front will jeopardies our overall development strategy. Government will take new initiatives in this critical area.

53. It is imperative to effect changes in our administrative system to bring it in tune with the objective of growth with social justice. Management in Government has to be imbued with a new social outlook. It is not a question of imposing something from above. The impetus to reform must come from within. The national community as a whole must debate issues affecting the working of the administrative system. A concrete agenda of action will thus emerge for implementation. Our watchwords must be improvement of efficiency and enforcement of accountability.

54. To safeguard the health and vitality of our basic political institutions, changes will be needed in our electoral and other laws. Government will hold wide ranging consultations with the leaders of political parts with a view to formulating concrete proposals to ensure cleaner public life.

55. The vision of a mighty Indian will be realised only in the actual lives of men and women who have strength of character, tenacity of purpose and commitment to

excellence. Government's strategy for human resource development aims at developing these qualities in our national life. The new education policy will be an integral part of this strategy. It will aim at the physical, intellectual, cultural and moral development of society in a harmonious fashion.

56. It is not enough to state objectives. A national mobilisation is essential to ensure that the resources required to implement the education policy are forthcoming. Even more important is the involvement of the youth, students, teachers, the intelligentsia, workers and farmers in giving a new direction to the national effort in this area. Education has to be transformed from an activity in the classroom to a social process for building the India of our dreams. It has to be integrated more closely both with production and our commitment to conserve and enhance our cultural heritage to make us proud to be Indian.

57. The years ahead are years of challenge. Government have take a number of measures to accelerate growth, to modernise the economy and to give new content to our programmes for achieving social justice. It is imperative to impart a sense of urgency to the task of implementation.

58. Much has been achieved this past year, and the hopes and expectations of our people are high. As their representatives, you have the onerous duty to fulfill their aspirations. Above all, people's representatives and organisations of all political persuasions should work together to strengthen the secular and democratic foundations of our society. The forces of violence and fanaticism have to be fought. The economic capabilities we have built up since independence have brought us to a point where determined and concerted efforts to take us forward and to remove poverty are feasible. Now is the time it ensure greater political cohesion so that the

battle against poverty and backwardness can be won. I wish you all success in the tasks ahead.

Jai hind.

Now let us examine how this address is covered by newsmen. The copy of this speech was made available to all correspondents when the President began to read it.

Given is the report of the speech published in the Times of India, New Delhi :

Isolate terrorists, says President

The times of India news service

New Delhi, February 20. The President in his traditional address to the joint session of Parliament outlining the agenda of the government today pointed to the "inevitability of hard decisions without which forward movement will to be possible."

The address promised a comprehensive agriculture plan to promote an optimal cropping pattern, a more effective strategy for family planning and sharpening of the anti-poverty programme.

Technology missions will be mounted to ensure drinking water for all villages, eradication of illiteracy, immunisation, oil-seeds production and improved communications.

New initiatives will be made for promotion of exports and tourism with a view to maintaining a viable balance of payments position.

There will be wide ranging discussions to formulate concrete proposals for changing electoral and other laws. Administrative reforms calculated to improve efficiency and enforce accountability will be introduced.

The joint session, with its usual ceremonial, was still shorn off the excitement and rapture which featured in the function only a year ago. Most non-Congress groups stayed away as announced leaving gaps in rows.

Not since 1973 have so many groups joined in such a boycott. Even Congress members did-not find any cause to cheer during the entire reading of the address. They thumped the desks only at the end as the president resumed his seat.

There was a moment so suspense when the President paused at the beginning. It was then noticed he was looking for his reading glass.

At the same time, the President' address made it plain that "hard decisions" were inevitable in the pursuit of self-reliance, economic independence and eradication of poverty.

"Sooner or later we have to face the realities of the situation. No one should be under the delusion that growth, social justice, price stability and self-reliance, Are achievable without efficiency, discipline and sharing of burdens," Mr. Zail Singh said.

The President began his speech with a reference to the "triumph of democratic process over terrorism in Punjab"- and held that the supreme task now was to isolate those resorting to violence.

He reiterated the government commitment to the fullest implementation of the Punjab and Assam accord.

He acknowledged that communalism continued to pose a serious threat to national unity. "It is being reinforced by religious fundamentalism and fanaticism. The reconstituted National Integration Council will have to act decisively and systematically to strengthen secularism," he said.

He recalled the policies and programmes of the government outlined in his address last year and claimed "these have been fulfilled in a substantial measure". He cited the anti-defection law, enunciation of a new national education policy, establishment of a central Ganga authority, creation of a wasteland development board as cases in point.

As for trends in economy, agriculture made steady progress with grain stocks going up nearly 15 per cent. He described the investment climate as buoyant. Power generation, fertilizer production, steel output have all gone up.

Tax Collection: He said tax collections have been buoyant, belying gloomy forebodings. The collection of direct taxes is up by about 23 per cent compared to the corresponding period last year indirect tax collection has increased by 22 per cent which is the highest in the last decade.

Looking for Facts

Interpretative reporting, as the phrase suggests, combines facts with interpretation. It delves into reasons and meanings of a development. It is the interpretative reporter's task to give the information alongwith an interpretation of its significance. In doing so he uses his knowledge and experience to give the reader an idea of the background of an event and explain the consequences it could led to. Besides his own knowledge and research in the subject, he often has to rely on the opinions of specialists to do a good job.

In the USA, thus first important inputs to interpretative reporting was provided by World War-I. Curtis D. MacDongall writes in his book Interpretation Reporting that when the First World War broke out, most Americans were taken by surprise. They were utterly unable to explain its causes. This led to changes in the style of reporting. The result was that when in 1939 the Second World War began, an overwhelming majority of the Americans expected it or at least knew it was possible.

MacDongall says that a successful journalist should be more than a thoroughly trained journeyman. With his reading of history, economics, sociology, political science and other academic subjects, an interpretative reporter is aware of the fact that a news item is not an isolated incident, but an inevitable link to a chain of important events. An interpretative reporter cannot succeed if he is hampered by prejudices and stereotyped attitudes, which would bias his perception of human affairs.

Interpretative reporting thus goes behind the news, brings out the hidden significance of an event and separates truth from falsehood. The biennial elections to the Rajya Sabha took place in July. The interpretative reporter would give the reader the breakup of the results and acquaint him with he impact they would have on the various political parties and on the composition of the upper House. He would, for instance, inform the reader that the Congress Party lost its majority in the Rajya Sabha, following the elections and that the Bhartiya Janata Party emerged as the main opposition, pushing the Janata Dal to third place. He will then explain the effect it would have on the working of the Rajya Sabha and on political party affairs generally.

The election of the new President of India took place in July. The interpretative reporter would not only convey the bare news of the victory of Dr. Shankar Dayal Sharma but analyse the reasons behind it and reflect on the consequences of his victory for the future of the Congress and opposition parties.

Making News

Deeply rooted in American journalism is the notion of the journalistic reporter. Reporters are trained in the journalistic method which gives them the tools and wherewithal to cover almost nay situation they may confront. Essentially journalistic training means knowing how to gather the news—how to sift through documents, do background research, interview sources, and so on-and how to write it using the usual news and feature forms employed by newspapers and broadcast outlets. In the midst of this seemingly routinised task, however, come all kinds of ethical issues (tactical decisions) including "checkbook journalism," fabrication of sources, false identification, lying. Some of these issues, being topical, come and go. But many are recurrent.

Different Sides

As with news-gathering methods and writing methods, competent reporters and editors are expected to handle tactical or ethical dilemmas. But do these problems require precise and differing tactics for different situations, or responses based on consistent and universal standards? While such questions are regarded as worthy of debate and discussion, most reporters believe that they have somehow internalized professional values, and competencies that will help them resolve any problems that may occur.

We come now to discuss a very real and important everyday convert of journalists: reportorial tactics, journalistic ways and means of gathering and writing stories. Should these tactics be situational and relative; should they be, as Professor Dennis will argue later, consistent and universal? we maintain that they are situational and relative; even more, we insist that they should or ought to be situational and relative. This position, of course, gets us into the realm of ethics.

Opposing my view, however, is a considerable theoretical tradition in this country, even if it fails to manifest itself in common practice. It is safe to say that an accepted truth in American journalism is that journalists should be consistent in their methods and their actions: that they should all subscribe to universal standards, and should, if they are responsible and "Professional," have a profound respect for predictable an consistent practice. Consistency and predictability, we are led to believe, are foundation stones of professionalism.

Unpredictability is associated, on the other hand, with amateurism, with inconsistency and relativity, which are seen by many as deleterious to journalism, harmful to the journalist, and frustrating to the audience. We would maintain just the opposite: that consistency in journalism—the journalist always using the same tactics and dealing with the elements of the story in the same way—makes for a deadly dull journalism, keeps the individual journalist from full self -realization, and prevents the audience from being exposed to the multifaceted, rich, and diversified aspects of similar (but different) stories.

Perhaps it is more comfortable and satisfying for journalists to have hard-and-fast rules as to tactics of reporting. Most printed codes of ethics fail because they present absolute and consistent rules or standards (or because they are so fuzzily written that they, in essence, say nothing meaningful). But, perhaps, the fact that they fail is paradoxically a good thing—for their failure assures that tactical situationalism and relativism will thrive in the absence of absolute ethical codes.

Ethics, of course, is very closely related to the subject of journalistic tactics. One cannot really separate them. Should I lie, either to get a story or while, telling the story to my readers or listeners? Should I reveal the source of certain statements or quotes which I use in my story? Should I give my readers or listeners all of the information which I have collected and verified?

These are just a sampling of questions that are both ethical and tactical. I might rephrase them thus:

- Should I ever lie as a reporter?
- Should I always reveal my sources? Or never reveal them?
- Should I tell the whole truth (as much of it as I have verified) to my audience?

Here we have introduced the possibility of tactical consistency of absoluteness. Such consistency has a notable appeal, If I am going to reveal the source in one case, why should I not reveal all sources? If I am going to lie in one case, why not in all? If I am going to withhold part of a story in one case, what would be wrong with withholding parts from any story?

Let me give an example of each of the two tactical positions.

1. *Absolute:* always identify victims of all crimes.
2. Relativistic identify victims in some crimes but not in others.

The first tactic (the absolute) does, indeed, simplify the journalist's decision making. If this tactic is accepted all that must be done is to identify all victims—juveniles, the mentally ill, rape victims, and so on. The second tactic (the situational) is more difficult because it forces the reporter to discriminate, to think. The reporter must see distinctions, think about consequences; is short, the reporter must decide that it is not only all right but good journalism to make exceptions—to have double standards, if you will.

The Distinctions

The reporter who is situational recognises that there is a difference, and a very important one, between a rape victim, for example, and a murder victim. Naming a rape victim can bring mental and emotional harm to the victim: naming a murder victim cannot harm the victim at all. The thinking reporter understands that the naming of a nine-year-old boy for shooting his father is quite different (in psychological, if not in legal, terms) than the naming of a 39 year-old adult for shooting his father.

The reporter believes that it is his duty to make certain editorial decisions impinging on what is and is not published. After all, he reasons, editorial decision is the nature of journalism: selection is made to some degree-among facts in every story that is written.

Reporter must play this tactical game rather loosely: that he must not strive for consistency in tactics: that he must consider the specific situation or circumstance. In short, the reporter (to be effective and in many cases to be ethical, too) must specifically determine not to be absolute and consistent, but rather to be situational and relative.

Case: A reporter cannot subscribe to a tactic of always revealing his source—even if he does, indeed, maintain that the people have a right to know. In some cases, to reveal sources would be counter productive as well as unethical. For example, the journalist may get information from a source who would be in great physical danger if his identity were know. The reporter not only wants to keep the source operative for another day, but also to avoid endangering his life. In other, similar cases, the reporter might want to keep his source from losing his job.

Case: A reporter is writing a rape story. He has the name of the person arrested on suspicion of committing the rape. He also has ascertained the name of the rape victim. He decides not to use the victim's name, although he does not hesitate to use the suspected rapist's name, although he does not hesitate to use the suspected rapist's name. Inconsistent? Yes. He is, in effect, withholding information from the reader. At the same time he is providing the name of another person connected with the case—even though this person may not have committed the rape. He feels no qualms about this procedure, even though it is inconsistent, reasoning that in this particular case it is tactically prudent to do as he has done. He justifies withholding verified information from the reader on ethical grounds—on a consideration of possible consequences to the victim.

The reporter in the above case is inconsistent. And he certainly does not subscribe to a "universal" tactic. A universal tactic in reporting would be: The reporter is obligated to report all the facts that he has, all that he has verified, and all that are pertinent to the story. In this rape story, certainly the name of the rape victim is pertinent to the story, as we will be told by our absolutist reporter. After all, the reporter has found out who the woman is: therefore should not the name be given—especially since the name of the rape suspect has been used?

Let us reply to the above question with another question: Why should the reporter use the victim's name? The reporter is wise to subscribe to relativistic tactics, to play the story the way he wants to play it in that particular case—after consideration of possible consequences. Why should the reporter always name names? Why should the reporter subscribe to the same tactics in every story? Straight jacketing oneself does not ,assure better reportage by the reporter. In fact, a relativistic or situational tactical program in reporting is what is called for. Consider the importance of the story. Consider each story. Consider consequences or implications for certain persons in the story (e.g., the rape victim in the example above).

Various Aspects

It may well be that when a reporter considers the importance to the public of a particular story, there will be a realisation that "usual tactics must be modified or changed." The reporter may decide that the story is important enough, for example, to steal files (or at least to make copies of papers and return the files). The reporter may even feel that in a particular case there is justification to pose as someone else. It may be that the reporter will decide to eavesdrop on conversations and report what he overhears, using or perhaps not using the names of those who said the things he is divulging. The reporter might decide to "bug" a room or wiretap a telephone in order to get some very important enough, for example, to steal files (or at least to make copies of papers and return the files).

The reporter may even feel that in a particular case there is justification to pose as someone else. It may be that the reporter will decide to eavesdrop on conversations and report what he overhears, using or perhaps not using the names of those who said the things he is divulging. The reporter might decide to "bug" a room or wiretap a telephone in order to get some very important information which he believes the public should know. The reporter might decide, in order to get some much-needed information, to tell a source that he knows certain things or that he has heard certain things from someone else (which he really has not heard) in order to get a response. The reporter might decide to make up quotes and drop them into a story so as to prompt someone connected with the story-someone he wants to make a statement— to come forward to refute or to enlarge on the "speculated" or fabricated quotes.

Now, we can justify these tactics by resorting to the "ends justifies the means" argument. We can say that we are thinking of the public, and the public's right to know. How can the public know unless we break through the barriers of secrecy with our situational tactics? So, journalists must resort to these tactics from time to time in order to do their job, to live up to their responsibilities.

We can justify relativistic or situation tactics by contending that they are more ethical; we can also justify them instrumentally or pragmatically by saying that they are needed to accomplish our ends. If we need a further rationale for inconsistency in journalistic practice, we can always fall back on press freedom in its editorial self-determinism sense. In other words, it is the right of a newspaper reporter to be inconsistent; if he wants to use a victim's name—(or any name) in one story and not in another, that is his right.

If the reporter wants to reveal the source of a quote in one story and not in another, that is his right. In fact, if the reporter wants to reveal the source of a quotation in one part of a story and make all the other quotes in the same story anonymous, that is his right.

After all, why should the reporter be consistent or use universal tactics? Even though there may not be any evidential basis for the belief, the reporter can contend that journalistic consistency is the "hobgoblin of little minds." Journalism, it seems to the relativistic reporter, is riddled with instances of inconsistency, most of which are considered valid journalistic practices. Here are just a few:

Using the lead in one story, but not in another.

Using indirect quotations only in one story, and using direct quotations or a mixture of indirect and direct quotes in another.

Giving the addresses of persons in one story, and omitting addresses in another.

Going directly to persons for information in one story, while going to someone for second hand information in another or using old information form the files.

Giving certain personal data (such as age, race, occupation) about some persons in some stories but not about other persons.

A list of inconsistent tactics could be extended easily. What is the alternative to these inconsistent tactics? Consistent and universal tactics, we are told. The intelligent and dedicated reporter can only scoff at such an alternative, seeing it as a definite voluntary placement of the reporter in a straight jacket with little chance to achieve a primary goal of journalism: obtaining the story.

The preceding discussion of news-gathering tactics defends the status quo in American journalism. Reporters do use relative and situational methods when gathering the news. However, there are many agreed-upon general standards and practices. These practical tactics for getting information are undergirded by ethical judgements that are self-contained, based mainly on the immediate situation rather than considered against the backdrop of long experience with similar cases. There is more than a slight temptation in reinvent the wheel with each ethical dilemma that arises.

That, in our opinion, summarizes one of the most serious problems in journalistic practice today—a thoughtless, seat-of-the-pants approach to reporting that eschews planning and thinking. It is the journalism of intuition. "Do what intuition tells you; apply common sense to the situation are accepted axiom. On the face of it this doesn't sound so bad, but consider the following:

A reporter for NBC News is asked how he knows when he has enough information to "go" with a story. "How," he was asked, "can" you be sure that your information is complete, that you are not missing major sources that would turn a story completely around, maybe with a different interpretation altogether?" The reporter replied, "You just know. There is, "he added, "no answer, things just click into place an it seems right." An editor for a metropolitan daily newspaper is asked by a Harvard Law professor how far he would go to get a story. "Would you lie? Would you steal?" Would you disguise your identity?" The editor thought for a moment, then responded, "Yes, under some conditions, I'd probably do all of those things even though I might personally find some of them reprehensible." The professor wanted to know, "How" do you make your decision; on what theory do you base your actions?" And the editor answered, "I have no theory, I just do what I think is right."

We would not accept this kind of thinking from other professional persons (say, doctors, lawyers, or architects) whom we expect to have standards, codes and a systematic basis for their decisions. We do accept it from journalists perhaps because we have no choice or because they convince us that news is unpredictable, a matter of timing that requires on-the-spot decisions governed solely by the facts of a particular situation. "You simply can't quantify these things," goes the incantation.

There is a prevailing myth in American journalism that planning news coverage runs counter to freedom of the press. Planning is thought to be dull and routine, not spontaneous and timely. It is further said that writers are creative persons who, if left to their own devices, will produce a better kind of journalism. And God forbid that journalists should have hypotheses. A hypothesis, which is an assumption that becomes an organizing principle, is thought to encourage bias and run counter to journalistic objectivity. There is also a prevailing view among many journalists that news really defies definition.

Working Theories

This kind of "every day a new beginning" theme in many newsrooms, the operational rule of the status quo, needs rethinking. While it certainly is not possible to always predict with scientific certainty what will happen on a given day, journalism is really much more routinized than most of its practitioners know or will admit. They may not know it because American journalism is insulated and parochial. Many journalists have little work-experience outside of their present assignments; few belong to national organizations where they come into contact with their journalists; few subscribe to professional publications or make any effort to keep up with the literature of their systematic research that gives us data about patterns and practices across many journalistic organisations.

Individual journalists may know their own organization intimately, but they often have little knowledge about the field generally. This situation is not unusual because many professionals are so busy doing their jobs that they have little time to think about them or to make comparisons with their colleagues in other places. For a field that is supposed to demand so much creative calibration, journalism is remarkably predictable, routinized, even stodgy. Send any five reporters to cover a city council story and you can predict with almost considerably certainty what they will write. Why? Because the coverage of public affairs, in particular, has been standardized. There is much agreement about the form and format of stories, about what essential facts should be included, and about what most editors will accept. Reporters know what is expected of them and generally they do it.

Of course there are stores that are more complex than routine meetings, but even with these the traditional methods of news gathering pretty much dictate what will eventually appear. And if this were not enough, we have "rewards and punishments" built into the journalistic system to guarantee conformity. At a positive level there are prizes (such as the Pulitzers) that honour imaginative work within the framework of traditional journalism. Journalism schools help out by promoting conventional approaches to news gathering through courses and books.

There is in American journalism a serious perceptual conflict. Journalist on the one hand believe that their work is unpredictable, situational, and relative. Communications researchers say this is not true, that reporting is not nearly as uncertain as practitioners think. In a sense both are right. While there may be great similarity in work patterns and output from day to day, journalist still think tat there is little formal guidance and there is considerable latitude for individual decision making.

They say that with regard to ethics, they live in a conceptual thicket which requires instant decisions of convenience if not conviction. They tend to justify what they do without worrying whether their choices about revealing sources or lying are consistent with what they did before. Scholars, on the other hand, because they are trained to look for patterns of organizational and individual activity, can see a method whether haphazard or well-though-out- in journalistic work just as they do in fire-fighters or farmers. The way the news paper or broadcast station is organized, the selecting of personnel, their training and socialization, all have a hand in shaping the news.

Interestingly enough, it is the once-similar (and now quite different) practices of journalists and social scientist that explain some of this discrepancy. As Philip Meyer, well known for his work in precision journalism and now a professor at the University of North Carolina, has written.

> "Social scientist used to be more like journalist. They relied on observation and interpretation, collecting the observations from public records, from interviews, from direct participation, and then spinning out the interpretations. Like many journalist they cheerfully accepted the American folk wisdom ... that anyone with "a little common sense and a few facts can come up at once with the correct answer on any subject".

But something changed. First with the development of inferential statistics and later with the advent of computers, social scientist no longer worked like journalist. Instead they used powerful quantitative tools to deal with unwieldy and massive data. Now, says Meyer, social scientist are doing "what we journalists like to think we are best at: finding fact, inferring causes, pointing to ways to correct social problems, and evaluating the effects of such correction". In short, he charge that journalism is being left behind because it lacks a systematic approach to news gathering.

The point of course, is that with an affective strategy for gathering information which systematically considers possible sources and mines them with care brings a far richer yield than old-fashioned, impressionistic reporting. It is now possible to determine how much information from what sources will be adequate-when enough information has been assembled and when writing can begin. This statement does not mean that journalists should be exactly like social scientist. Press people have greater time pressures and are more concerned about immediacy.

It is one thing to develop a strategy for news coverage that list the tactics to be employed, another to actually do it. No situation is ever perfect and no prearranged rules ever work in all situations. For this reason some journalist throw out the rules altogether and make expedient decisions. It is threatening to ask: Is the information complete? Have I mined all possible (and reasonable) sources? Is the evidence strong enough to warrant the conclusion actual or implied? Are various interpretations and leaps in logic justified?" If such questions could have been avoided in the past, such is no longer the case.

Way of Working

Systematic news gathering tactics are not simply a theory for journalism schools to trumpet, but something being demanded by the rests of society. One of the most compelling calls comes in the courts. Frequently in libel suits news organizations must offer evidence that the story is not marred by "knowing falsehood" or "reckless disregard" of the truth.

How is this honesty of intent determined?" By showing that reasonable efforts, consistent with national news gathering standards, were employed. If they were not and the paper admits it, there is the possibility for a whopping libel judgement. Sloppy reporting is expensive. Of equal or grater importance is the fear that journalist will not have the credibility they need and deserve unless their methods are respected by the audience.

People who argue against ethical standards or moral imperatives in news gathering tactics usually suggest that each case is so different that rules will strait jacket the reporter. They add that general guidelines are so vague that they are meaningless. I disagree. We need a theory of journalistic ethics, a fundamental framework for reporters to base their decisions on. This framework requires general understanding about ethical behaviour, whether in reporting or everyday life. It means having a clear notion about how specific journalistic dilemmas ought to be handled. This general ethical understanding does not mean that rules cannot be modified or tempered to meet particular situations. We need a thoughtful policy that serves as a conscience for individual journalist and their organizations.

Such a policy should spell out standards of conduct for information gathering. One minimal standard, we think, is that journalist should obey the law. In most instances this principle means they should not lie, steal, or cheat. They should not wiretap or break into places not otherwise open to them. In rare instances, a right-thinking reporter may want to be civilly disobedient, to deliberately break the law as a matter of principle because it will lead to a greater social good. In all instances where ethical questions arise, if there is not a clear answer, reporters should consider alternatives, not simply rush to judgement with the easiest solution. If the decision runs counter to conventional wisdom and standard ethical codes, there ought to be a clean and compelling rationale for making it.

In most instances it is regarded as ethical to reveal one's sources in a news story. This strengthens the credibility of the story and ties information to attributed sources. If revealing names will put sources in great danger or make them reluctant to talk, a different decision may be appropriate. If it is determined that a source benefit, clearly agreed upon and understood by the reporter's supervising editors os that they can defend the actin later. And the reporter, if summoned by the courts, must be ready to go to jail if it comes to that.

The problem today is that many reporters do not have solid ethical training and do not have the kind of foundation necessary of ethical decision making. Again, constancy is terribly important both for accountability to one's bosses and perhaps ultimately to the courts.

Journalists have gotten in trouble for being inconsistent in recent years with regard to fair-trial-free Press codes. The press was a signatory to such codes, which list tactical guidelines for covering criminal proceedings from initial investigations of crimes to court judgements. Reporters generally agree to withhold some information in the interest of not prejudicing a jury and assuring the defendant of a fair trail. This is a social compact between the press and the legal system. When the press violates this agreement or decides onto to abide by a particular provision of the code, there ought to be a good reason (beyond curiosity seeking or pandering) to justify its action. If not, reporters and editors may have to answer in court. This happened in 1981 in a notable case in the state of Washington where a newspaper was held accountable for violation of the fair-trail-free-press code.

And this example indicates, it is always possible to substitute a "greater social good" argument or a "humanitarian" argument to explain why an individual journalist or publication may deviate from an accepted rule. We believe such exceptions should be justified on the basis of devotion to the public interest, rather than petty or self-serving reasons.

Similarly it is quite appropriate to reconsider rules the are regarded as journalistic conventions or articles of faith. Printing he names of persons accused of rape has been mentioned. This practice would seem potentially unfair both to victim and accused.

The press usually prints the name of the accused. But is it really necessary? The reasons for printing names has to do with keeping the courts open so the they do not become secret tribunal. Thus, we know who is being tried, for what, and why. But as long as the courts are open to the press and to spectators, why not defer printing this material until the trail is over? No great social good is done by heralding names of victims or accused persons in advance of trial with some obscure exceptions.

Some newspapers have abandoned the practice of printing names of persons in civil litigation cases where the truly important story is the effect of the decision on similar cases in the future. If one person is suing another to establish a legal principle and if revealing names would prove embarrassing, it may serve no purpose to do so. Some wise editors are changing their policy in this area.

Consistent and universal standards of reporting with necessary escape clauses for unusual or unique situations will do much to enhance journalistic practice in America. Such standards, if widely known land the press can virtually guarantee this with adequate coverage) will do much to strengthen public confidence in the fairness and completeness of reporting. It will also have real advantages of individual newspapers and broadcast stations in an increasingly litigious society. Haphazard, thoughtless conduct that meets no standard but blunders along willy-nilly is neither appreciated nor rewarded by the courts. One of the most effective ways to put the journalistic house in order is to establish coherent policies and consistent practices. This the essence of professionalism performance and distinguishes competent from rank amateurism.

11

Art of Reporting

The news is the timely report of events, facts, and opinions and interests a significant number of people. It is a new piece of information about a significant and recent event that affects the audience and is of interest to them. The definition of a news item is dependent on:

(a) the size of the community,

(b) the periodicity of the publication,

(c) the social character and economic base of the community,

(d) the focus of attention of community.

Jhon Bogart pointed out that unusual events fall under the purview of the news. Later, Joseph Pulitzer, publisher of New York World defined news as "original, distinctive, dramatic, romantic, thrilling, unique, curious, quaint, humorous, odd and apt-to-be-talked about". Walter William, the founder of the first school of Journalism, defined news as, "News in its broadest sense, is that which is of interest to the readers-the public....."

The former-managing editor of the New York Times said that the news was "..... anything you can find out today that you didn't know before."

Thus, the news is Perishable; of interest to a large number of people; of unusual events and happenings; what is new to the public; an event put forward by a reporter.

Hard News and Soft News : These are the two main categories in which the news is mainly divided.

Hard News is mostly event-centered. It is a narration of an event. The Hard news items are centered on, "what, when, where and why".

No doubt, the major thrust of a daily newspaper is the hard news. The main task of the dailies is to provide information to the readers. Mere accounts of events however do not satisfy the readers. They would like to enter beneath the upper crust of hard news. This type of news is called soft news. Thus, soft news goes beyond what has happened. It analyses, interprets and draws logical conclusions. It is becoming a very important segment of the daily newspaper.

Determining Factors

Timeliness : News must be timely and new. It loses interest if it is already known.

Nearness : People are more interested in what happens under their nose. They are more concerned in the occurrence of an immediate impact on them.

Conflict : People gather in a street if and when there is a fight. Conflicts of all kinds are part of life and make good copy.

Prominence : What happens to important persons makes news. The value of the news increases with the prominence of the person involved. What the prominent people say, is also grist for a reporter's mill, particularly if they make some announcements which have an impact on the common people.

Government Action : The passing of a law or other orders concerning general people, cabinet meetings, parliament and assembly sessions, notifications about new rules and regulations are news worthy.

Development Projects and Issues : This is not news about government action, activities, though sometimes it will also qualify to be covered. The intention of a high-yield variety rice and its success in changing the lifestyle of a community will be of interest to people who will financially benefit from it.

Weather and Sports : Both the weather and sports have great news value. Also entire page is devoted to sports in many newspapers.

Follow-up : The news item become very interesting for the general public when the issues are followed and updated. It is important to remember that follow-up of news events will keep the interest of the readers alive.

News Values : News values differ from community to community, country to country. News values are also different for developing and developed countries. For the industrialized and individualised societies of developed countries, communally provocative speeches and incidents may be reported word for word, blow by blow. But the same treatment would be suicidal in a developing country.

One should take all possible care in reporting such developments keeping in mind the volatile nature of the audience and the reach of one's publication. One must follow some journalistic ethics and at times some self-censorship. Freedom of the press is not a licence to damage or destroy any one's reputation.

Basic Traits

Accuracy : Accuracy is basic to any news item. When you fail in accuracy, you lose credibility. Cross check your facts and information. Check figures, names and facts. Make sure that the meaning is not changed and the statements are not quoted out of context. Exclude rumours or gossip from your report.

Balance : To be balanced in reporting, is as important as being accurate. While writing about a controversy, both sides of the story should be given. A story may appear to be 'imbalanced' and thus biased, if it has too much of government views, or tends to give too much of foreign news which has little relevance to readers.

Objectivity : Your opinion should not be mixed in the story. Report only facts and other peoples opinions. You should be a disinterested observer, reporting events without taking sides.

Clarity : Your introductory sentence should be short and in active voice to the maximum extent possible. The ideal length of each para may be 3-4 lines containing one-to-three small sentences to facilitate easy comprehension.

Impact : Whenever you do a news report, consider the impact your story should have. Will it induce some changes somewhere for the better? Develop a "nose for news", particularly news that will make an impact.

News Sources : A reporter, to be successful, should have a variety of reliable and highly placed contacts. There are some of the useful 'sources' for his information. Among the news sources, some are available to all reporters, such as public meetings, monitoring of radio and television programmes, press conferences, news briefing, seminars and other functions. But the contacts are sources of exclusive information for the reporter. They may be in the government, public or private sector business or just anywhere. Some of the contacts may like to be quoted for the story as it gives them publicity.

In case of a critical story, they may not risk their neck. In that case, the story may have to be distributed to 'sources' only. It is the responsibility of a reporter to ensure the truthfulness of a report. In such cases, it will be advisable to keep some documents or audio tape to prove your story.

In the business of collecting the news, particularly of critical and investigative nature confrontation with the government is inevitable. A journalist chronicles daily events, places facts before the public, and tries to communicate that he considers truth. This may not suit the politician all the time, hence confrontation may occur. In case, a confrontation becomes inevitable, a reporter should face it. He should also treat his sources as 'sacred'. There may be pressure on the journalist from the government and the judiciary at times to disclose the sources. Protecting one's source is a cardinal principle of journalism.

News Reporting

Here is a description about news reporting and the main components of a news report-the body and the lead.

The Lead : The lead should contain the essence of the story. It should give the reader an idea of what the story is about and help the copy desk to pick a suitable headline for the story. A good lead should arouse the reader's curiosity and force him on to read the rest of the story. It should be precise and made up of short, simple sentences. The lead should answer the five W's-Who, What, Where, When and why and How.

The Body : While the lead should arouse the reader's interest, the body should sustain it. The body should flow smoothly and logically from the lead. The body should be as complete and as tight as possible and should provide all the relevant information within the shortest space possible. The essence of good journalistic writing is brevity and simplicity. Do not use a complex or long word where a short word would do.

Types of Reporting

Objective Reporting : A reporter is essentially a short story teller and he should tell the story in an objective and truthful manner, without lacing it with personal opinions or subjective comments. He should be fair and impartial and present both sides of the story. Complete objectivity is a mere concept. The reporter is a human being and he has certain ideas, feelings, attitudes, opinions and prejudices. However, a good reporter should try to rise above them and tell the facts as he has collected them in his search for truth. Objective reporting is, of course, not synonymous with dullness. It means fair and impartial reporting that is free from personal bias or prejudice.

Interpretative Reporting : It combines facts with interpretation. It delves into reasons and meanings of a development. His the interpretative reporter's task to give the information along with an interpretation of its significance. In doing so he uses his knowledge and experience to give the reader an idea of the background of an event and explain the consequences it could led to. Besides his own knowledge and research in the subject, he often has to rely on the opinions of specialists to do a good job. Interpretative reporting goes behind the news, brings out the hidden significance of an event and separates truth from falsehood.

Investigative Reporting : It is difficult to define the term 'investigative' journalism. In one way, of course, investigative journalism is a redundant concept, since all stories require some kind of investigation on the part of the reporter. However, the investigative reporter is expected to dig deeply beyond the facts stated in the hard news. Though we may face difficulty in defining the term, we can not ignore the concept of investigative journalism. Investigative reporting has made great leaps in western countries. In India, it is still in its infancy.

Attempts at investigative reporting, to quote one eminent Indian editor, arc like drilling for oil. A fair amount of wastage of effort has to be taken for granted. But when the oil is discovered and becomes marketable, the sense of achievement is usually more than in any other sector of journalistic enterprise. In India, investigative reporting started making a mark after the end of internal emergency in 1977. With governments becoming increasingly secretive and corruption spreading its tentacles far and wide, the need for investigative reporting can not be over emphasized.

Investigative reporting requires hard and sustained work. The investigative reporter should be combination of a crusader, super detective and blood bound and should have the necessary time and finance to carry out his work. The best thing of Investigative Reporting is that which keeps the public interest in mind. It may highlight an injustice, expose corrupt practices or unmask dishonest politicians and bureaucrats.

But experience shows that unless an investigative reporter or a crusading reporter gets the support of the judiciary, the executive or the legislative, can not bring his reports to logical ends.

Crime Reporting : There is tremendous public interest in crime stories and no newspaper can afford to ignore them without damage to its circulation and credibility. Crime is a part of life and it is newspaper's duty to inform the readers of what crimes are going on in their city, state or country.

Crime reporting is a highly responsible and specialised job. The reporter should not only have the ability to shift the grain from the chaff, and the truth from lies, he should also have good contacts in the police and other departments of the administration as well as working knowledge of the penal codes and law on libel and other relevant matters. Besides, he must observe a code of honour. He should not suppress news of public interest. Nor should he seek to settle personal scores with police officers or lawyers or judges. And he must be careful that in the course of this work, he doesn't necessarily invade a citizen's privacy. The crime reporter must never violate standards of decency and good taste.

Crime as News : There are several types of crime news-murders, fires, accidents, burglaries, fraud, blackmail, kidnapping etc.

Fires : The reporter must get his facts correct about the essential elements of a fire story-the number of persons killed or injured, the extent of damage, to property, the loss of valuables. He should question eye-witnesses about any act of bravery or cowardice. All these are essential ingredients of a fire story.

Homicides : In cases of a major murder, the reporter should rush to the scene as soon as possible and gather all the relevant facts. Their dependence on police information often hampers their search for truth. In reporting dowry deaths or alleged dowry deaths, the reporter should refrain from levelling uncorroborated statements by one party or the other.

Accidents : Most accidents are reported on the basis of police bulletins or information supplied by police spokesmen. However, wherever possible the crime reporter must rush to the scene of a major accident to give authenticity to his story.

Major Traits

A journalist must possess and uphold certain noble qualities in order to be professional. Integrity of character, commitment to the truth and a reasoning power of mind are essential to any reporter. These qualities also contribute to the credibility of the reporting organization. Besides, a journalist has to be truly responsible. A journalist is responsible to the audience as much as to the news organization. Again a journalist is always responsible to the sources who reveal information. A reporter must also have a healthy respect for news values.

Role of a Reporter

It is said that a reporter is both eyes and ears of a news organization. It is not possible to strictly prescribe qualifications which a good reporter must possess. However, novice reporters must train themselves informally for the job so that they would be able to discharge their responsibilities with confidence, courage and competence. To be a successful reporter and to accomplish your job competently, you must be able to perceive, predict, calculate and plan your action appropriately in anticipation of a news event.

Chief Traits

A Nose for News : The reporter is the most important functionary of a newspaper. So one must know what constitutes news in order to be able to gather news. A reporter's job of discovering the news has been simplified in one, way and rendered difficult in another sense, in this age of information. While there are the usual press notes on which news reports can be based, there are other sources of information on a variety-of news event. But quite often, most of the material before a news reporter may just be a publicity matter. Therefore, as a reporter, one must check the material and squeeze the news that would interest one's reader. A sharp sense of observation may also help one to gather amusing sidelights of interest to one's readers. This alertness will help one to discover contradictions and problems.

Outgoing Nature : Professional journalists are never arm chair writers. Introverts normally make poor reporters. Reporters have to move about meeting people, making their acquaintance and winning their confidence. This would help them to establish contacts, which in turn helps in writing well-investigated reports. This is the era of investigative reporting and readers are keenly interested to know what is going on behind the scenes. To get that kind of stories, one has no alternative but to be outgoing. One has to develop an affable temperament and an easy-going nature.

Ability to Establish Contacts and Develop Sources : An outgoing nature is the basic quality to establish contact and develop sources. You must have the ability to win the confidence and respect of those who may be potential sources of news. During the course of your regular duties, people may voluntarily offer you information.

Alternatively, this might not be the case when you are working on an investigative story. People may hesitate to talk on sensitive matters. They may like to reveal, yet are afraid to in case it were to affect them adversely. It may be quite difficult to win their trust. While you are establishing contact, there may be some among them who may want to plant information on you to serve their vested interests. Such information may consist of half-truths and even lies. So, you must have other independent contacts through whom you can verify the information. What matters is the alertness and ability to pursue your sources to get the right lead.

Ability to be an Unprejudiced Observer : The reporter must be an unprejudiced observer of events, one who presents the facts to the reader in a balanced, objective manner. It has been said that reporters mix comment with fact and so their reports are quite subjective. The reporters should not allow personal opinions at any place in the copy. One must be able to throw light on unclear aspects if any, of the news event. At the same time, the news reporter must endeavour to write a report which is only a statement of facts.

Thus, the first thing is to source your copy properly, to assure the reader that what you are passing on as news, is not your opinion. Even when you are not able to quote the sources, you must ensure that the story is balanced, by giving adequate coverage to all the sides of the subject. You should also ensure that the information you are presenting is true, which can be done by counter checking.

But remaining an unprejudiced observer does not mean adopting what is known in American journalistic parlance as 'man from the Mars' stance, i.e., seeing each event afresh, unconnected to any previous expectations or future possibilities and passing them on untouched by interpretation. In many cases, this would mean an irresponsible attitude, a refusal to make the reader understand the event in its proper context and realise its significance.

Clarity of Expression : Your command, as a reporter, over the language must be such that you can explain even the most complicated issues in simple terms to any general reader. In addition to specialised subjects such as science and technology, even government press notes are written in complicated language, burying the news point. You must be able to simplify it and bring out the news point.

***Team Spirit* :** Except for routine coverages which can be handled by one person, many investigative stories have to be handled by a team. You must be able to work as a member of such a team. And you must pool your talents, sources and contacts into the team and work under a leader. In the course of time, you may rise to head such a team. Working under a team discipline will certainly be of help to you later.

***Ability to Cope with Pressure* :** With investigative journalism seeking to bring out scandals and exposures, there is bound to be pressure on journalists to keep someone's wrong doings hidden from public view. The 'pressure' on journalists is exerted in the hope of preventing exposure. The concerned journalist may also be bribed with attractive favours in return for silence on the matter.

The pressure could be used to make you change the news or 'kill' a story. This constitutes censorship. Pressure could also be applied with the hope of inducing journalist to volunteer the change or omission which is then equal to self-censorship.

There are three ways of coping with pressure: fighting it, giving in or anticipating the pressure and taking preventive measures.

Preventive measures to fight pressure could be legal steps, like seeking a court stay on any law or ordinance that could affect the freedom of the press.

Different Liabilities

The reporting profession is unlike any other profession. At times, some slight carelessness in doing one's duty, can cause incalculable harmful repercussions, both for the news organization and society. A slight laziness in cross checking certain facts could endanger the credibility of the news organization.

Responsibility towards the News Organization : As a reporter, you have to follow the character, style and policy of your newspaper or magazine or news agency. There are conservative papers which may prefer to stick to routine coverage, not bothering about investigation of scandals. In such papers, you have to stick to their policy even if it cramps your style.

But in a news organization with a more dynamic approach to news, you must develop the skills of an investigator. Whatever you do as a reporter will affect the newspaper and its reputation. So you must take pains to ensure accuracy and objectivity in your stories.

Responsibility towards the Sources : Your sources are sacred. Your credibility in their eyes could be a major factor in your performance as a newsperson. There are sources with whom you will have to take great pains to establish your credibility to make them open up towards you. You will have to assure them that no harm will come to them, and if they so desire, you must keep their identity a secret.

Responsibility towards the Reader and Society : As a news reporter, you have a duty to provide accurate, unbiased and objective information to the reader. Every effort must be made to ensure that the news is accurate, free from prejudices and that all sides of the news event are presented fairly.

To maintain your credibility with the reader you have a duty not to accept things or favours or pursue any activity that might compromise your integrity.

However, in these days, publicity seekers including those in private business, organize press conferences and conduct tours with attractive gifts and other incentives. While private firms depend mainly on advertising for publicity, they sometimes want their activities to be carried as news items since news carries greater credibility than advertisements. News reports are written by newspapers who are supposed to be independent and objective.

Ability to Talk

A very authentic way of gathering facts, figures and opinions on various issues is to interview the persons concerned. The interview is a very useful input for all the media-print and electronic. It depends on how one would like to use an interview.

It may be used as a programme to make the audience/reader get information/facts from the source directly. The interview can form the basis of an article, a feature or a commentary.

How to Prepare for an Interview : The most important part of the interview is to know your subject as completely as possible. It is imperative for you to not only fully research the information you want from your subject, but also the person behind it. You should also have all the essential background information on the interviewee which will help you to build an instant rapport with the interviewee.

Research : It is most important to research your subject matter. It could be a subject in which you neither have any interest nor adequate knowledge. But once you are fully armed with the basic and important information acquired through books, newspapers, journals or magazines articles, you will be much more comfortable and should be successful in your venture.

You must know your subject matter as well as the person whom you intend to talk to about the subject matter.

Editing Interviews For Use : Two fundamental factors are to be remembered by all journalists-First, all interviews are subject to editing. So there is no harm in culling more information than you can use. The information that you need to buttress an argument or to refuse another or to make a point, can be used at the appropriate place. The rest can be stored for use in future.

Second, no statement made in the interview is allowed to be used out of context. If the authority interviewed does not generalise it, the reporter or, sub-editor is debarred from generalising it.

Strategy : It is important to establish contact with the interviewee much in advance of the interview. More often than not, where important interviewees are concerned, there is a channel you will have to go through. It could be the private secretary or the members of the family referred to as the "protector of the interviewee".

So, the first thing to do is to establish a rapport with the protector. To get to your subject-matter or the person, you must be able to play to the gallery to defeat all the obstacles imposed by the "protectors".

What You Want from the Interview : If the first thing is to establish contact and to build up a rapport, the most important part of the preparation is to decide what you want to get out of the interview. May be you want substantiation of a fact you have discussed; or the refutation of something; or may be you want the interviewer's views on some, proposition you or someone else is making.

It is vital for an interviewer to decide what he wants out of the interview. It is not a fishing expedition in which you net whatever you get. It is a hunt where you go after a target and get it.

Also one has to keep his senses on full alert and the antenna unfurled to each nuggets of news which have a knack of falling from the lips of the interviewee at the most unexpected moments.

Preparing Yourself : It is important and essential to make a deep study of the individual you plan to interview. Paying attention to his minute, apparently insignificant, matters really helps in contusing the interview smoothly. You must build a personal rapport to begin with, so you may start the interview comfortably.

Physical Preparation : If it is a television interview, then you need the cameraman, sound recordist, lighting technician and sound technician.

The other way in which the interview is to be held in a studio, then arrangements should be made accordingly in the studio. For the radio studio interview, a good recording machine is required, a lip microphone is used which prevents extraneous sound from getting injected into the microphone.

How to Get an Interview : Getting an interview can often be difficult, because the interviewer is generally viewed with suspicion. The interviewer labours between two competing factors. One, the public has the right to know and you are the tool employed to gather the information. Two, from the legal point of view nobody can be forced into talking hence, the job can be tiresome and at times, very frustrating.

It is very important that one's own participation in the interview is secondary. One must let the interviewee do most of the talking. To make this happen smoothly, a number of skills have to be deployed like :

(a) There is the direct approach-to telephone and tell the interviewee what you want.

(b) The end round: A secretary in a business or government office will generally try, and give you the 'brush off'. The attempt of the interviewer should be to try and make the secretary one's friend.

(c) When faced with repeated failure, find out the person's hide-out and with an overdose of apology, just barge in.

(d) Sit in: It pays to just 'sit and wait' till the subject of interview shows up in spite of secretaries saying that 'the boss has no time to see you'.

(e) The appeal: As soon as you get the glimpse of the reluctant interviewee, make your appeal as quickly and strongly as possible.

(f) Be courteous and polite: Tell the interviewee that there are two sides to every story, and we want to know yours. Thus, you arouse the interviewee's curiosity and attention.

In many cases, it pays to tell the interviewee of the other side.

Do's and Dont's for an Interview

(a) Be operational on time for the interview. This is very important. It shows the importance of the interviewee and that he has not been taken for granted. In a nut shell, you must be ready right on time to start the interview.

(b) Outline your reasons for being there, unless you are working on something very sensitive.

(c) Start the interview with a broad question. This helps you to size up the person and also collect your thoughts. It also helps to receive information you may not have anticipated.

(d) Do not interrupt until the interviewee has relaxed. Avoid making the interviewee uncomfortable at the outset. It would be of little value.

(e) Let him speak at length on his favourite topic/ achievement/ feat. You will get nuggets of information. The irrelevant facts can always be edited out.

(f) Grunt and chuckle occasionally.

(g) Stick to your subject.

(h) Avoid commenting except to egg him on to top more. Let the interviewee do most of the talking.

(i) Do not end the interview till you have the basics-how does he spell his name, official title, age etc. Preferably get the details in advance from his staff and then get it confirmed by him.

(j) Be understanding. Do not be insensitive. Make the interviewee feel important. Keep the interviewee at ease.

Interviewing Skills : Advance preparation for the interview by way of well-thought out questions and a thorough consideration of approach is very helpful. One need not fear that the final outcome will sound stilted with no natural spontaneity. Usually the reverse is true.

Taking Notes : Taking notes is an essential part of interviewing. Some take down everything, even irrelevant and redundant remarks. Take down only what is important. People sometimes stop talking when you start writing and so taking down only the important remarks may not be possible. And you don't always know what is relevant until you have written it all down and reviewed it.

(i) Write as fast as you can.

(ii) Keep hand and mind together, listen to key phrases. A tape recorder helps you to review the interview *in toto*. It is a must for a question and answer story.

Conducting An Interview : Know your subject. Read the person's eyes and mannerisms since these offer a reliable clue on how an interview is to be handled. Since the interview rarely goes as planned, therefore the interviewer requires a lot of instinct.

How to Establish Rapport with the Interview :

(a) In many small and big ways, try to make your interviewee feel nice, cheerful and important.

(b) Outline your reasons for being there. Bring the interviewee up-to-date on what you are looking for.

(c) Start with a broad question. This helps you to see the person and collect your thoughts. It also gives you an opportunity to receive information which you may not have anticipated.

(d) Stick to the subject. Do not ramble or chit-chat. Neither is it advisable to beat around the bush. So go ahead and simply ask your questions straight-away.

(e) Doodling or writing down a lot of useless matter in your notebook can be helpful. Those who have important information to transmit, like to feel they are being recorded.

You might be asked to show what you have taken down. For all that, jotting down points helps you to prepare the transcription of the interview-session for publication.

(f) Listen. Listen. Listen. Not only does this make the interviewee feel good and wise, but it also helps you to control the interview. An interviewer might start speaking with good intentions and slowly digress. You can bring him back to point. "You were saying something about the time you were in college, prison, etc. When was that?" And you are back on the track.

(g) Be understanding. Nobody likes insensibility. The interviewee is often quite nervous while discussing his/her wrong doings, sin or tragedy. Help him/her to relax. If your mind goes blank, just say, "Excuse me. I forgot where we were and what I need to ask"

12

Editor's Role

Press is an opinion making institution, a newspaper should not confine its energy only for printing the news accurately, but it should also comment editorially on important matters and events. An editor of a newspaper can exert a lot of influence for the social good of the society. In fact, the editor of a widely circulated national newspaper is the keeper of the public conscience. The editor of a newspaper should always use his paper's influence to improve the lot of the people, to suggest reasonableness when passions are aroused, to remove corruption from public administration and political life and take the administration to task for its failures. No doubt, this is a very important responsibility of the editor of a newspaper which he should discharge sincerely.

The editorial policy of a newspaper should be based upon fairness and accuracy. It should not only be applied to the editorials but it should also be applied to the news items published in the newspaper. Such a policy will increase the popularity of the newspaper as well as create a lot of confidence among the readers of the newspaper.

Of course, the aim of a newspaper is to serve the public

interest. In a popular newspaper the news is given an accurate and fair treatment, its editorials are straight, even if a little partisan. A good newspaper will give an honourable treatment even to its opponents. Thus, the editor of a big newspaper can exercise a lot of influence in making his newspaper popular.

Although much of the time of the editor is occupied in the direction of the complex machinery of newspaper as well as attending the conferences with heads of departments, yet he can enthuse the spirit of honesty and public service in all the staff members of his newspaper. The editor commissions writers to write articles for his newspaper, he decides the subjects for the leaders and the lines upon which they are to run, especially when they concern some controversial topics. Some editors also contribute leaders and specials to their columns two or three days a week. In this way, we see that the life of an editor is not an idle one.

Nobody can deny the fact that a good newspaper influences the minds of the people to a great extent. No doubt, a pernicious influence is always more easily exerted than a good influence. Therefore, it is the responsibility of the editor that he should have a good influence on the people by conducting his newspaper in a clean and honest manner. Although the editorial opinion expressed in the editorial may not have a direct influence on the minds of the public, yet it is a fact that if there is a continual reiteration of a certain set of truths, it is bound to make an impression upon the minds of the readers sooner or later.

Public opinion is largely influenced by the newspaper's opinion indirectly. On controversial issues people generally adopt the arguments given in the leading articles on the subject in the different newspapers. In fact, like all subtle influences, a newspaper's opinion is imbibed subconsciously by the readers and therein lies its strength.

Undoubtedly, a newspaper chiefly makes its influence felt on its readers, especially in the political field, by means of the leading articles. In fact, leader writing occupies a very important place in any newspaper. A leader writer should have the quality to write an article on any subject with equal facility. In a way, he is the editorial handy man who should be able to express the considered judgement of his newspaper without being influenced by his personal views. There is no doubt that the leading articles of a newspaper can be used for a lot of good by starting a campaign against many social, political and economic evils existing in the society.

An editorial should always be written in an independent style. Generally, the important national papers take an independent line editorially on all things and matters about which they write. Such newspapers do not write their leading articles regarding political controversy in a partisan manner. In fact, the editorials of these newspapers are written in a broad-minded and unbiased manner. The editorial columns of a good newspaper are always interesting. They are full of life and compel attention. The leading articles should be thought-provoking and instead of being biased and partisan they should be independent and full of inspiration for all the readers.

Art of Writing

A leading article in a newspaper should appeal not only to the few but to the largest number of the readers. A leading article should be the true leader of thoughts in a newspaper. It will not be wrong to say that the best newspaper is that which has the best editorials. Some people believe that the leading articles are read by a microscopic minority of the readers. And, sometimes, jokingly it is said that the leading article is read only by the proof reader who is paid to do so. Apparently, this is not the correct thing. In fact, good editorials are read with the same interest as any other part of a newspaper.

Some people feel that the leader writers generally make too much use of political topics for writing their editorials. According to these people the ordinary citizens are not interested in boring politics all the time except at election time. The common citizens prefer to read articles on general topics which concern the day to day life. Therefore, it is a good policy that from time to time leading articles should also be written on such topics as are of interest to the average readers and which concern their day to day life.

Sometimes, a newspaper editor has to speak about the truth in the columns of his newspaper, even at the risk of some danger. While doing so, the editor should do his utmost to retain the goodwill and respect of his readers, otherwise his plain speaking on a topic which is considered a taboo by the people may make his paper suffer.

However, the editor should always keep the public interest supreme in all these matters. There is no doubt that a newspaper editor who is afraid to write, even when he knows certainly that this is the right course to pursue, is unworthy to hold his high post. An editor who tries to adopt the easier and safer path whenever faced by such a decision to take a bold step in support of a true cause, will prove himself a coward and will condemn his paper to eternal mediocrity.

The editor of a newspaper should maintain certain high ideals of his newspaper worthy of being followed by his juniors. The newspaper editorials should be free, fearless and outspoken, as far as the rooting out of social and economic evils is concerned. He should also be fearless to write against the prevailing corruption, both in the social and the political life of the country.

Similarly, he must not be afraid of writing against the administration or the government to safeguard the rights and the freedoms of the people. An editor must maintain the high principles of honesty and integrity to enhance the reputation of his newspaper. In fact, an editorial is just like the heart of a newspaper and it is to a great extent responsible for the success or failure of a newspaper.

Why Advertorials and Booklets? : Most publications are on the look-out for ways of increasing their circulation and some are also looking for extra revenue. This means that both the editors and the promotion department of a particular publication may be interested in 'advertorials', associated booklets, competitions and special offers. The fact that a particular publication does not offer these types of promotion on a regular basis does not mean that it will not be interested in discussing a bright idea. And though it is usually consumer publications that are involved there have been some notable exceptions among even the more staid members of the trade press.

These promotional tools can be extremely useful to the discerning PRO, particularly for products and services which have passed their first peak of interest. The first advantage to the participating company of all of these types of activity is that they are not seen by the reader as advertising but as part of the editorial content of the magazine and therefore as having the endorsement of the editorial staff. This is true even though the approach may vary from a fairly soft sell in the 'advertorial' to quite a strong sales pitch in the special offer.

The second advantage is that such promotions enable the name of your organization or its brands to be included in the copy, which can be very important in publications which would not normally use such names.

The choice between the different types of bought space outlined below will depend partly on the product or service in question and partly on the available budget. It will also depend upon which type of promotion the editor is prepared to tolerate in his or her pages, for the choice of medium is as important here as in many other parts of the media programme. The best advertorial in the world will be of no value at all if it is aimed at the wrong audience.

Advertorials: Advertorials are paid-for editorial material and though they must be labelled as advertisements they are designed to look as much like the editorial pages of the publication as possible. The difference is, of course, that the copy has been supplied by a PRO and the photography and space have been paid for by the PROs organization or client.

Advertorials may take the form of single or double spreads in the magazine or they may be more elaborate booklets which are bound into each copy of the magazine. They are particularly useful to PROs who have the unenviable task of promoting everyday products such as soup, shampoo, paint, weedkiller or garden tools. The products are good enough to need little in the way of revamping and apart from the odd addition to the range or a change of packaging little of any interest happens to the product. But the PRO is charged with keeping it in the public eye. Even fashion products such as nail polish or lipstick, which do have regular changes of colour, can benefit greatly.

News Material

In theory an advertorial could be put together on almost any subject appropriate to the magazine and to the sponsor. In practice it has mainly been used in the fields of food, cooking and beauty. But there is no reason why an enterprising PRO might not put together any package which would be of interest to the general consumer. A gardening magazine might be interested in advertorials on growing certain types of plant on different soils or on dealing with pests. Obvious sponsors might be seed merchants or weedkiller manufacturers. Similarly, holiday route guides or DIY maintenance might be of interest to motoring magazines, with car or accessory manufacturers as sponsors. Home decorating and colour scheming advertorials might be offered by paint and wallpaper companies; indeed the opportunities are many and varied.

The Methods

The mechanics of the advertorial vary. Some editors try to avoid them altogether, others only include them under pressure from their promotions departments. This means that the copy and photographs are usually provided by the sponsor. Do not make the mistake of trying to write the piece yourself. It is better to hire a freelance expert who can write to the style of publication concerned and who will avoid the kind of PR cliches so beloved of the marketing department.

Remember that every time you use outside writers, whether for articles, advertorials or booklets, you will need to draw up a contract to cover all aspects of copyright.

Where photography is involved-and it usually is-it is even more important to get the style right. After all, the advertorial is intended to look as much like the other editorial pages as possible. Arrange a briefing meeting with representatives of the magazine and the sponsor, the author and the photographer to make sure that everyone knows exactly what is required.

The cost of any advertorial will depend upon the publication and the size of its circulation. If the cost is higher than your budget will stand it is possible to collaborate with one, two or even three other manufacturers to put together a bumper bundle. One national women's magazine recently carried an advertorial with no fewer than ten participating, but of course non-competing, manufacturers. However, you might well think that some of the impact is lost in such an exercise.

The Booklets: Associated booklets distributed with a magazine are another form of bought space, though they are a little less subtle in approach in that they are not bound into the publication and may have a different format. However, the editorial endorsement may still be fairly strong in that the booklet may carry the name of the magazine in its own title such as the 'Modern Woman's Guide to House Buying'. It may or may not go on to say 'produced in conjunction with brand X or company Y'

The content of such a booklet is very similar to that of an advertorial. There is a relatively soft sell of the company's products or services and the copy is as useful as possible. The idea is to create goodwill by producing a really helpful guide or a series of ideas which will be of use to customers and potential customers. However, the shape and length of the booklet may be planned with effective presentation in mind. It will not be as limited by the size and shape of the magazine as the advertorial.

Distribution in conjunction with a particular publication can be expensive both in the distribution fee and in the cost of producing so many copies. It might therefore be worth considering the alternative of independent production and printing, relying on editorial mention for distribution. Booklets can be very popular indeed and some booklets have been taken up in large quantities.

Checklist for Advertorials and Booklets

1. Choose a subject which will be of interest to the readers of the magazine concerned and which will illustrate the best use of your organization's range of products.
2. The content must, first of all, be useful to the reader. Any attempt to introduce the sponsor's range of products must be low-key. This is not an advertisement in the usual sense.
3. Consider who is best qualified to write the copy. An independent or outside expert may be the answer.
4. Make sure that the photography or drawn illustrations are in keeping with the editorial image of the magazine.
5. Look at the costs involved and if these seem too high for your budget, consider joining with non-competing manufacturers.
6. Before committing yourself compare the various costs, advantages and disadvantages of advertorials against booklets.

PARTICULAR MATTERS

Special offers fall into two main categories: those which are really free give a way or are very cheap indeed and those which offer relatively expensive items at a discount.

FREE INVITATIONS

Free giveaways are almost always associated with new products and form part of the sampling operation which is often necessary for the public to acquire a taste for them. They may be physically attached to the front cover of the publication, slipped between the pages or offered on the editorial pages. Items which are physically attached to the front cover gain in that they could not really be more prominently displayed and are bound to reach all the purchasers of the magazine. But they do need to be small enough to fit on the cover without taking up much space, and light enough not to tear the paper. Packaging can also cause a headache.

Slipping between the pages of a magazine may work for a sachet of shampoo or for a soup mix, but the product can very easily slip out again and the end purchaser may not receive the sample. Offers made on the editorial pages need to be particularly attractive or the readers will not take the trouble to send off their stamped addressed envelope. With all these promotions you must be prepared to give away large numbers of the product. The magazine may have a circulation of half a million or more. Even with editorial offers the magazine will want to be sure that stocks will not run out too soon, or there will be many disappointed readers.

CONCESSIONAL INVITATION

Special offers involving a discount, on the other hand, can both promote the product and bring in some revenue. However, magazines will drive a hard bargain and if you are to enjoy the advantages of full-page coverage you will have to offer a very good discount, guarantee stocks and pay a handling fee.

A problem arises with sample offers if you are not geared up for individual direct mail dispatch. Of course, you can hand the whole thing over to a direct mail house but there may still be additional and expensive packaging to design and pay for.

For some companies special offers are more difficult because their product may only be used by professionals, such as hairdressers, or it may be perishable and not suitable for selling through the post. Money-off vouchers are one answer, but they are not very popular with magazines and may not be well received by suppliers either. If you do try to use them you must be very sure that they will be honoured or you will be generating bad rather than goodwill.

Checklist for Special Offers

1. Does the cost of the product in question point to a free offer or a discount?
2. Is the product or sample small enough to slip between the pages of the magazine or can it easily be attached to the front cover?
3. Are you prepared to fulfil quite large demands for the sample or offer?
4. How is the discounted product to be dispatched and how is it to be protected en route? What is the cost of this?
5. If vouchers are under consideration will retailers be happy with the redemption system?

RACE FOR EDITORSHIP

A competition is another device for promoting your product or services by name in terms of both write-up and pictures. Most types of publication and indeed some radio stations will consider competitions. They are fun for their readers or audience and offer a chance to win something for nothing or at least for a very slight effort. Of course, the prizes are crucial. Ideally they should be associated with your product or services. They are also the means of 'buying' your way into the publication. Publications which run editorial competitions on a regular basis usually have a set price level, which may vary from as little as £100-£500 value for a small provincial weekly to around £25 000-plus for a national women's magazine. There may also be a handling fee.

13

Relevance of Media

The rapid development of industrialisation gave rise to new technologies which were instrumental in bringing about a change in the process of communication. The process of communication was fast and receipts of communication and the feedback were ensured. Mass Media and Communication technologies have become integral parts of our life and our society.

Work Set-up

Education : Media are used to add new information to human knowledge and keep on upgrading it. Ignorance can not be eradicated without adequate information supply. The overall development is directly related to education. Media enable the spread of education through conventional as well as unconventional methods. The desire to have access to media increases the level of education and knowledge among the population.

Economic Growth : Increase in media use increases the level of education. Thus, people's demand for education has given rise to the need for greater access to informations which has further boosted the media hardware production causing an unprecedented growth in the economy. This, in turn, has stimulated the expansion of communications industry including media industries.

Entertainment : The mass media has -monopolised the leisure industry. Transactional media giants have started invading the continents via the sky, using satellite slots. The competition for audience attention has become fierce.

Public Watchdog : Mass media have also played a leading role in shaping, guiding and reflecting the public opinion. These functions of media help to establish democracy. Use of media in a democratic polity creates critical awareness among the people. The media may not be able to perform these functions unless the access to them is ensured to a large section of our population.

Information : Access to media means access to facts and documents which help one acquire information and knowledge. In comparison with individuals, media have more access to sources of information due to their reach and institutional character. Media power makes access easy.

Safeguarding Democracy : Media access is important in the political sphere. Access to media is access to public opinion, so essential to protect and preserve democratic institutions. It is advantageous to both the leaders and masses. Leaders can address masses depending upon their convenience. They reach widely dispersed masses simultaneously through the electronic media in particular.

Liberty of Expression

As technological innovations improved, as the spread and reach of the press expanded, attention was focused on diffusion of information upholding the right of the public to the freedom of information. Originally, the freedom of information meant the people's right to information. In simple words, it was the right to know whatever affected the individuals themselves. New information technology has posed new dangers to the freedom of media person as well as media consumers. In theory, everybody enjoys the right to freedom of expression, but the huge capital needed for investment in new media of mass communication, has negated the whole concept since only the very-well-to-do, the elite can afford to launch the media ventures.

India is a classic example of communication contradictions. Certain media are allowed in the private sector while others are controlled by the Government. Newspapers in India have traditionally uphold the freedom of press. In India, with a low literacy level, the influences of print media are limited to the urban centres. Further, most Indian newspapers being privately owned, are supposed to guarantee free and unbiased reporting. Several defects have been identified. Most of the largely circulated newspapers are owned by big business and industrial houses, and thus political interests take precedence over any other human interests. A study conducted by the IIPA, Delhi, revealed that out of 54 dailies selected, 27 newspapers were owned either partially or totally by business and industrial houses and controlled about 50 per cent of the total circulation. For the purpose of unbiased and objective performance, delinking the ownership of newspapers from large industrial houses was suggested.

However, inspite of all this, the Indian Press enjoys credibility with reading audiences. Public opinion is reflected either in the editorials or letters to the editor published in newspapers. But, with 85% of the population totally unexposed to the press and its accessibility limited to just the elite, it is questionable how accessibility to the media can be a criteria for its high credibility. Further, how can editorials or letters to the editor from the literate few, constitute feedback of the entire nation.

Government controlled electronic media are anathema to the very concept of an open society. Frequent political interference has eroded the credibility of both AIR and Doordarshan. Added to this, bureaucratisation has affected professional aspects of their functioning. These two powerful media can cross the barriers of illiteracy and their reach is the reason why political authorities keep a stranglehold on them.

Community Participation : A community is an assembly of people in an identified geographical area. A community's development hinges on effective communication. The increased use of local media makes communication a vital input of every community development programme. Community participation in media programmes accentuates free flow of information. Consequently, the democratic process acquires more meaning and relevance. Community participation in mass media can be both at the level of decision-making and management.

The mass media are very important component of society. Their use in a developing country like India is considered most crucial in the challenge to mobilize people for development activities. Therefore, there must be a communication policy. The policy should give direction to the programmes which are channeled through various mass media networks.

Functional Problems

Technology-oriented Problems : The mass media systems may fail to perform their functions when unplanned use of such technology creates problems. For instance communication resources can be concentrated in a few centres alone. The mass media may be misused by the owners to exercise their power, or the media content may be manipulated to give as a result of the communicators biases. All these problems forced the formulation of a viable communication policy. If the policy itself becomes outdated in the face of technological developments, it will have to be suitably changed.

Problems of Research : Traditionally, communications research in India has shown a remarkable orientation towards social problems. Studies on propaganda techniques, attitude change, effects of mass media, personal influence, diffusion of innovations, flow of information, media uses and gratifications and the economics of communication have been motivated by practical problems faced in society. These studies focus on the need to understand the role of communication in those problems and the desire to apply the knowledge gained from research to solve them.

In spite of a great deal of empirical research, no systematic knowledge about the nature, frequency and origin of communication problems in India is available. However, the situation is changing now. Demands are being made for improving existing regulations, resource allocation principles, institutional arrangements, and defining the rights and responsibilities of professional communicators, commercial communication organisations and the bureaucracies. A communication policy must give importance to these issues. The policy, in effect, is built on the body of knowledge developed by research.

Formal Aspects

A Policy is a set of principles, rules and guidelines to help in the tackling of problems which may be faced by a society in any particular field. A communication policy is formulated in response to the challenges of new communication technologies. We can define communication policy as action-oriented principles, outlining objectives and means of achieving objectives, focusing on what needs to be done and what is to be avoided in dealing with current and anticipated communication problems in society. The policies are formulated on authoritative guidelines.

Role of Communication Policy : Given the centrality of communication in modern society, one should rightly expect that communication policy would have a distinct and independent role to play. It would take into account the problems that crop up when using communication in varied activities. Communication policy should be based on an understanding of the totality of communication problems. Such a policy should aim at achieving society's goals and expectations regarding the applications of communication.

Objectives of Communication Policy : The priorities according to which the developed and the developing countries formulate their policies differ, sometimes even contradict each other. The technologically advanced countries like USA and Japan are concerned with mobilizing world markets for their communication goals and services. The developing countries like India, on the other hand, are concerned with building and expanding their communication systems with indigenous and appropriate technology.

One major objective of their policy is to eliminate the vestings of colonial dependency. A major thrust area of communication policy of developing countries is the implementation of viable alternatives to the one-way flow of information into their societies. Most of the developing countries are busy waging a constant battle against poverty, malnutrition, illiteracy and indebtness. Thus, communication development receives scarce priority in their national objectives.

Mass Media Policy Formulation : The mass media can be tools of cultural enrichment, national cohesion and advancement. The media policy makers in India first have to bridge the gap between ground realities and ideal situations. Certain paradoxes exist in the field of communication which need to be considered by policy makers. Some of these realities are elucidated here :

(a) Whereas there is an urgent demand to realise the right to equal access to information, there is a widening of the information gap between the richer and the poorer sections of society.

(b) There is misappropriation of the mass media for commercial and political purchases, when the need of the hour is to apply the media to the task of propagating culture, education, information and leisure time entertainment.

(c) There is predominant use of media to impose foreign values.

(d) In India, by and large, the communicators don't desire to find out the reactions of the audience to their programmes.

(e) The increase in the number of channels is not matched by any corresponding increase in the standard of programming.

(f) While communication satellites remove the barriers to information and education across the national boundaries all over the world, the same technology pave the way for cultural imperialism and new communication colonialism.

Policy versus Practice and Performance : The Doordarshan has always suffered from the dichotomy between policy pronouncements and the continuous drift and departure from them in actual practice. In developing and democratic country like India, access to television and the social benefit accruing from it, is a crucial test of the social relevance of such an expensive medium. The importance of utilising TV is not just for the idle entertainment of the elite but for the uplift of the poor. But in effect and in actual practice, the purchase of a TV set is seen as wholesale investment in entertainment which obviates the bother and expense of going to an auditorium or a stadium.

Commercialism vs Social Good : From inception, broadcasting in India has been looked upon as a public service for the promotion of social objectives. The concept of advertisements for the promotion of consumer goods was also considered incompatible with the prevailing philosophy of the "socialistic pattern of society". In a developing country like India, radio and TV should be viewed as a national resource for the uplift of the masses. It is only through a strong media network that the eight kind of information and education can be imparted to the people. But the media in our country, like elsewhere in the world, have buckled under the pressure of commercial interests. Mindless entertainment with little or no educative value defeats the very purpose of building up a strong media network.

Performance of Indian Press : The press in a democratic country plays a vital role in creating, moulding and reflecting public opinion. It is a fundamental institution of our society. Though the press in India is free, it suffers from many ills. There are a few in-built handicaps such as vast geographical area, illiteracy, poverty, multiplicity of languages and absence of adequate communication facilities. Some other bottlenecks exist like :

(a) the linking of ownership of newspapers with other industrial or commercial enterprises.

(b) limited newspaper ownership with closely held share interest.

(c) Urban-oriented expansion of newspapers leaving the vast country side population untouched.

(d) inadequate and expensive newsprint.

(e) the lack of local advertisement support.

Speech and Expression : Man's greatest invention is language. The invention of the script has helped mankind to preserve human thoughts and learning. It has helped society to conquer both space and time. An important product of the script was the book. The books helped older civilisations like the Chinese and the Indian civilizations to preserve heritage. Books spread ideas which set people thinking, as a prelude to individual and group action. For this reason, they met opposition from guardians of political and religious doctrines.

Plato argued that wise men alone could rule and the state would control education. For Machiavelli, the security of the state was supreme. Hegel regarded state as embodiment of morality. John Milton (1608-1674) in Areopagitica gave a solid reason for the freedom of the Press. In his essay on liberty (1859) John Stuart Mill (1806-1873) proclaimed that liberty was the right of the individual.

Today freedom of expression and speech are internationally reorganised rights. The league of nations made the first organised attempt at the international level to proclaim rights of speech and expression by launching a series of conferences. In just a few years of its birth, the United Nations approved the UN Declaration of Freedom of Information (1946) and the Universal Declaration of Human Rights (1948).

With the gaining of independence, freedom of speech and expression were recognised as fundamental rights and were included in the Indian Constitution. They are provided in the Article 19(1) of our constitution. Article 19(2) provides reasonable restrictions on freedom of expression.

In U.S.A., freedom of the press was very clearly recognised for the first time in the Virginia Bill of Rights in 1776. Unlike U.S.A., Britain has no written constitution. But it has been the fountain of all philosophy concerning freedom of speech, expression and the press, as John Milton did most of his work in Britain. The rights of free speech, expression and the press are in a constant process of evolution.

Freedom of the Press : In general press freedom means freedom, unless specifically prohibited by law, together, print and publish information and to set up technologies in pursuit of such objectives, to claim and gain access to information. In practice, freedom of the press means freedom of the owner of a newspaper. Journalists enjoy only that much freedom as is given to them by the owner of their newspaper/magazine.

From the beginning, freedom of the press was sought and obtained on the ground that it was a prerequisite to democracy. The press demand freedom because of the functions they discharge for the benefit of the society. In today's context, freedom of the press is only an extension of the citizen's right to freedom of speech and expression. It is the press alone which can thwart the attempts of any government to deny this right to the citizen. Today, the press, the electronic media, wherever they operate privately, have information-gathering networks spread all over the world. They are the eyes and ears of the people everywhere.

In connection with the limitation, the very first thing is that the right of the freedom of the press is only an extension of the citizen's right to freedom of speech and expression. Therefore, all those laws imposing restrictions on this right of the citizen apply to the press too. It has no special privilege that the citizens do not enjoy in this area. In all western societies and in India, the constitutions as well as the general laws of the countries, set the limits for the exercise of freedom of the press. It goes without saying that with regard to freedom, the press is not on any higher footing than the ordinary citizen. Since the press is also a business and an industry, all those laws which apply to business and industry, also apply to newspaper organizations.

Responsibilities and Social Obligation of the Press : The theory of responsibility is simple that everyone is responsible for the consequences of his actions. 'No Rights without responsibilities'. Therefore, freedom of the press is also linked with responsibilities.' At least, the freedom should not be abused.

Responsibilities and its Rationale : When we say that somebody is responsible, we mean that he has a duty to do something, when we say someone is accountable, we mean that if he fails to do what his duty is, he is accountable to some person or institution. Thus, the right to freedom of speech and expression carries with it, a duty not to disturb public peace. If he so disturbs it he is accountable to the state for such breach of responsibility. Since media circulates information for the consumption of members of the society, it is natural that they should be responsible in the dissemination of the information. With every increase in the power of media, this responsibility towards the society also increases.

Unwritten Understanding : Editors and others often say that they have a right to inform the public. These are self-imposed responsibilities. These arise from an unwritten understanding between the media and society. On the basis of the responsibility of the media to inform the public, media have fought for and gained the right to free speech and expression.

But state has also imposed some obligations on media like not to publish anything that leads to, or has a tendency to lead to, a breakdown of public order. These are responsibilities imposed in addition to, and sometimes in contrast to, self-imposed responsibilities.

Government at Work

The First Press Commission was appointed in 1952, because after independence the role of the press was changing. It was fast turning from a mission to' business. The commission founded that there was a great deal of scurrilous writing often directed against communities or groups, of indecency and vulgarity and personal attacks on individuals.

It felt that the best way of maintaining professional standards of journalism would be to bring into existence a body of people principally connected with the industry whose responsibility it would be to arbitrate on doubtful points and to ensure the punishment of anyone guilty of infraction of good journalistic behaviour. Second Press Commission was appointed in 1978 and it wanted the press to be neither a mindless adversary nor an unquestioning ally. It wanted the press to play a responsible role in the development process. From the role that the two commissions recommended for the press, we can summarise the responsibilities of the Press thus :

— Help the country in its development process both by making constructive suggestions as well as criticism of delays and distortions in the development process.

— Give the widest possible access to people, reflecting the pluralistic composition of Indian society.

— Maintain internal stability and safeguard external security.

— Prevent and deflate social conflict.

Code of Conduct for Journalists : Complaints are heard throughout the world that a section of the press functions without regard to its responsibilities to the society. There is a vast area not covered by any legal regime. Media ethics apply mostly to cases not specifically concerned by law.

Code of Ethics : The Second Press Commission observed that one of the functions entrusted to the Press council was the building up of a code of conduct for newspapers, news agencies and journalists in accordance with high standards of journalism. The second Press Commission lists a number of codes drafted in India, the USA and Britain have through the years. The All-India Newspaper Editors' Conference formulated a Code of Ethics and a Charter for Editors in 1953. The National Union of Journalists (1981), the All India Small and Medium Newspapers Association (1975) had all drafted similar codes. But the Editors Guild of India refused to draft any code arguing that responsible people do not need such a formal code.

The second Press Commission said that it would not be desirable to draw up a Code of Ethics for newspapers. The Code of Ethics (1953) of All India Newspaper Editors' Conference asks journalists to serve and guard public interest, to be alive to fundamental human and social rights, to observe restraint in reports dealing with tensions leading to or likely to lead to public disorder, to assume responsibility for all information published, to respect confidence, not to exploit their status for non-journalistic purposes, not to allow personal interest to influence professional conduct, to correct inaccurate information, not to demand or accept bribe. The National Union of Journalists' Declaration of 1981 is also largely on similar lines.

Ombudsman : The idea of an Ombudsman is of Swedish origin. In Sweden the Press Ombudsman at the national level is appointed by all the newspaper organizations together. Ombudsman generally means an intermediary, investigating complaints by private citizens against government officials or agencies. However, at present private or voluntary organizations are also having Ombudsmen to decide public complaints made against themselves or their members. In India, the Lok Ayuktas in some states are Ombudsmen.

Although this concept first originated in Sweden, but it was first adopted by the Press in USA.

Press Council : The world's first Press Council took its birth in Sweden in 1916. In USA, a Press Council (National News Council) worked for 11 years and today there are nearly 50 Press Councils all over the world. The Press Council of India was set up on July 4, 1966 and Justice J.R. Mudholkar, was its chairman. It consisted of 25 members who were editors, working journalists, proprietors etc. In 1970, news agencies were also put under its jurisdiction. The council has powers to levy a graded fee on newspapers and news agencies to meet its expenditure and to reduce its dependence on government's financial support.

The countries of North and South are separated by an enormous gap in their respective communication capacities. The developed countries continue to exercise considerable political, economic and technological control on information flows. Nearly 80 per cent of the information disseminated in the world originates from five largest transnational news agencies as told before. About 15 great media corporations dominate the production of the radio sets, television sets and printing equipment, ten of these corporations belong to the U.S.A. Due to our dependence on the media delivery systems of the West, we also become dependent on the West.

Need for Self-reliance : Self-reliance in news and information distribution, both in disseminating news to the outside world or in getting news and information from various places in the world, for internal consumption, is essential for the following reasons :

(a) To provide the media a national identity and personality.

(b) To facilitate the analyses of the world events not from the perspective of the West but from the national perspective.

(c) To foster better understanding among the developing countries, which is far more essential now than ever before.

(d) To prevent the unwarranted entry of foreign and alien ideas, cultures and life-styles, that always tend to contribute to shaping public opinion in favour of foreign countries, particularly of the West.

(e) To provide an objective account of the news and developments that were considered newsworthy by the indigenous media.

Non-aligned News Pool : As per the directives of the UNESCO to establish a news pool or consortium of news agencies, the 'pool' of news agencies of the non-aligned countries was formally launched in July, 1976 at the New Delhi Conference of Information Ministers and Representations of the news agencies of the non-aligned countries.

The objective of the pool is to expand the mutual exchange of information among the non-aligned countries in a spirit of collective self-reliance.

The Non-Aligned News Pool is not a transnational news agency, but a system of exchange of agency information, based on co-operation and co-ordination among individual news agencies taking part in these activities. The Pool is not based on any formal membership. The Pool has no single directing centre, nor does it have its own budget.

The Restraints

Communication Restraints : Many of the developing countries do not have an extensive and elaborate telecommunication network. For some, high tariffs are major barriers. Optimum information exchange depend on the level of development of communication systems in the individual non-aligned countries.

News Flow : A few year ago, about 85% of the news items received by PT1 from the Pool partners were spiked. The reasons for this were given as delay in news reception, poor quality, low news value, or propaganda material.

Lack of Training : The lack of proper training among the non-aligned journalists and their inability to match the professional standards of the journalists of the transnational news-agencies, are the reasons for the poor quality of material put out by the Non-Aligned News Agencies Pool.

Political Constraints : In many of the non-aligned countries, the news agencies are under the strict control of the governments. The first casualty of such a solution is the objectivity of the news and information put out by their agencies.

The Media's Lukewarm Attitude : The editors of private-owned newspapers in the democratic countries like India, either are not convinced of the need for such an inter-regional co-operation or they do not respect the news coverage of several agencies, which are participants of the pool.

The Systems : While there has been a continuous effort to establish alternative news and information distribution systems in the world, the recent global changes have had a deep impact on the information scene. The West has been for a long time using the concept of 'Freedom of Information' as an ideological weapon, and successfully deploying it to deflect the 3rd World from its pursuit of a new world information and communication order.

In the matter of broadcasting, the Western powers insist upon the 'open skies' policy, which they claim to be consistent with the principle of freedom of information. On the face of things, this seems a plausible argument. Open skies, seems to connote a situation of an unfettered information exchange of knowledge flowing freely across the national boundaries. On the contrary, the same western countries, show a complete disinclination towards free trade by imposing heavy tariffs to protect their own products.

These developments call for a greater unity among the 3rd World countries to come out of the dependence and dominance in the field of information, and promote self-reliance. The existing world information order provides an opportunity to the richer nations to use the scarce global natural resources, and exclude the poor nations from using the same. An attempt is made through the on going GATT talks to impose stronger forms of monopoly control over the content of information flows.

Scene in the World

The developing nations campaigned for a 'new order' in the field of international information and communication, which would facilitate a 'free and balanced flow' of information capable of breaking through the stereotypes created and nurtured for over 50 years by the western media empires. The new order, they maintained, would create a new international information climate that would foster a closer and better understanding among nations and individuals. The most important step in this direction was the launching of the Non-Aligned News Agencies Pool, in 1975.

The 'free flow' concept was amended to 'free-and balanced flow', when a declaration on the role of the media in the promotion of international understanding and peace was approved by the UNESCO in 1978. 'The right to know' was transformed into 'the right to communicate'.

The non-aligned nations coined the phrase, New International Information Order (NIIO). The MacBride Commission broadened the sphere by substituting the term 'world' for 'international' and incorporating 'communication' along with 'information'. Since then the phrase the 'New World Information and Communication Order (NWICO) has been widely used.

Free Flow Ideas : A major factor that helped the growth of US agencies was the wireless transmission technology, which reversed the world communication imbalance to the overall advantage of the American interest. Another factor was a general realization in the US of the advantages that world communication control bestowed on foreign trade and commerce. Following such realizations, ideas on unrestricted How of communication between nations began to crystallize in the US.

Demand for NWICO : The following overlapping and mutually complementing factors are at the base of the demand for a new order in the field of information-

(1) The emergence of new nations following the dissolution of the colonial empires after World War II.

(2) The asymmetrical economic relationship between the new nations and the western industrialized nations which, while strengthening the latters' wealth and power, perpetuated the new nations' dependency, not merely economic but political and cultural as well.

(3) The coming together of the new nations under the umbrella of non-alignment in the wake of aggressive bloc-building by the US and the USSR.

(4) The new nation's realization that their under-development was related to their dependence on rich nations followed by a firm resolve to assertive actions to correct imbalances in world trade and commerce, and cultural exchanges.

(5) Their gaining in strength in international organization, such as the UN and the UNESCO. Four stages can easily be identified in the history of the NWICO. The first stage (1973-76) marked the evolution of a new order. The second stage (1976-79) saw the accumulation of data and empirical evidence to give credence to the new order demand. The third stage followed the publication of the MacBride report in 1980. The fourth stage is the period following the adoption of the NWICO Resolution in the UNESCO.

Generally, the evolution of the new order concept is credited to the NAM. Much of the credit for the enlarging communication agenda of the UNESCO in the 1970s goes to the Non-Aligned Movement, which saw communication, at least in the early 70s, as a means to an end, the end being economic development of the poor nations.

The Algiers Summit of the non-aligned countries, held in 1973, is a major landmark, in the history of NWICO, for it was here that communication concerns were addressed directly in more than one paper in the context of their economic development programmes.

The 19th UNESCO General Conference adopted a resolution inviting the Director General to undertake a review of the problems of communication in modern society. Director General constituted a 16 member commission for the study of communication problems.

The 20th UNESCO general conference, held in 1978 was marked by a spirit of compromise. The new Mass Media Declaration (MMD) text now retitled as 'Declaration on Fundamental Principles Governing the contribution of the Mass Media in strengthening Peace and International Understanding and in combating was Propaganda, Racialism and Apartheid' was approved.

Character and Content of NWICO : The 21st general conference of the UNESCO, held in 1980, accepted the MacBride report and unanimously adopted Resolution outlining the basic character and content of the NWICO.

The establishment of the NWICO depended upon five major factors : (1) the will of the developed and developing countries to bring about changes in all areas of communication within their respective regions; (2) Co-operation between the developed and developing nations for removing all obstacles to a two-way and balanced flow of news and information among nations; (3) sharing of communication resources, including technologies, for countering monopoly of the international news flow by a few; (4) cooperation among the developing countries to correct imbalances with their own regions by increasing horizontal flows and (5) Co-operation between the media-rich and media-poor for mobilization of resources to strengthen communication infrastructure in the latter's region.

The 21st General Conference of the UNESCO approved the establishment of a news agency, the International Programme for the Development of Communication (IPDC) within the framework of the UNESCO to reduce the gap between the developed and developing countries by strengthening infrastructure and services through international cooperation and assistance. The objectives of the IPDC cover all facts of communication development.

Problems and Prospects of NWICO : The withdrawal of the US on December 31, 1984, and Britain and Singapore a year later, from the UNESCO, was not a deterrent to the objectives of the NWICO. Today, the evolving goals of the NWICO rest with not just the UNESCO, but a large number of international organizations such as the Organization for Economic Co-operation and Development (OECD), the International Telecommunications Union (ITU), the IPDC and the Third World and its organizations for moving the aim of the NWICO to a higher plain. The IPDC has done its best to help develop communication capabilities of the media-poor regions.

Between the second session in 1982 and the seventh session held in January 1986, it had allocated US$ 9.74 million for some communication projects in the developing countries. Those included 3 regional news agency projects Pan Africa News Agency (PANA), the Agencia Latino American De Servcios Especiales do Information (ALA SEI) and the Asia-Pacific News Network (ANN) and 14 national news agency projects in different 3rd World countries. These agencies and news exchange arrangements operating within the developing countries, no matter how inadequate they are, indicate that the NWICO has set itself on its evolutionary path. But there is more to be achieved.

Imbalances in the flow of news and information at international level have not ceased to exist. The one-way flow is still very much in evidence. Most of the news flowing through the transnational agencies into the developing regions concerns the developing world. The agencies continue to view the developing world's events and issues from their own perspectives. As a result, news everywhere is seen through the prisms of the West, the developed world. The Western media giants continue to set the world's news agenda.

Measures to be Adopted : The developed countries should be more open to redress the ever-increasing asymmetrical economic relations between them and the poor countries. This calls for hastening the pace for the establishment of the NIEO as it is linked with the NWICO. The developed world could make available resources for communication specific projects in the poor regions of the world. New technologies needed to be viewed as resources for the benefit of the mankind, and not as a new tool for exploitation of the disadvantaged.

Steps are needed to establish a balance in the information flow by devoting more space and lime to news and issues concerning the developing countries. The developed countries should join hands with the developing countries in making the telecommunications tariffs more suitable for a better use of existing systems.

The developing world, on the other hand, needs to formulate communication policies, without which the media development would get hampered. The press must make conscious efforts to free itself from the attitudes fostered by the Western news criteria.

Free Flow of Information : The free flow of information is a Western concept, by which almost all western countries rationalise the operation of their media and information agencies. The term means that any person or persons and any organization or organisations can own and operate any media or information agency, gather any information, and disseminate the same, if they so desire, to any target audience, wherever and whenever they want. The concept is basic to the history, culture and life of the liberal capitalist western society. Any challenge to this concept is rejected on grounds that it is undemocratic, inhuman and even uncivilized.

The philosophy of free flow resulted in the consolidation of the centres of information gathering and dissemination in the western countries. The socialist and the 3rd World countries could see that they were not represented objectively in the western media. Significant happenings in their countries were paid scant attention and whatever done, those were only half truths coloured by the Western perceptions.

Slowly, this situation got concretised, and the leaders of the 3rd World countries endured the situation as they were unable to take steps to change the situation. The 3rd World countries had no infrastructure or active network to make a difference.

Concept of Imbalance : There is imbalance in the flow of information between the developed West and the developing 3rd World countries, which can not have any say on the mechanism of gathering information as they do not own and control the technology of the giant information agencies of the West. Moreover, the 3rd World countries, knowing fully well that the information disseminated from these agencies doesn't represent all the truths about them. The imbalance is in terms of volume of information, flowing into the 3rd World countries, when compared to the volume of information flowing out from them.

The root of the problem goes back to the late 1950s and 1960s, when the concept of 'Development Communication' was born. The communication specialists thought that what the West achieved in centuries, the 3rd World could achieve the same in a matter of decades if aided by the mass media. Two eminent western scholars-Daniel Lerner and Wilbur Schramm-were in the forefront to suggest this theory.

Their theories were tried in many 3rd World countries. It was assumed that mass media used for creating a stable and sustainable democratic nation and implementing programmes to uplift the living conditions of the common man in society would transform the developing societies into modern, vibrant and stable societies.

However, a decade later, it was found that most of the social problems remained unsolved. Instead more problems were created. The western media organizations focused the negative developments of the developing society.

In such a situation, an American author, Herbert Schiller articulated something very new. He said that the free flow of communication was essentially meant to safeguard the economical growth of the West. And any attempt to regulate the flow of information beyond borders is seen as a threat to the western economies. Thus, it is termed as interference with the basic human right. Hence, the concept of 'imbalance' is an economic issue, and the international flow of information is just another fact of this issue.

Although the flow is still imbalance, exchanges of TV programmes, specially educational programmes, are quite frequent. More western programmes are seen on the TV screens of the 3rd World countries. Despite the large scale changes brought about by technology, imbalance persists in the media and coverage of the development west vis-a-vis the developing countries of the 3rd World.

Bibliography

Alice, G. : *Agents of Power : the Role of the News Media in Human Affairs,* Longman, New York, 1984.

Anthony, Smith : *The Newspaper—An International History,* Thames and Hudson, London, 1979.

Aronson, James : *The Press and the Cold War,* Beacon Press, Boston, 1970.

Baehr, H. : *Women and Media,* Pergamon, London, 1980.

Berger, C.R. : *Handbook of Communication Science,* Sage Publications, London, 1987.

Bernard, H. W. : *Principles of Journalism : A Basic Text*, Allied Publishers Private Ltd., New Delhi, 1998.

Bhattacharjea, A. : *The Constraints of Development Reporting,* Har Anand, New Delhi, 1994.

Bhattacharya, Bhabani : *Gandhi the Writer,* National Book Trust, New Delhi, 1969.

Brewer, J.M. : *Journalism as Guidance*, MacMillan Co., New York, 1998.

Campbell, Jeremy : *Grammatical Man : Information Entropy, Language and Life,* Simon and Schuster, New York, 1982.

Care, G. : *Modern Journalism,* Holt, Rinehart and Winston, New York, 1962.

Carrol, L. : *Occupational Information*, Prentice Hall, New York, 1961.

Cattell, B.B. : *Media Structure, Growth and Action*, Houghton Mifflin Co., Boston, 1999.

Chalapati, M. : *The Romance of the Newspaper,* National Council Educational Research and Training, Delhi, 1975.

Chandra, Navin : *Principles, Practices and Challenges,* Kanishka Publishers, New Delhi, 1998.

Chaturvedi, J.F. : *The Indian Press at Crossroads,* Media Research Foundation, New Delhi, 1992.

Chauhan, S.S. : *Principles and Techniques of Journalism*, Vikas Publishing House, New Delhi, 1982.

Christopher, C. : *Dynamics of Journalism* , Anmol Publications Pvt. Ltd., New Delhi, 2000.

Cohen, B.C. : *The Press and Foreign Policy,* Princeton University Press, New Jersey, 1963.

Critchfield, Richard : *The Indian Reporter's Guide,* Allied Pacific Pvt. Ltd., Bombay, 1962.

D'souza, Y. K. : *Encyclopaedia of Communication Media*, Discovery Publishing House, New Delhi, 2001.

Defleur, M. L. : *Fundamentals of Human Communication,* Mayfield, London, 1993.

Eisenstein, E. : *The Printing Press as an Agent of Change,* Cambridge University Press, New York, 1978.

Elizabeth, Grey : *The Story of Journalism,* Longmans Young Books, London, 1968.

Emery, Edwin : *The Press and America,* Prentice-Hall, New Jersey, 1997.

Eraser, F. : *An Introduction to Journalism,* MacMillan Co., New York, 1958.

Fiske, J. : *Introduction to Communication Studies,* Methuen, London, 1982.

Frederick, C. : *Communication in India : Experiments in Introducing Change,* NICD, Hyderabad, 1969.

Gagne, R.M. : *The Conditions of Learning*, Holt Binsort and Winston, New York, 1965.

Gandhi, M.K. : *Young India* (1919-27), Tagore & Co., Madras, 1922.

Garret, A. : *Interviewing: Its Principles and Methods*, Family Service Association of America, New York, 1942.

George, A. : *News Writing,* Kanishka Publishers, New Delhi, 1999.

George, A.L. : *Propaganda Analysis,* Peterson & Company, Illinois, 1959.

Gerbner, G : *Mass Media Policies in Changing Cultures,* Wiley, New York, 1977.

Giner, S. : *Mass Society,* Martin Robertson, London, 1976.

Gupta, V.S. : *Media and Development,* Har-Anand, New Delhi, 1994.

Hachten, W.A. : *The World News Prism : Changing Media of International Communication,* Iowa State University Press, Iowa, 1996.

Harris, G. : *Advertising on the Internet : Let Your Fingers Do the Talking,* Atlantic Publishers, New Delhi, 2001.

Hercleread, A.V. : *Instruction : Materials and Methods*, Mc Graw Hill Book Co., New York, 1964.

Hohenberg, John : *The Professional Journalist,* Holt, Rinehort and Winston, New York, 1969.

Holsti, O.R. : *Content Analysis*, Amerind, New Delhi, 1969.

Huda, Anwar : *The Art and Science of Cinema,* Atlantic Publishers, New Delhi, 2004.

Hynds, C. : *American Newspaper in* 1980s, Hastings House, New York, 1980.

Jag, M.C. : *Selected Editorials and other Writings of M. Chalapathi Rao*, Young Asia Publications, New Delhi, 1976.

James, S. : *The Politics of the Developing Areas,* Princeton University Press, Princeton, 1960.

Jasra, S. : *Information Technology in Journalism*, A.&M. Publishers, Delhi, 2002.

Jayapalan, N. : *Journalism*, Atlantic Publishers, New Delhi, 2001.

Jaylor, & Esa : *Imagologies Media Philosophy*, Routledge, UK, 1996.

Jhingan, M.L. : *The Economics of Development and Planning*, Konark Publishers, New Delhi, 1994.

John, A. : *The Asian Newspaper's Reluctant Revolution*, The Iowa State University Press, Iowa, 1977.

Joseph, M. K. : *Textbook of Editing & Reporting*, Dominant Books, New Delhi, 2000.

Julian, Harriss : *The Complete Reporter*, MacMillan Co., New York, 1942.

Kamath, M. V. : *Professional Journalism*, Vikas Publishing House, New Delhi, 1997.

Kerlinger, F.N. : *Foundations of Behavioural Research*, Rinehart and Winston, New York, 1973.

Kichar, R. S. : *Electronic Media and the Library Services*, Discovery Publishing House, New Delhi, 1999.

Kipling, Rudyard and Bonamy, Dobree : *Realist and Fabulist*, Oxford University Press, London, 1967.

Klapper, J.T : *The Effects of Mass Communication*, Free Press, Illinois, 1960.

Kothari, O.S. : *Report of the Indian Education Commission, 1964-66*, Concept, New Delhi, 1966.

Krippendorff, K. : *Content Analysis : An Introduction to its Methodology*, Sage, California, 1980.

Krishnamurthi, Nadig : *Indian Journalism*, University of Mysore, Mysore, 1966

Krouse, H. : *Media Technique with Youth*, Charles and Mervil, Ohio, 1990.

Krug, R.E. : *Ability Testing in Developing Countries: A Handbook of Principles and Techniques*, Praeger, New York, 1972.

Kumar, J. : *Mass Communication in India,* Gyan Books Pvt. Ltd., New Delhi, 2000.

Lawrence, R. : *How to Report? and Write the News,* Prentice-Hall, Englewood Cliffs, New Jersey, 1961.

Lawrence, R. : *Investigating Communication : A Introduction to Research Methods,* Prentice Hall, New York, 1991.

Leland, D. : *Editing the Day's News,* MacMillan Co., New York, 1947.

Lerner, D. : *The Passing of Traditional Society : Modernising, the Middle East,* Free Press, New York, 1958.

Long, L. and Mehta, P.M. : *First Mental Measurement Handbook for India*, NCERT, New Delhi, 1967.

MacDougall, Curfis D. : *Interpretotive Reporting*, MacMillan Co., New York, 1957.

Madhavan, P. K. : *Careers in Publishing,* Vikas Publishing House, New Delhi, 1997.

McClelland, D.C. : *The Achieving Society,* Princeton, New York, 1961.

McQuail, D. : *Towards a Sociology of Mass Communication,* Collier MacMillan, London, 1969.

McWhinnie, Donald : *The Art of Broadcasting*, Faber & Faber, London, 1961.

Mehta, D.S. : *Mass Communication and Journalism in India,* Allied Publishers, Bombay, 1979.

Melkote, S.R. : *Communication for Development in the third World : Theory and Practice,* Sage, New Delhi, 1991.

Merton, R.K. : *Social Theory and Social Structure,* Free Press, Glencoe, Illinois, 1957.

Mody, Bella : *Designing Messages for Development Communication,* Sage, New Delhi, 1991.

Mohanty, J. : *Educational Broadcasting : Radio & Television in Education*, Sterling Publishers, New Delhi, 1984.

Moraes, Frank : *Witness to an Era,* Vikas Publishing House, Delhi, 1977.

Mosan, N.N. : *Indian Education in the Emerging Society*, Sterling Publishers, New Delhi, 1982.

Moven, Kiran : *Studies in Educational Broadcasting*, Deep & Deep Publications, New Delhi, 1996.

Myers, G.E. : *Principles and Techniques of Vocational Education*, Government of India, Department of Labour, Manager of Publications, Delhi, 1972.

Narayana, Andal, : *Communication : Theory and Model,* Himalaya Publishing House, Delhi, 1999.

Natrajan, J. : *History of Indian Journalism*, Publication Division, Government of India, New Delhi, 1999.

Natrajan, S. : *A History of the Press in India,* Asia Publishing House, Bombay, 1962.

Nichols, S. : *Precision Journalism : A Practical Guide,* Sage, New Delhi, 1987.

Ottaway, A.K.C. : *Press and Society*, Routldge and Kegan Paul, London, 1962.

Pachori, Sudhis : *Jan Sanchar Madhyaam : Bhasha,* Rohit Publishers, Meerut, 1990.

Pandey, K. S. : *The Muzzled Press : Introspect and Retrospect,* Kanishka Publishers, New Delhi, 1998

Panickkar, K.M. : *The Foundation of New India,* George Allen & Unwin, London,1963.

Parikh, R.D. : *The Press and Society,* Popular Prakashan, Bombay, 1965.

Parthasarathy, R. : *History of Journalism in India,* Sterling, New Delhi, 1991.

Paul, Wingate : *Newspaper History : From the 17th Century to the Present Day,* Constable, London,1978.

Persons, A. : *The Making of Energy and Tele Communication Policy*, Praeager, London, 1995.

Philip, O. : *Journalists' Notebook on Live Radio-TV News,* TAB Books, Blue Ridje Summit, Paris, 1978.

Phillips, W. : *Mass Communication Research : Major Issues and Future Directions,* Praeger, New York, 1974.

Rati, Balsara : *The Working Journalist's Guide to Substance and Style,* Dominant Books, New Delhi, 2003.

Rayudu, C. S. : *Media and Communication Management,* Himalaya Publishing House, Delhi, 1990

Righter, R. : *Whose News? Politics, Press and the Third World,* Times Books, New York, 1979.

Robert, Gunning : *The Technique of Clear Writing,* McGraw Hill Book Co., New York, 1999.

Roland, E. : *Journalism in Modern India,* Asia Publishing House, Bombay, 1964.

Rostow, W.W. : *The Stages of Economic Growth : A Non-communist Manifesto,* Cambridge University Press, Cambridge, 1960.

Sanjay, B.P. : *The Eighteenth Elephant : Udayavani's Experiment in Development Jouralism,* Udayavani Press, Manipal, 1990.

Saraswat, R.K. : *Mass Media*, NCERT, New Delhi, 1998.

Sarkar, N. N. : *Public Relation,* Sterling, New Delhi, 1998.

Schramm, W. : *Development Communication—History and Theories*, Oxford University Press, New York, 1989.

Shaw, David : *Journalism Today*, Harper's College Press, London, 1977.

Singh, J. K. : *Media Cultural and Communication,* Manohar Publishers, Delhi, 1999.

Srivastava, K. M. : *News Reporting and Editing*, Sterling, New Delhi, 1997.

Tahmankar, D.V. : *Lokmanya Tilak,* John Murray, London, 1956.

Thorndike, R.L. : *Media Psychology and Education*, Wiley Eastern Pvt. Ltd., New Delhi, 2001.

Vajpayee, Rama : *Press : Inside Outside 2002,* Gyan Books, Pvt. Ltd., New Delhi, 2003.

Valdivia N. : *A Companion to Media Studies,* Blackwell, New Delhi, 2004.

Verma, J.S. : *Media and Cultural Environment*, Methuen, London, 1969

Vernon, P.E. : *Personality Assessment*, Methuen, London, 1964.

Viner, George : *The Practice of Journalism,* Heinemann, London, 1963.

Walton, Paul : *Language, Image, Media,* Basil Blackwell, Oxford, 1983.

William, L. : *The Opinion Makers : The Washington Press Corps,* Beacon Press, Boston, 1967.

Willian, Charvat : *Handbook for Writers,* Prentice Hall, New Jersey, 1962.

Woollacott, J. : *Mass Communication and Society,* Edward Arnold, London, 1977.

Young, J. : *The Manufacture of News,* Constable, London, 1973.

Zaller, R. : *The Nature and Origins of Mass Opinion,* Cambridge, New York, 2001.

Index

C

D

E

F

G

H

I

J

K

L

M

N

O

P

Q

R

S

T

U

V

W

Y

Z

❑❑❑